The Early Caliphate

by

Maulānā Muḥammad Ali

English Translation
of Maulānā Muḥammad Ali
Urdu work, *K͟hilāfah Rās͟hidah*
by Maulānā Ya'qūb K͟han

The Aḥmadiyya Anjuman Is͟hā'at Islām

Lahore — U.S.A.

First edition 1932
Reprinted 1947, 1951, 1983

The *Ahmadiyya Anjuman Isha'at Islām* (Ahmadiyya Assocation for the Propagation of Islām) was founded at Lahore, Pakistan, in 1914 by the prominent followers of Hazrat Mirza Ghulam Ahmad. It exists to promote a liberal, tolerant and peaceful picture of Islām, as found in the Holy Quran and the life of the Holy Prophet Muhammad. It has published a vast quantity of highly-acclaimed literature on Islām in various languages, and has branches and members in several countries.

Information, books and free literature on Islām may be obtained by contacting:

Ahmadiyya Anjuman Isha'at Islam Lahore (or A.A.I.I.L.)
1315 Kingsgate Road, Columbus, Ohio 43221, U.S.A.
Phone (614) 457-8504
Fax (614) 457-4455
e-mail aaiil@aol.com

PRINTED IN CANADA

ISBN 0-913321-27-3

Preface

The *Early Caliphate*, which is a record of thirty years of ideal Islamic rule, is a natural sequel to *Muḥammad the Prophet*, in which I offered a picture of the life of that great benefactor of humanity, the Prophet Muhammad, who of all the world's great men is the most misunderstood. Two reasons have prompted me to undertake this task. The first is that, just as the Holy Prophet brought about a transformation which is unparalleled in the history of the world, to his immediate followers it was vouchsafed to contribute not only "the most amazing story of conquest in the whole history of our race"* but also wonderful moral and spiritual uplift of humanity. The second reason is that in all histories of this period written by either Muslim or non-Muslim writers, there exist many misunderstandings about the great and noble deeds of the most righteous monarchs that the world has ever produced.

In the *Early Caliphate* I have dealt with the period of thirty years that followed the death of the Holy Prophet. In Islamic history this period is known as *Khilāfah Rāshidah* or the rightly directed Caliphate, the underlying significance being that the men who were chosen to steer the temporal bark of Islām during this period were also models of righteousness and that they led the Muslim nation onward both temporally and spiritually. In a hadīth of the Holy Prophet, this period of thirty years is specially called *Khilāfah* or Successorship to the Holy Prophet as distinguished from *Mulk* or the Kingdom of Islām which came after it. In the last phase of the Holy Prophet's life he was both prophet and king, a spiritual guide of his people as well as their temporal head, and therefore the later phase of the kingdom of Islām in which the king was only the temporal head does not fully represent the idea of successorship. *The Khilāfah Rāshidah* or the Early Caliphate, however, is in both aspects fully representative of successorship to the Prophet, and it

---

* *A Short History of the World* by H.G. Wells.

is for this reason that I have included in the history of the Caliphate an account of the lives of the four Caliphs whose reigns constitute the Early Caliphate, viz., Abū Bakr, ‘Umar, ‘U<u>th</u>mān and ‘Alī.

I would draw attention to two salient points about which there prevails great misconception. The first is the general impression among Muslims as well as non-Muslims that, though the battles which the Holy Prophet had to fight were defensive and not aggressive, yet the wars of the Early Caliphate were undertaken with no other object than the expansion of Islām and the territorial extension of its kingdom. In this short history I have shown that this is quite an erroneous view, and that Muslims never sallied forth to impose their religion or even their rule on the neighbouring empires; or to offer what has frequently been represented as the alternatives of Islam or *Jizyah*. This question has been fully dealt with in the lives of Abū Bakr and ‘Umar. The second point to which I wish to draw special attention relates to the equally great misconception as to internal dissensions of the times of ‘U<u>th</u>mān and ‘Alī. The example of greatness set by Abū Bakr and ‘Umar are not wanting in ‘U<u>th</u>mān and ‘Alī; only they are revealed in a different sphere.

The book was written originally in Urdu in the form of a simple history. The element of the lives of the Caliphs was added in a second edition, and it is now that second edition that is being presented in English garb. The translation has been done by my able and esteemed friend Maulana Muḥammad Ya‘qūb <u>Kh</u>ān, Editor of *Light*, to whom my sincerest thanks are due for his labour of love. I must also thank him for the help he has given me in reading the proofs.

MUḤAMMAD ‘ALĪ.
President

Ahmadiyyah Anjuman I<u>sh</u>ā‘at Islam,
Ahmadiyyah Buildings,
Lahore, 12-9-32.

Contents

Page

Preface iii

Abū Bakr 1

Early Life 1
Conversion to Islām and services 2
He is persecuted 4
His daughter 'Ā'ishah is married to the Prophet 4
Flight to Madīnah 5
Services in Madīnah 6
Part in warfare 6
Abū Bakr as Imam during the Prophet's last days 8
The Prophet's demise 9
Abū Bakr's election as Caliph 10
Abū Bakr's statesmanship 11
Abū Bakr's address to the people 12
'Alī and Abū Bakr 13
Abū Bakr duly elected Caliph 14
Usāmah's army despatched to Syria 15
False claimants to prophethood 16
Aswad 'Ansī 17
Musailimah 17
Tulaihah 18
Sajāh 18
The Apostasy movement 19
Refusal to pay zakāt 21
The Defence of Madīnah 22
Rebel attack on Madīnah repulsed 23
Despatch of expedition to different quarters 24
Object of expeditions 25
Khālid defeats Tulaihah 26
Mālik ibn Nawairah 26
Khālid defeats Musailimah 26

Bahrain rebellion crushed 27
'Umān and Mahrah cleared of rebels 28
Yaman and Hadramaut restored 28
Conflict with Roman Empire and Persia 28
Insurrection called for fortification of frontiers 30
Abū Bakr's motives in sending expeditions to frontiers 31
The strength of the Caliphate as compared with the two Empires 32
Aggression on the enemy's part 33
Trouble in Arabia fomented by Persia and Rome 35
Muthanna's expeditions 36
Khālid reinforces Muthanna' and assumes command 37
Hirah taken 37
Jizyah and charge of loot 38
Conquest of Anbar and 'Ain al-Tamr 40
Expedition on the Northern frontier 40
The battle of Ajnadain 42
Abū Bakr's illness and death 42
Simplicity of his life 43
The collection of the Qur'ān 44
The collection of zakāt 46
Government by counsel 47
Position of the Ruler 48
Treatment of enemies 49
Strength of character 49
Appearance and character 50

'Umar 52
Early life 52
Conversion to Islām 52
The Flight 53
Help rendered to the cause of Islām 55
The Prophet's death and after 56
'Umar pursues the Frontier policy of Abū Bakr 57

Objection against early Muslim conquests 58
The safety of Arabia the sole motive of the Early Caliphate wars 59
Defeat enhanced Persia's and Rome's passion for revenge 60
A necessity of war 62
Islām, jizyah or the sword 62
Significance of the alleged message 64
Persian forces under Hurmuz 67
Muslim General's appeal to Caliph 67
Hirah lost and regained. Battle at Namāraq 68
Battle of Jasr 69
Persia again defeated at Buwaib 70
Sa'd appointed generalissimo 70
Battle of Qādisiyah 72
Sa'd's advance on Madā'in. The western part evacuated by Persians 73
Fall of Madā'in 73
Persians' advance on and defeat at Jalūlā 75
Battle of Takrīt. Christian tribes embrace Islām Mosul occupied 76
Baṣrah and Kūfah founded 76
Damascus conquered 77
Battle of Fihl 77
Battle of Ḥimṣ 78
Battle of Yarmūk 78
Jerusalem capitulates 80
Treaty of Jerusalem 81
Greek efforts to expel Muslims from Syria 82
Conquest of Jazīrah 83
Removal of Khālid 84
Plague of 'Amwās 85
Egypt invaded 86
Fall of Fusṭāṭ 87
Fall of Alexandria 87
Library of Alexandria 88

The Suez Canal 88
Campaign in Khūzistān 88
Hurmuzān becomes Muslim 90
Ban against advance on Persia withdrawn 91
Battle of Nihāwand conquest of Persia 92
Death of ‘Umar 93
Reasons underlying the great conquest of ‘Umar’s reign 93
Weakening of the Roman and Persian Empires 94
False charge of love of loot 95
Glorious deeds of the Muslim soliders 96
Muslim’s sense of duty 98
Strength of character of Muslim soldiers 100
Solidarity of Islām 103
Democratic spirit 104
Simple life and concern for the ruled 106
Treatment of non-Muslims 107
Condition of women in the time of ‘Umar 109
Gradual abolition of slavery 109
Equality of man 110
Works of public good 111
Spreading of Islām and knowledge of Qur’ān 112
Soldier and Administrator 113
A true successor of the Prophet 114

‘Uthmān 116
Early Life 116
Conversion to Islām 117
Emigration to Abyssinia 117
Services rendered to the cause of Islām 118
‘Uthmān’s part in warfare 118
Part played in earlier Caliphate 120
Elected Caliph 120
Revolt in Persia leads to extension of Empire 122
Roman attack on Syria and further conquests 123
Cyprus occupied 123

Roman invasion of Egypt and further conquests in Africa 124
Causes of the discontent in ‘Uthmān’s Caliphate 125
Appointment and dismissal of Governors 127
Uthmān’s impartiality in the choice of Governors 129
Ibn Sabā leads agitation against ‘Uthmān 130
Agitation gains strength 131
Disaffection spreads among Beduins 132
Deportation of Abū Dharr 133
Burning of unauthentic copies of the Holy Qur’ān 133
Mischief started 135
Enquiry into grievances 136
Governors’ Conference 137
Seditionists gather at Madīnah 138
Seditionists’ entry into Madīnah 140
The Caliph is maltreated and imprisoned in his house .. 142
Madīnah Muslims were averse to shedding Muslim blood 143
Annual Pilgrimage 145
The Caliph is slain 146
‘Uthmān sacrificed his life for the unity of Islām 147
Prophet’s great qualities mirrored forth in the first four Caliphs 149
‘Uthmān took nothing from the Public Treasury 149
‘Uthmān’s reign 151
Administration 152
Standardization of the Qur’ān 153
Manners and morals 153

‘Alī 155

Early Life 155
Conversion to Islām and determination to help the cause 155
Flight to Madīnah 156
Marriage with Fāṭimah 157

Martial exploits 157
As an envoy and preacher of Islām 159
At the Prophet's death 160
Oath of allegiance to the Caliph 160
'Alī becomes the Caliph 161
Dissensions within the house of Islām 162
Demand of retribution against 'Uthmān's assassins 163
Appointment of new Governors 164
War preparations against Mu'āwiyah 165
'Ā'ishah, Ṭalḥah and Zubair demand retribution for 'Uthmān's murder 166
Purity of their motives 167
'Ā'ishah captures Baṣrah 169
'Ā'ishah was against fighting 171
'Alī's attack on Baṣrah and negotiations with Ṭalḥah and Zubair 173
Battle of Jamal 173
Affectionate relations in warfare 175
Kūfah as capital and calling Mu'āwiyah to submission 176
Relations between 'Alī and Mu'āwiyah 176
Battle of Ṣiffīn 177
Desertion of 'Alī's troops 179
The arbitrators' award 180
Battle against the Khawārij 181
The Khawārij cause further trouble 182
Mu'āwiyah captures Egypt 182
Later period of 'Alī's reign 183
'Alī's martyrdom 184
'Alī's reign 184
No better choice of Caliph could be made 186
'Alī's learning 187
'Alī's devotions 188

Chapter 1
Abū Bakr

Early Life

'Abd Allāh was the name given to Abū Bakr by his parents. Abū Bakr was his *kunyah*[1] before Islām, while he received the title of *Ṣiddīq* (lit., the most truthful) and *'Atiq* (lit., generous, excellent, or free) after his conversion to Islām. His father's name was 'U<u>th</u>mān, but he is generally known in history by his surname Abū Quhāfah. Umm al-<u>Kh</u>air Salma was the name of Abū Bakr's mother. Both of Abū Bakr's parents belonged to the Banī Taim clan of the tribe of Quraī<u>sh</u>. This clan occupied a position of eminence in Arabia, and questions relating to blood-money in murder cases were referred to it; Abū Quhāfah, Abū Bakr's father, being entrusted with this important function.

---

1. Among Arabs, a surname, generally indicating relationship to male offspring (*Ar. kunyah*) was looked upon as a title of honour. The *kunyah* was especially taken from the name of the eldest son, to whose name the word *ab* (lit., father) was added, and it was thus generally *father of so and so*. But *kunyah* did not always express paternity; in some cases it was taken from some characteristic of the person, and the reason of this was that the word *ab* has a wide significance. Thus Abū Hurairah (lit., father of kittens), the famous reporter of Ḥadī<u>th</u>, was so called from his kindness to cats. Abū Bakr literally means *father of the youthful camel*, and there is no indication in any report as to why he assumed, or was given, this particular *kunyah*. It may have been due simply to his kindness to, or love of, camels.

Abū Bakr was born in the second or third year of the Elephant[2] and was thus two or three years younger than the Holy Prophet Muḥammad. In his youth he was well-known for his high morals and commanded universal respect. Such noble virtues as helping the poor and the needy, doing good to kith and kin, rendering relief to the afflicted, hospitality and truthfulness, were all found in him in abundant measure. From his very childhood he had not so much as touched liquor. All these are precisely the virtues of which, as history tells us, the Holy Prophet was possessed before the Call. This shows that in a way Abū Bakr had a natural affinity to the Prophet. He had, however, received some education. He could read and write, and was a specialist in knowledge of the genealogy of the Quraish clans. People held him in very high esteem both for his knowledge and his ripe experience. By profession he was a cloth merchant and this business made him quite a rich man. At the time of his acceptance of Islām, he had 40,000 gold dirhams in hard cash. According to one of his own statements, he was the wealthiest of all the Quraish traders.

Conversion to Islām and services

When the Prophet received the Divine Call and invited people to join him, Abū Bakr was one of the first converts to embrace Islām. His zeal for Islām was so great that no sooner did he join its ranks than he applied all his energy and wealth to promote the sacred cause. Many were the souls that saw the light of Islām through him. Such great men as ‘Uthmān, Zubair, ‘Abd al-Raḥmān ibn ‘Auf, Sa‘d ibn Abī Waqqās, were converted by his preaching.

2. Before the Muslim era known as *Hijrah*, the Arabs used to reckon dates from the year of the "Elephant" which was the year in which Abrahah, the Christian Governor of Yaman, led an attack on Makkah, with the intention of demolishing the Ka'bah. This army had one or more elephants in it and hence the name. The year of the Elephant was the year of the Holy Prophet's birth. The Hijrah came 53 lunar years after this.

His own mother, Umm al-Khair Salma, one of the early converts, also owed her conversion to him. His father, Abū Quhāfah, however, heard the call much later, after the conquest of Makkah in the 8th year of Hijrah.[3] Many slaves of both sexes, who were persecuted and tortured by their masters for their acceptance of Islām, were purchased and set free by Abū Bakr. Of such, history has preserved the names of seven, including the famous Bilāl. Of his wealth he spent liberally in the cause of Islām, so that at the time of the Hijrah only 5,000 dirhams remained of his fortune. The Prophet himself acknowledged his valuable services when he said: "No one's wealth has benefited me so much as the wealth of Abū Bakr." Within the courtyard of his house, he had built a small mosque. Here he would sit and recite the Qur'ān in strains that captivated the hearts of listeners. The Quraish objected and demanded that he should cease reciting the Qur'ān in a loud voice because it attracted their womenfolk and children, who might be led to renounce their ancestral faith. But Abū Bakr did not yield on this point and left no stone unturned to spread the light of Islām. During this period the ties of affection between him and the Prophet grew ever stronger. His monetary and missionary services endeared him all the more to the Prophet, so much so that the Master would in person call frequently at the house of his disciple. And when at length there came the time of Hijrah, it was Abū Bakr whom the Prophet chose as a comrade in a critical hour.

---

3. *Hijrah*, which is generally rendered as the Flight, means originally *cutting off* from friendly intercourse or *forsaking*, and in the history of Islam it has come to signify the migration of the Holy Prophet and his Companions from Makkah to Madīnah, to which he was compelled on account of the growing opposition of his enemies and severe persecution of Muslims by them. The Muslim era is named after it and dates from the first day of the first month (Muḥarram) of the year in which the Hijrah took place, that event itself taking place more than two months after the commencement of the year. The year of Hijrah probably coincides with 19th April 622 of the Christian era, while the Hijrah itself took place on 20th June.

He is persecuted

Abū Bakr was held in great respect not only for his noble birth but also for his personal worth, his high morals and his wealth. He could not, however, escape persecution in the cause of Islām. In connection with the conversion to Islām of his mother, Umm al-Khair, it is recorded that one day Abū Bakr began openly to preach the new faith. This was the time when the Prophet himself confined his activities to secret preaching in the house of Zaid ibn Arqam, where prayers were also said in secret. When the Quraish saw Abū Bakr openly preach Islām, they fell on him and beat him into insensibility. His own kinsmen took him up and carried him home. On recovering consciousness, the first question he asked was, "Where is the Prophet?" His mother ascertained the Prophet's whereabouts, and immediately both went to the house of Zaid ibn Arqam, where the mother accepted Islām. When the people of Makkah put Muslims to severe persecution, the Prophet counselled them to emigrate to Abyssinia. Abū Bakr was one of those who chose to bid farewell to their native land. On the way he met a chief, Ibn al-Daghnah, who asked him where he was going. "My own people's persecutions have driven me out of hearth and home," replied Abū Bakr. "A man like you," said the chief, "certainly must not be exiled — you help the poor, you are kind to your kith and kin, you render succour to the distressed and show hospitality to the wayfarer." And, bringing him back to Makkah, he had it proclaimed that Abū Bakr was under his protection. This protection, however, did not last long. As usual, Abū Bakr started his loud recitation of the Qur'ān in the mosque which he had built in the yard of his house, which happened to be on a public thoroughfare. The Quraish were not prepared to tolerate this and so Ibn al-Daghnah had to withdraw the protection he had pledged. Abū Bakr was unmoved. Careless of the withdrawal of protection, he continued his usual recitations.

His daughter 'Ā'ishah is married to the Prophet

In the tenth year of the Call, the Prophet lost his faithful wife Khadījah, who at the time of her death was sixty-five years of age. During the many hard trials through which the Prophet had passed, she had been his greatest comforter. This bereavement, therefore, was a great shock and told heavily on him. Seeing him greatly depressed, a Muslim lady suggested to him that he should marry, and proposed the name of Abū Bakr's daughter, 'Ā'ishah. The young girl had already been betrothed to Jubair, son of Mut'im, and when the lady in question mentioned her proposal to Abū Bakr, he was glad to strengthen his already strong ties of affection with the Prophet, but wanted first to settle the matter with Jubair. This being done, the *nikāh* (marriage ceremonial) was performed, though consummation was delayed for five years on account of 'Ā'ishah's age, which was only nine at the time of *nikāh* according to a report of Ibn Sa'd.[4]

Flight to Madīnah

At last the Makkans' persecutions reached their climax. Under the Prophet's order, Muslims began to emigrate to Madīnah. Abū Bakr also made ready for emigration, but the Prophet told him to wait till he (the Prophet) should receive Divine permission to go. The Muslims removed themselves one by one. Abū Bakr and 'Alī were the only two who remained behind with the Prophet. At length there arrived the hour when plans to assassinate the Prophet were matured in every detail. Then did the Prophet receive the Divine word to leave. He informed Abū Bakr, accordingly, to get ready and, leaving 'Alī in his own bed departed from his house in the dark of night and passed unnoticed through the would-be assassins who had surrounded it. Three miles away from Makkah, there was a cave known as the cave of Thaur. There the two refugees took shelter. Abū Bakr was the first to go in. Dark as it was, he cleaned the cave with his own hands, and then asked the Prophet to enter. In the morning the Quraish began the search and followed the track right up to the mouth of the cave. From within the cave

4. *Tabaqāt*, Vol. VIII, p. 42.

the refugees could even see the feet of their pursuers. This overwhelmed Abū Bakr with grief, but the Prophet consoled him saying, "Fear not, for God is with us." The pursuers saw the cobweb of a spider over the mouth of the cave and turned back. Food arrangements had been made beforehand by Abū Bakr. He had instructed his servant to drive his herd of goats, while grazing them, to the mouth of the cave. The milk of these goats was all they had to live on. Thus they subsisted in hiding for three consecutive days and nights till, on the fourth, they mounted the camels which Abū Bakr had arranged for and left for Madīnah.

Services in Madīnah

Islām's needs, limited in Makkah, grew with its advent in Madīnah. When money was wanted to build a mosque, Abū Bakr paid for the site from his own pocket. But the greatest need of the community was the conduct of a hard struggle against numerous enemies who were bent on annihilating it by the sword, and Muslims had therefore to put up a fight in self-defence. The carrying on of incessant war against an ever-increasing foe necessitated the utmost sacrifices from the adherents of the cause, and here, too, Abū Bakr was the foremost as he was at Makkah. On one occasion, 'Umar offered one half of his savings for the cause. This time at least, he hoped, he would out-do Abū Bakr. Presently there came Abū Bakr bringing with him all that he had. "What have you left behind at home?" enquired the Prophet. "God and His Prophet," came the reply. On his poor relations, too, Abū Bakr spent most liberally of his wealth.

Part in warfare

In Madīnah Abū Bakr was the Prophet's right-hand man in the affairs of state. He also took an active part in fighting and was never absent from any battle in which the Prophet himself took part. The first battle was fought at Badr in the second year of the Hijrah. The enemy's numerical strength was thrice that of the Muslims but their fighting strength was greater still, for they were well-equipped and experienced warriors. The Prophet retired to a hut and prostrated himself in supplication before God. "O God," said he, "if this day this handful of Thy servants perish, there will be none to worship Thee on this earth." Abū Bakr kept guard at the entrance and heard his Master's fervent prayers. At last he spoke out. "O Prophet," he said, "God will undoubtedly come to thy help as He has promised." Then they sallied forth into the field of battle and Abū Bakr displayed great valour. The Muslims won. Seventy prisoners of war fell into their hands. Abū Bakr counselled the Prophet to release them on payment of ransom money. This was done, as it was quite in accordance with the Quranic teachings.

At the battle of Uḥud in the third year of the Hijrah when the Muslims were trapped and suffered a heavy loss, Abū Bakr firmly stood to his ground. The Quraish shouted: "Is Muḥammad there in the midst of the people? Is Abū Bakr there in the midst of the people? Is 'Umar there in the midst of the people?" "They are alive and here to bring you down," shouted back 'Umar at last, on which the enemy left the field. The very next day they were pursued, Abū Bakr taking part in the chase.

Then came the battle known as the Battle of the Ditch in the fifth year of the Hijrah. Here again Abū Bakr was seen working as a common labourer, digging the ditch to protect Madīnah from the on-rush of the enemy. Madīnah remained in a state of siege for thirty days, after which the enemy retreated. He was also present at Ḥudaibiyah, when a truce was concluded. The Muslims were much upset about it as they thought that the terms were humiliating to themselves.[5] 'Umar was particularly agitated and came to Abū

---

5. Two of these terms were particularly distasteful: (*a*) Muslims shall not take with them any Muslim already living in Makkah, nor shall they stand in the way of any one from among themselves should he wish to stay at Makkah. (*b*) Should any of the Muslims at Makkah go over to Madīnah, the Muslims shall hand him over to the Makkans, but if any of the Madinite Muslims should rejoin the Makkans, the latter shall not restore him to the Muslims.

Bakr, saying, "Why must we submit to terms so humiliating, if our cause is a righteous one?" Abū Bakr replied that the Prophet must have acted in obedience to the will of God. "Did not the Prophet say," argued 'Umar, "that we would perform the pilgrimage?" "Indeed, he did," rejoined Abū Bakr, "but he never said we should do so this very year." This was the same reply that 'Umar got from the Prophet when he put a similar question to him. In the first stages of the battle of Ḥunain the Muslims were forced to retreat under pressure from the enemy's archers. Here again Abū Bakr kept firmly to his ground and the battle was ultimately won. When money was needed for the Tabūk expedition, Abū Bakr placed the whole of his wealth at the disposal of the nation. In the ninth year of the Hijrah, he was put at the head of the pilgrim party to Makkah.

Abū Bakr as Imām during the Prophet's Last Illness

About the end of the tenth year of Hijrah, the Prophet went to perform a pilgrimage. This is known as the *Hajjat al-Wada'* or the Farewell Pilgrimage. It was revealed to him on this occasion that the religion of Islām had attained perfection, and that his time was drawing nigh. On his return to Madīnah, some two months and a half afterwards, the Prophet was taken ill. Notwithstanding his illness, he attended the mosque and conducted prayers personally so long as he could. But he was too weak to talk much. One day in a sermon he said, "God has given to a servant of His the choice between this worldly life and the life with Him. The servant has chosen that with the Lord." This brought tears to Abū Bakr's eyes. The hint was clear enough. The Prophet's life was coming to an end. Then the Prophet ordered that all doors opening on to the mosque should be closed with the exception of Abū Bakr's door. Gradually he became too weak to come out to the mosque. One day, word was thrice sent to him to come to prayer but he could not muster enough strength. So he directed that Abū Bakr should lead the prayers. 'Ā'ishah submitted that her father was too tender-hearted and while reciting the Qur'ān would burst into tears. This would make his recitation inaudible. The Prophet did not accept this excuse and insisted that Abū Bakr should lead the prayers. Consequently, for the last three days of the Prophet's life Abū Bakr acted as the *Imām*. This was, in a way, an indication that the Prophet considered Abū Bakr to be the fittest person to succeed him.

The Prophet's demise, Rabī I, II A.H. (June 632 A.D.)

It was Monday, the 12th of Rabī I in the year 11 A.H., when Muḥammad, may peace and the blessings of God be upon him, breathed his last. He had been bed-ridden for twelve days and had passed through some very critical moments, but only that very morning he had felt much better and had spoken with several persons. It was believed that the crisis was over and Abū Bakr who had so far kept by his bed-side, had taken permission to go home to Sunḥ, where he lived. Few, therefore, were prepared to believe the news when it came. 'Umar regarded it as a piece of mischief by some hypocrite and, sword in hand, he stood in the mosque to stop this disquieting news from getting abroad. Abū Bakr heard the news and forthwith hastened back and went straight into 'Ā'isẖah's chamber. It was there that the Prophet had been nursed. He found that he was really dead. He kissed his forehead and gave voice to his sorrowing love in these touching words: "Sweet wert thou in life and sweet art thou in death." Then he came out into the mosque and communicated the news to the congregation in the following words:

"Listen ye all! Whoever worshipped Muḥammad, then certainly Muḥammad has passed away, and whoever worshipped God, let him know that God is Ever-living and He never dieth."

Then he quoted the following verse of the Qur'ān: "And Muḥammad is no more than a Messenger; all messengers before him have passed away" (3 : 143). This convinced the people that the news of the Prophet's death was true.

Abū Bakr's Election as Caliph

Abū Bakr and 'Umar were still in the mosque when someone from among the Anṣār[6] (Helpers) came with the news that the Anṣār had assembled in the Thaqīfah Banī Sā'idah, a place used as a council hall by the people of Madīnah, and were discussing the election of a successor to the Prophet. It was a critical moment. Had the Anṣār succeeded in setting up a man of their choice and the rest of the people disapproved of that choice, the solidarity of Islām would have been shattered. No time was to be lost. Abū Bakr and 'Umar hastened to the council hall. On arrival there, they found that Sa'd ibn 'Ubādah had just finished his speech and that the Anṣār had agreed to elect him as a successor to the Holy Prophet. On the arrival of Abū Bakr and 'Umar, one of the Anṣār stood up, and in further confirmation of the choice, dwelt on the claims of the Anṣār and their virtues. Abū Bakr in reply said that so far as service to the cause of the Faith was concerned, there could be no two opinions about the Anṣār. But the people of Arabia, he reminded them, would not submit to any king other than a Quraishite.

This was perfectly true. Never before in her history had Arabia known allegiance to a king. Every clan, every tribe, had been independent, and none had ever been under the sway of a rival clan or tribe. In the first place, the Arabs were temperamentally averse to owing allegiance to one king or overlord. Love of unfettered freedom had by birth and breeding become part and parcel of their nature, and every tribe prized its undisputed sovereignty above all else. And again, even if they could be reconciled to the idea of a central authority, they could never agree that that authority should be vested in any tribe other than the

6. The Muslims living at Madīnah were either the Muhājirīn, i.e., those who had fled from Makkah and settled at Madīnah or the Anṣār (lit. helpers) i.e., the residents of Madīnah who had invited the Prophet to live among them. The Muhājirīn belonged generally to the tribe of Quraish, whose supremacy was admitted throughout Arabia on account of their guardianship of the Ka'bah. The Anṣār belonged to two tribes, the Aus and the Khazraj.

Quraish, whom they had learnt by long-established tradition to venerate by virtue of the fact that to this tribe belonged the sacred privilege of the custody of the spiritual centre of Arabia, viz., the Ka'bah, and to whom belonged the additional distinction that from it came the Prophet himself. Abū Bakr's statesmanlike foresight at once grasped the situation and he put it before the assembly of Anṣār. It was thereupon suggested by the Anṣār as a solution of the difficulty that instead of one there might be elected two successors, one from among themselves and another from among the Quraish. But this meant the disruption of Islām. After much discussion, the Anṣār came round to Abū Bakr's point of view. One of them stood up and said:

"For the pleasure of God and in obedience to His will alone have we been sacrificing life and property, and now that the best interests of Islām so require, we submit to the election of a successor from among the Quraish. Just as we stood by the Prophet, even so do we pledge ourselves to stand by his successor."

And so saying, he took hold of Abū Bakr's hand and swore allegiance to him. According to some reports, the first to do so were 'Umar and Abū 'Ubaidah, and thereafter the Anṣār, group by group, came forward to make the pledge at the hand of Abū Bakr. Sa'd ibn 'Ubādah was the solitary exception.

Abū Bakr's statesmanship

It was thus due to the prudence of Abū Bakr and 'Umar that a calamity was successfully averted. Had it not been for their speedy action in reaching the council hall, Islām would have found itself in the grip of a most formidable dissension within its own house which would have ended in the total destruction of its power at that early stage. On the one hand, there was the funeral of the man for love of whom they had for a quarter of a century sacrificed their lives, their property and their all, the man whose separation they could not for one moment bear; it was their duty to see the body of their Master to its last resting-place. On the other hand, there was the duty to save Islām from disruption at this critical moment when one false step at the council hall, which had almost been taken, would have sealed the doom of Islām itself. And this call of national duty was too urgent, too imperative, to permit of delay. The temptation to remain close to the Prophet's body, irresistible as it must have been, had to be sacrificed; and the sacrifice was made without a moment's hesitation. For thus saving Islām at a critical point, posterity must ever remain indebted to these two great men. Abū Bakr's words on his own death-bed show that it was only to save Islām that he left the dead body of the Prophet. Calling 'Umar to his death-bed, he gave him directions regarding reinforcements for Muthannā in the following words: "Command a levy for al-Muthannā. Tarry not. If I die, as I may this day, wait not till the evening; if I linger on to-night, wait not till the morning. Let not sorrow for me divert thee from this service of the Lord. Ye saw what I myself did when the Prophet died, and there could be no greater sorrow for mankind than that; truly, if grief had stayed me then from girding my loins in the cause of the Lord and of His Prophet, the Faith had fared badly; the flame of rebellion had been surely kindled in the city."[7]

Abū Bakr's address to the people

The spark of dissension which may have blazed into a conflagration and consumed the entire fabric of Islām having been thus extinguished, the Prophet's body was with due solemnity interred the following day. The question of where the grave should be dug gave rise to a difference of opinion. This, too, was settled by Abū Bakr who decreed that a prophet must be buried on the very spot where he dies. So 'Ā'ishah's chamber became the Prophet's tomb. Then came the ceremony of general pledge-giving at the hand of Abū Bakr as Caliph. After all had sworn allegiance, Abū Bakr delivered an address in the course of which he observed that nowhere in the depth of his heart was there any desire to be elected Caliph, and that he had accepted the responsible office only in obedience to the will of the community. He also expounded principles of caliphate or rulership which, if acted upon by the

7. *The Caliphate*, by Sir W. Muir.

world of Islām, would have saved its world-wide empire from the decomposition and decay which later overtook it. "Help me," said the Caliph, "if I am in the right. Set me right if I am in the wrong!" In other words, he laid it down as the very corner-stone of government that all power is ultimately vested in the people themselves. If a ruler administered this power in the best interests of the people, it was the duty of the people to render him every help. If, however, he worked against the good of the people, he forfeited his claim to the latter's loyalty and support. In the same address, he gave in most pithy words the main function of all governments, viz., the preservation of peace and order and safeguarding the rights of citizens: "The weak among you shall be strong in my eye till I have vindicated his just rights, and the strong among you shall be weak in my eye till I have made him fulfil the obligations due from him." He also told his people in what lay the secret of their life and prosperity: "No nation abandoned Jihād (struggle) in the path of God but God abased it." And he concluded with the beautiful words: "Obey me as long as I obey God and His Prophet. In case I disobey God and His Prophet, I have no right to obedience from you." Each word of this splendid address contains volumes of wisdom and may well serve as a beacon to the Muslim world in these dark and dreary days of universal decay. A Head there must be in any scheme of national organisation, call him king, Caliph, president or Imām; one outward symbol of national unity and solidarity there must be. But the will of this Head of the nation ceases to be binding on the people the moment he transgresses the limits laid down by God and His Prophet.

'Alī and Abū Bakr

There are reports to the effect that for six months 'Alī did not take the oath of allegiance. Their authenticity is, however, doubtful. There are others, on the contrary, which say that he took the oath the same day. It appears that 'Alī and Zubair were not present at the general pledge-giving ceremony at the Mosque. Abū Bakr expressly sent for them from their homes, and remonstrated with them for their staying away which might have led to a split in the camp of Islām. Thereupon both made the formal pledge, accepting Abū Bakr as Caliph. It is just possible that Abū Bakr's verdict against Fāṭimah in the dispute over the Prophet's inheritance might have offended 'Alī as it did the noble lady herself, and the slight rupture between 'Alī and the Caliph on this score might have lent a handle to the report that 'Alī did not take the oath. But the fact that when Madīnah was attacked by hostile forces within a couple of months after the Prophet's demise 'Alī and Zubair stood loyal and steadfast by Abū Bakr and actually participated in the defence operations under the Caliph's orders should suffice to give the lie to all such reports.

Abū Bakr was duly elected as Caliph

Abū Bakr's election settled once and for all the all-important problem of succession to kingship in Islām. Under the constitution of Islām, it was demonstrated for the guidance of posterity that the head of the State must be elected by the people. This golden rule ceased to be the guiding principle of Muslims after the period of the four rightly-guided Caliphs when kingship became a private inheritance. This went a long way to undermine the vigour of the body-politic of Islām. The words in some accounts that pledge-giving to Abū Bakr "came all of a sudden" need not mislead anybody. They certainly do not imply that he was not duly elected. Election, as shown above, was regularly discussed, and after consideration of the pros and cons of the question from diverse points of view choice fell by popular consent on Abū Bakr. The words convey no more than that the election was precipitated. Ordinarily, the first and foremost thing to receive attention should have been the Prophet's funeral and burial. But the separatist activities of some of the Anṣār in the council hall thrust the question of election to the forefront and it was in this sense that it overtook the people by surprise. Even if not thus precipitated, and if an all-Muslim conference had been summoned subsequently, the choice must just the same have fallen on Abū Bakr. He was the right man for this great office. The Prophet himself had during his sickness appointed him to lead the congregational prayers.

In point of experience of men and matters, foresight and physical prowess, he also possessed a testimonial from the Prophet himself inasmuch as the latter had, at the time of emigration, selected him as his own companion.

Usāmah's army despatched to Syria 11 A.H. (632 A.D.)

Abū Bakr's first act on his accession to the Caliphate was the despatching of Usāmah's army to the Syrian Frontier, orders for the expedition having been given by the Prophet himself before he fell ill. The Eastern principality of the Christian Roman Empire was a source of constant trouble to the peaceful Muslim population on the borders of Arabia, and it was to check its depredations that the Prophet had given the orders. The command was entrusted to Usāmah, a young man of twenty, whose father, Zaid, had met martyrdom in an earlier Syrian expedition at the battle of Mūtah. Distinguished men like Abū Bakr and 'Umar were to serve under the youthful general. In this, the Prophet had set a practical example of the lofty ideal of the equality of man for which Islām stands. Zaid was the son of a slave, yet in the house of Islām he was as good as any other, and such illustrious scions of the Quraish as Abū Bakr and 'Umar were required to serve under his command. In person the Prophet had made all arrangements, and bound the banner for the army. Usāmah was encamped outside Madīnah, ready to start, but in the meantime the Prophet's illness took a turn for the worse. Usāmah, therefore, had to postpone the departure of his army. On assuming headship of the government, Abū Bakr directed that the Master's last command must be carried out and ordered Usāmah to proceed. These were, however, critical days at home. The whole of the peninsula of Arabia was in a state of unrest and disorder. Towards the close of the Prophet's life, false prophets such as Musailimah, Aswad and Ṭulaiḥah had already arisen among the Banī Ḥanīfah, the Yamanites and the Banī Asad respectively and created disturbances in the country by beguiling the people. News of the Prophet's death spread like wild fire, and several tribes under the influence of the pretenders rose in revolt against the central authority of Madīnah. Wild rumours had disturbed the peace of the whole country, and Madīnah itself was in danger of attack. An expedition to the Syrian frontier was hardly to be thought of under the circumstances. The companions approached the Caliph to withdraw his orders. To deprive Madīnah of the army protection, they argued, might tempt the insurgents to fall upon the capital itself and put an end to the Caliphate. "Who am I to withhold the army that the Prophet of God himself ordered to proceed!" — was the firm reply of the Caliph. "Come what may," he said, "Madīnah may stand or fall, the Caliphate may live or die, but the Prophet's word must be fulfilled." Representations were also made to him through 'Umar that Usāmah was only a young man and the command of an expedition so great must be entrusted to someone of riper experience. "How can I set aside a man whom the Prophet himself put in command?" was the Caliph's stern reply. At last the army set out, Abū Bakr accompanied it on foot to see it off. Usāmah, who was on horseback, insistently implored the Caliph either to let a horse be brought for him or to allow Usāmah to dismount and walk with him. But to no avail. Thus did he say good-bye to the army consisting of some of the most prominent of the companions. He could not spare 'Umar, but as 'Umar was a soldier of Usāmah's army under the Prophet's orders, the Caliph asked Usāmah to leave him behind.

False claimants to prophethood

The expedition to Syria left Madīnah practically defenceless. The peninsula was in a state of disorder. The main cause, as already stated, was that false prophets had sprung up in different places. Before the advent of the Prophet, Arabia had witnessed no such claimant, but the success of the Prophet's mission fired many a heart with ambition, and several pretenders arose in various parts of the country with claims to Divine mission. As many as four of these pretenders raised their own standards, and to each rallied a large army from among their respective tribes. Yet, within a short time, each one of them met with utter failure, though Islām itself was in a state of helplessness at the time.

Aswad 'Ansī

Of these pretenders, Aswad 'Ansī was the first to arise in Yaman. He was the chief of his tribe and a wealthy man. By giving out that he was in communication with the spirit-world, he began to exercise influence over the people. At the same time, he entered into secret alliance with the neighbouring chieftains and, when he had gathered enough strength he rose in open revolt against Islām and turned the Prophet's deputies out. This was in the year 10 A.H. Aswad fell upon Najrān and annexed that province. He also took possession of Ṣan'ā, the capital of Yaman, slew the Governor, Shahr ibn Bāzān, and married his widow. Thus he subjugated the province of Yaman and the whole of southern Arabia. News of this was brought to the Prophet who commissioned Mu'ādh ibn Jabal and other officials to quell this rising. At length, one night a near relative of the slain governor of Yaman, Firoz Dailmī by name, stole into Aswad's palace and killed him. This happened a day or two before the Prophet's demise, but the news was received in Madīnah after Abū Bakr had been proclaimed Caliph. When, however, reports of the Prophet's death reached Yaman the flames of revolt, subdued to some extent by the murder of Aswad, blazed up once more and the standard of rebellion raised by Aswad was kept flying.

Musailimah

Musailimah was another pretender who set himself up as a prophet. He came of the tribe of Banī Ḥanīfah and was one of the deputation of his people that waited upon the Prophet at Madīnah. On his return home, he began his propaganda by laying claim to prophethood. He composed some clumsy sentences which he gave out as revelations from God and also pretended that he could work miracles. In an epistle to the Prophet he wrote that he had been made a co-partner with him in his Divine commission, and rulership of the peninsula was to be equally divided between the Quraish and his own tribe. In reply, the Prophet wrote to say that, as regards the land, it belonged to God, Who bestowed it on whomsoever He pleased and as regards the hereafter, it was awarded only to the righteous. The Prophet also sent an emissary to Musailimah to dissuade him from his false pretensions. The latter, nevertheless, raised his standard of revolt in Yamāmah and was at length killed in action against the Muslims during the regime of Abū Bakr. The Holy Prophet had once seen in a vision two bracelets on his hands which he had blown off with a puff of breath. This he observed, referred to the two pretenders, Aswad and Musailimah. The interpretation was later on amply borne out by events. Of the four pretenders that rose in Arabia, Aswad and Musailimah were the only two that were killed. The remaining two, Ṭulaiḥah and Sajāḥ, ultimately embraced Islām.

Ṭulaiḥah

Ṭulaiḥah was the chief of the Banī Asad and a famous warrior of Najd. Once it so happened that his tribe was crossing a desert and could not find water. Ṭulaiḥah, pointed out a certain place where, he said, water would be found. This proving true, Ṭulaiḥah laid claim to prophethood calling this his miracle. On the Prophet's death he rose in open revolt but, defeated by K͟hālid, he fled to Syria. Subsequently when amnesty was granted to his tribe, he also returned and joined the fold of Islām. In the reign of 'Umar, he distinguished himself by his valour and feats of arms in Mesopotamia under the banner of Islām.

Sajāḥ

Sajāḥ, a woman, was the fourth pretender who laid claim to a Divine message. She came of the tribe of Banī Yarbū' in central Arabia. Her people had, however, settled in Mesopotamia among the Christian tribe of Banī Tag͟hlib. Thus she was brought up as a Christian. When she heard that the whole Peninsula was in a state of unrest, she seized the opportunity and, entering into alliance with neighbouring Christian tribes, marched against Madīnah at the head of a large army. Reaching Banī Tamīm, she invited her ancestral tribe, the Banī Yarbū' to join hands with her and promised them a share in the rule of the land. Her offer was accepted and the Banī Yarbū' rallied to her standard under the leadership of Mālik ibn Nuwairah. The rest of the tribes of Banī Tamīm, however, rejected her offer and she attempted to overpower them by force of arms. Being repulsed, she directed herself towards Yamāmah to fall upon Musailimah. The latter was in no mood to give battle. He sent her presents and made overtures for peace. She consented to pay him a visit and, during the interview, each confirmed the other's claim to prophethood and a temporary marriage seems to have been the result. After a stay of three days with Musailimah, she retraced her steps to her own people, the Banī Taghlib. The Muslim army was too strong and her courage failed her. She would not risk an encounter. She embraced Islām in the reign of Mu'āwiyah.

The apostasy movement

Here arises a question of great importance. How was it that as soon as the Prophet closed his eyes tribe after tribe renounced the faith and rose in revolt? Was it because their conversion was the result of pressure and, when the Prophet's demise afforded an opportunity to throw off the yoke, they eagerly seized it? How to account for this wild conflagration that spread over the entire length and breadth of the country and threatened to consume all? That some of the tribes did apostatize is no doubt true, but that apostasy affected the whole of Arabia is not borne out historically. The fact is that such Muslims as had embraced Islām some good time before the Prophet's death, and were thus well-grounded in the teachings and spirit of the faith, never wavered in their allegiance. Their devotion was put to the most crucial tests but was never found wanting. Through thick and thin they stood by Islām, staunch and steadfast, and knew not a moment's hesitation to bear the brunt of any hardship in vindication of the faith. Even those who were of no more than a couple of years' standing were devoted, heart and soul. Hence it was that, whereas the countryside all around was in flames, Makkah was perfectly calm and quiet. There was not a single case of apostasy and not a little finger was raised against the authority of Islām. But the vast bulk of the people had only just joined the fold when the Prophet passed away. That they had done so of their own free choice is a clear historical fact. But it is one thing to profess a faith and quite another to become imbued with its inner spirit. This latter they had had neither time nor opportunity to do. They were like children just put to school when the Master passed away, and without his teaching and control they drifted rudderless. Unlettered and of uncouth manners as these Beduins were, it was no easy task to work any appreciable transformation in them in the course of the few months that they had been in the new faith. That the whole of the peninsula, barring a sprinkling of Jews and Christians here and there, abandoned their idolatrous and polytheistic creeds and voluntarily embraced Islām is undoubtedly a most mighty revolution — a revolution without parallel in the pages of history, both sacred and secular — and redounds to the unrivalled glory of the great man who wrought it. Nevertheless, it was a physical impossibility to arrange in the few months that the Prophet lived thereafter, for the proper education or training of the masses scattered over a vast territory with very scanty means of intercourse and communication. Those who came in deputation to the Prophet from distant desert tribes took back with them a deep impress of Islām, but they were only a drop in the ocean. The Prophet did all that could possibly be done to see that the vast masses might receive education in the teachings of Islām. From amongst those who had imbibed the spirit of the faith by sojourn in the Prophet's company, he sent out missionaries to distant parts. But the supply of such qualified men was by no means adequate to meet the demand. Towards the close of the Prophet's life, tribe after tribe sent deputations to declare their allegiance and Madīnah had not enough men to meet the demand. Nor was it desirable to deplete the seat and centre of the movement of all eminent men. The Qur'ān too had forbidden such a course and advised that, rather than disintegrate the force, it must be concentrated, that Madīnah must serve as the centre of learning to which selected men from different tribes should come and receive their education and imbibe the spirit of the faith and thus, duly qualified, go back to their own respective tribes and there kindle the light of Islām.[8] But obviously a scheme on these lines could not but take some time to mature, and the Prophet had hardly had any time to do it. The result was that large numbers of these children of the desert, who had only latterly joined the ranks of Islām and were ignorant of its true worth and spirit, lapsed again into their tribal creeds and once more challenged the authority of Islām.

Refusal to pay Zakāt

It is not historically true, however, that the whole of Arabia renounced Islām. There will still many people who were true to the faith but whose connection with Madīnah, through the temporary ascendancy of the pretenders, was cut off. They were neither apostates nor the confederates of the rebels though, owing to the pressure of the latter, they could not openly side with the central government. There were many others whose only contention was that no zakāt[9] should be levied on them. Born in freedom and bred to freedom, these dwellers of the desert were utter strangers to notions of a state on a national scale with power and authority centralized in one place, to which all must owe allegiance. Their own individual tribal independence they prized above all else. Long centuries of unfettered freedom had rendered them intolerant by temperament of any authority other than their own. Islām, however, stood for the welding of these numerous disjointed and discordant fragments into one harmonious whole. Out of the scattered sands of the desert, so to speak, Islām wanted to build the edifice of a

---

8. "And it does not beseem the believers that they should go forth all together; why should not a company from every party from among them come forth that they may apply themselves to obtain understanding in religion, and that they may warn their people when they go back to them so that they may be cautious" (9 : 122).
9. Zakāt is a tax levied on the rich from among the Muslims for the help of the poor. It is generally one-fortieth of the annual savings when they are above Rs. 52.50

nation, strong and solid. This the tribes could not understand. They could not appreciate the value of a central public treasury for purposes of nation-building: hence their objection to the payment of zakāt. Taking advantage of the general confusion, they refused to pay this tax. But Abū Bakr was particularly strict on this point. National unity, national solidarity, was his foremost concern, and refusal to pay taxes, if unchecked, was bound to dismantle the whole of the fabric. The safety of Islām as a faith was bound up with that of the Muslims as a nation. Hence the Caliph's resolve at all costs to suppress this no-tax movement. He issued an ultimatum to all such tribes as had with-held zakāt that war would be declared against them unless they duly paid. Refusal was tantamount to revolt. There were thus three different causes that contributed to the general confusion at the Prophet's death. Firstly, there were those who were the dupes of false prophets. Secondly, those who objected only to payment of taxes into the central treasury, and as such were confused with the rebels. Thirdly, there were those who were true to Islām but cut off from Muslims: not possessing the strength to fight the insurgents, they remained practically neutral.

The defence of Madīnah

Such was the state of Arabia when Abū Bakr took the reins of government in his hand. Hemmed in by difficulties and dangers, he yet stood undaunted and sent out the best of his men on the Syrian expedition in obedience to the orders of the Prophet. To deplete Madīnah of all troops and thus leave it defenceless at such a critical time may took unstates manlike. Nevertheless, the bold action brought the Caliph's extraordinary force of conviction into the most prominent relief. Their leader's example could not but inspire Muslims with daring, and the handful left behind undertook the defence of the capital. All man-power available in Madīnah and its suburbs was mobilized, and all the approaches to the capital were carefully guarded day and night. Ṭulaiḥah, one of the false prophets, sent his brother to rouse the Beduin tribes to the north of Madīnah. A large army was raised, but these people were neither hostile to Islām nor did they mean to fight for Ṭulaiḥah. They had their own axe to grind. Sending a deputation to the Caliph, they requested that they might be exempted from payment of zakāt. The Madinites considered this as a godsend, and many were of opinion that under the circumstances it would be wise to grant their demand. Abū Bakr was, however, more far-sighted. He could see the far-reaching and disastrous effect of yielding on this point. Exception in one case would open the door for similar demands from other quarters, and Islām would ultimately lose its hold on the whole of the peninsula. Moreover, payment of zakāt was a most imperative injunction of the Qur'ān, and it was not for a Caliph to waive an obligation imposed by God. Hence, unmoved by all considerations of policy, Abū Bakr stuck to his resolution in the face of war clouds on all sides. "If even so much as a string to tie a camel is withheld from zakāt," he replied, "they shall have war." This resolute refusal rendered the plight of Madīnah all the more critical. The Caliph had all Muslims summoned and told them to be on their guard every minute. At any moment the town might be stormed. 'Alī, Zubair and Ṭalḥah were put in command of the garrison.

Rebel attack on Madīnah repulsed

The insurgents gathered and encamped at a place called Dhu-l-Qaṣṣah. After three days, they advanced on Madīnah. The Madīnah advance guards at once sent word to the town, and immediately the Muslims were on the march to meet the invaders. The Beduins were hardly prepared for such a reception. They were under the impression that Madīnah was absolutely defenceless, the troops having been despatched to Syria. Thus confronted with a bold front, they turned their backs. The Muslims kept up the pursuit some distance and then returned. During the night, however, Abū Bakr got his men together, and early in the morning, while it was yet dark, fell upon the Beduins again. Not able to resist the onslaught, they took to flight. The Caliph, after stationing a detachment at Dhu-l-Qaṣṣah, returned to the capital. This encounter had a great moral effect. The Muslims took heart and the Beduins had a most salutary lesson. The central government at Madīnah, they now perceived, was strong enough to curb any insurrection, notwithstanding the absence of regular troops on the Syrian expedition. This went a long way to restore the prestige of Madīnah, with the result that zakāt money came pouring in from several quarters. Rebels and the pretenders lost their spirit. This was all due to the unshakable rock of faith on which Abū Bakr took his stand. To him is due the credit of piloting the bark of Islām to a haven of safety in such foul and stormy weather.

In the meanwhile, Usāmah returned from his Syrian expedition. The Caliph put him in charge of the defence of Madīnah and himself marched at the head of a small army to Rabdhah[10] which was now the rendezvous of the rebels. Being defeated, the latter fled and joined the forces of Ṭulaiḥah.

Despatch of expedition to different quarters

Abū Bakr now embarked on the extermination of the insurrection, root and branch. Dividing the army into eleven battalions and putting each under the command of a tried veteran he directed the campaign simultaneously on various fronts. Khalīd ibn Walīd was deputed to march first against Ṭulaiḥah and then against Mālik ibn Nuwāirah; 'Ikrimah, son of Abū Jahl, was sent against Musailimah; Shuraḥbīl was to reinforce 'Ikrimah; and Mahājir ibn Abī Umayyah was to invade Yaman and Ḥaḍramaut. One battalion was despatched to keep guard on the Syrian frontier; two were sent out to suppress the rising in 'Umān and Mahrah; one was required to curb the tribe of Quzā'ah, and yet another to fight the Banī Salīm and Hawāzin. Upon himself Abū Bakr undertook the duties of generalissimo with Madīnah for his base, from where he watched and directed the campaigns. He also sent a proclamation to his officers as well as to the tribes, directing the former that they must be moderate and kindly in their dealings with the latter,

10. A place about three days' journey from Madīnah.

that before engaging in action they must first invite the belligerent tribe to Islām, that they must desist from fighting should the tribe concerned accept their invitation, and that in case of refusal alone they were to resort to fighting. The usual call to prayer, the instructions continued, was to be considered sufficient evidence that a particular tribe was Muslim.

Object of expeditions

It must be clearly understood that the object of these campaigns was no more than the suppression of rebellion. It is legitimately open to every government to punish rebels, to execute their ring-leaders and, if necessary, to declare war on them. But over and above this, there were several other reasons that called for action. In the first place, these rebels had wantonly shed the blood of peaceful Muslim citizens here and there, causing disorder and disturbance. Again, they were out to extirpate the rule of Islām. The slightest leniency would have added enormously to the fury of the conflagration. And yet again, in the midst of these rebel tribes there were clans that were loyal to the Government but were cut off from intercourse with Madīnah. Even in such far-off parts as Ḥaḍramaut and Baḥrain, the loyalists were there side by side with the rebels. In several places, if one clan of a tribe had risen in revolt, there was another that refused to join hands with the rebels. Under the circumstances the Caliph's proclamation that before starting the operation, it must be ascertained whether or not the particular tribe was Muslim was perfectly justified, and must on no account be considered as anything in the form of conversion by force. As a matter of fact, it was indispensable that such a notice should have been broadcast among both the officers and the tribes in order to discriminate between rebels and loyalists. It was just a precaution lest seeing a tribe in revolt, all its component clans should be mistaken as rebels and dealt with as such. And to extinguish the fire of revolt was the paramount call of the moment. Had the task not been undertaken, it would have been a matter of days for the rebels to reduce the power of Islām in Arabia to ashes.

Khālid defeats Ṭulaiḥah

First of all, let us follow Khālid on his expedition against Ṭulaiḥah–Khālid at once a soldier and a general whose peer it is difficult for the history of heroism to produce. At the head of his men, he marched against Ṭulaiḥah who had now been joined by the tribe of Ghaṭafān under its chief 'Uyainah. Some people of the tribe of Banī Ṭay had also made common cause with him. Khālid's negotiations, however, succeeded in winning over the Banī Ṭay to the side of Islām, and his army defeated Ṭulaiḥah in the field of Buzākhah. 'Uyainah was taken prisoner and brought to Madīnah, where he declared his repentance. Ṭulaiḥah escaped to Syria. Khālid encamped here for some time and established peace. He forgave the Banī Asad but punished those who were guilty of murder. The tribes that had been cut off from the main body of Islām owing to the revolt of Ṭulaiḥah also rejoined the forces of Islām.

Mālik Ibn Nuwairah

Having suppressed Ṭulaiḥah, Khalīd next advanced against the Banī Tamīm. To this tribe belonged the clan Banī Yarbū' which had, under its chief, Mālik ibn Nuwairah, joined hands with Sajāh, the false prophetess. The rest of the clans of Banī Tamīm one by one offered their loyalty to Khālid. Banī Yarbū' alone kept away. Khālid attacked them but found that they hastily decamped. Some Muslims were of opinion that they should be left alone, but Khālid gave chase and took several prisoners. Mālik ibn Nuwairah being one of the captives. Through misunderstanding of an order of Khālid some of these prisoners including Mālik, were put to the sword. A complaint against this was made to Abū Bakr, who summoned Khālid for trial. When, however, the whole truth came to light, he was found not guilty and acquitted.

Khālid defeats Musailimah

After restoring peace and order in this part, Khālid was instructed by the Caliph to march against Musailimah. This expedition had originally been entrusted to the command of 'Ikrimah and Shuraḥbīl, but Musailimah's hosts far outnumbered the Muslim troops. 'Ikrimah acted rashly, resorted to a hasty attack and suffered defeat. Consequently the victorious troops of Khālid were now ordered to proceed against Musailimah, while 'Ikrimah was ordered to 'Umān. Musailimah had a large army sixty thousand strong, and Khālid had a comparatively much smaller one, but the deficiency in numbers was made up by the strength of faith of the Muslim troops. A fierce battle was fought at Yamāmah, one of the most important battles in the history of Islām. Much valour was displayed on both sides. Several times the Muslims were repulsed but every time they fell back, they returned to the attack with renewed spirit. Musailimah's troops were at length put to flight. They took refuge in a garden with a high rampart. This stronghold was, however, speedily stormed and won. One of the Muslim soldiers, Barā' ibn Mālik, displayed remarkable valour on this occasion. He asked his comrades to lift him up, and thus, he scaled the rampart, without hesitation he jumped down into the garden among the surging masses of the enemy, and with his sword cut a way through them rushing right to the gate of the garden and flinging it wide open. Musailimah was killed by a Negro slave, Waḥshī by name, and his army took to flight. In all, seven thousand Muslims fell in this battle, including a large number of those who had committed the whole of the Qur'ān to memory. The loss in human life on the other side was much greater. The Banī Ḥanīfah surrendered. When a deputation from that tribe visited Madīnah to pay homage to Abū Bakr, the Caliph was curious to know what the teachings were that Musailimah had given them. On their reciting a few sentences, he expressed his astonishment that they had accepted such nonsense.

Bahrain rebellion crushed

While Khālid secured victory on this front, putting down the insurrection at its strongest centre, the rest of the expeditions of Muslim troops in other parts of the country met with similar success. Baḥrain was another such part. Shortly after the news of the Prophet's death reached Baḥrain, the Muslim governor of the province, Mundhir, also died. This gave rise to disorder. One of the tribes, Banī 'Abd al-Qais, stuck to Islām, but the other Banī

Bakr, renounced the faith and rose in open revolt. A battle ensued between these two tribes. The Banī Bakr asked for help from Persia, and the Banī 'Abd al-Qais from Madīnah. A contingent of Muslim soldiers was despatched under the command of 'Alā ibn al-Ḥaḍramī to their assistance. The combined forces of Banī Bakr and the Persians were defeated. They took shelter within a fort but were scattered by the Muslims. Thus was Baḥain totally cleared of rebellion.

'Umān and Mahrah cleared of rebels

Insurrections at two other places, 'Umān and Mahrah, were likewise crushed. This expedition was led by Ḥudhaifah. 'Ikrimah after his reverse at the hands of Musailimah was also sent to Ḥudhaifah's help. At 'Umān a certain man, Laqīt ibn Mālik, had laid claim to prophethood and had raised a large army at Dabā', the capital of the province. The Muslim army was victorious. Leaving Ḥudhaifah at 'Umān, 'Ikrimah proceeded against Mahrah, and restored peace and order there.

Yaman and Ḥaḍramaut restored

Ziyād ibn Labīd was the collector of zakāt for Ḥaḍramaut and Kindah. On the Prophet's death, Ash'ath ibn Qais turned apostate along with his tribe, and raised the standard of revolt at Ḥaḍramaut. Ziyād rallied the loyal tribes and gave him battle, but was defeated and fled to Madīnah. From there, he was sent back assisted by Muhājir, but no decisive battle took place. 'Ikrimah, who had in the meantime put down insurrections at 'Umān and Mahrah, was consequently sent to Ḥaḍramaut to reinforce the Muslim troops. Ash'ath was besieged and taken prisoner. He was brought to Madīnah where he embraced Islām. In the meanwhile, the province of Yaman had also been purged of rebellion.

Conflict with the Roman Empire and Persia

Within a year, Abū Bakr crushed all the forces of disorder and revolt in the territory which had, during the Prophet's lifetime, come under the sway of Islām. Having set his own house in order, the Caliph next addressed himself to the strengthening of the Persian and Syrian frontiers. This gave rise to the long chain of wars that ended, during the reign of 'Umar, in the subjugation of the Roman and Persian Empires by the Muslims. In the rebellion of Baḥrain, it will be recollected, the rebels sought the help of Persia which actually sent its forces against the Muslims. This was an act of open hostility and a declaration of war against the Caliphate. This is a point that must be specially borne in mind; for this, in fact, was the starting point of the war against Persia. It was Persia that assumed an aggressive attitude by penetrating into the territory of Islām and actively helping the rebels against the government of Islām. Furthermore, from the side of Mesopotamia where Persian influence was strong, there was another incursion into Arabia by Sajāḥ, who pretended to be a prophetess. She was actually out on an expedition against Madīnah, the capital of Islām, and only turned back after coming as far as Yamāmah in Central Arabia. It is unthinkable that a woman representing an insignificant tribe should have the audacity to march on the heart of Islām, unless instigated and backed by its powerful neighbour. Anyway, the fact that a tribe on the Persian border and under Persian influence should invade Arabia is enough to incriminate Persia of another act of grave aggression. It was but natural under these circumstances that the government of Islām should anticipate danger on the Persian border and, in self-defence, address itself to strengthening it. Consequently the first expedition were all confined to the Arab colonies to the west of the river Euphrates. As a matter of fact, the Muslims would have been perfectly justified even if they had pushed forward to Mesopotamia. The rules of morality as well as international law would have been on their side. War had actually been declared against them and, what is more, Persian troops had already encroached upon Arabia to help the insurgents. It would have been suicidal on the part of the Muslims to sit still. Historians who have accused Abū Bakr of deliberately provoking hostilities with the neighbouring empires in order to keep the Arab tribes busy and divert their attention from internal disorders have obviously ignored these hard facts of history. The explanation seems to have been prompted by the common obsession of a certain class of writers that Islām was propagated at the point of the sword. Not finding a single incident in the life of the Prophet, warranting such a charge, they turned to the period of the Caliphs in quest of material. There they saw wars waged with the neighbouring empires and, in their impatience somehow to strengthen their preconceived notion, jumped to the conclusion that these wars were inspired by a spirit of proselytism, forgetting that the initiative in them all was taken by the other side.

Insurrection called for fortification of frontiers

A cursory glance at contemporary events in Arabia is enough to exonerate Abū Bakr of the charge that in waging these wars he was moved by his zeal of conversion or love of conquest. A most dangerous insurrection which threatened the very existence of Islām had just been put down. It was but common foresight and obvious precaution to keep under proper control all the forces of domestic disorder. And Abū Bakr had hardly strong enough army to do it. It must be remembered that Abū Bakr never resorted to drastic measures against insurgents, measures which are adopted even today, in the name of discipline and prestige, by the most civilized nations. When once order was restored, not a single individual was molested. Not a man was killed simply because he had taken part in the rebellion. Even the ringleaders were granted amnesty. Under such circumstances, it was the paramount duty of the Caliph to establish strong garrisons in the affected areas to prevent a relapse to disorder. The elements of trouble were still there and might burst out again at any moment. Demonstration of military power alone could hold them in check. To maintain peace and order, therefore, should have been the foremost anxiety of the Caliph and this could be done only by strong military posts scattered all over the land. How fantastic to allege that under conditions such as these, when he wanted every available man for service at home, his expeditions on the frontiers of Arabia were inspired by lust of loot or territorial extension! The flames of a terrible insurrection had just been brought under control, and to entertain such ideas at such a moment would have been absurd on the face of it. That he actually sent out his troops to strengthen the frontiers only shows the extremity of the danger at those points. There was in all truth enough danger at home but, it seems, that danger from abroad was even greater and required immediate action. It was thus not the so-called loot-lust of the Caliph but his far-sightedness that urged him to grapple without the least delay with this major threat, even at the risk of ignoring the minor danger at home. And it speaks much for his statesmanship. Unless immediately countered and nipped in the bud, the tide of mischief on both Persian and Syrian frontiers must have engulfed Arabia once more and plunged it into the chaos from which it had just been extricated; and that to an extent beyond the control of the government of Islām.

Abū Bakr's motives in sending expeditions to frontiers

The idea that the expeditions against Persia and the Roman Empire were intended to keep the Beduin tribes occupied with the lure of loot, thereby diverting their attention from fostering trouble at home, is a mere myth. It is inconceivable that men with such scant fidelity to the throne of Islām should have been entrusted with the most vital function of opposing two most mighty empires. Contemporary history bears testimony to the fact that for a considerable period the tribes that had participated in the insurrection were debarred from military service. A historian like Sir William Muir, by no means friendly in his attitude towards Islām, admits that when these expeditions were first launched, Abū Bakr forbade the enlistment of all who had taken part in the rebellion. This ban continued throughout his rule. The same historian records that while the Caliph was on his death-bed, word was brought from Muthannā, who was then in Mesopotamia, that the danger on the Persian frontier was on the increase, and, therefore, in order to raise additional forces to cope with the threatening situation, permission should be given for enrolment of members of the tribes that had taken part in the rebellion. Yet in the same breath it is contended that the Persian and Syrian campaigns were intended to lure away these rebel tribes from home politics! How could this be so when the door of military service was shut against them? This clearly shows that the accusation is absolutely baseless. No doubt a time did come when the ban was removed and the door to military service was opened to the rebels. But this was at a much later period when, in view of the vast hosts put in the field by Persia and Rome, it became necessary proportionately to multiply the forces of Islām. To judge Abū Bakr's motives at the launching of these expeditions by subsequent developments is certainly bad logic. The only permissible data on which any such judgment can be based would obviously be the events and conditions that preceded these expeditions, not those that followed as a later development, mostly during the reign of the second Caliph.

The strength of the Caliphate as compared with the two Empires

In order to discover the true causes that led to these wars we must view them in the context of the state of things obtaining at the time. At a cursory glance historical facts show that the Arabs could not dare invade two such mighty empires as Persia and Rome. The Caliph could not dream of such an undertaking. Persia and Rome were far too formidable and their very name inspired terror in the heart of an Arab. The power of Arabia was comparatively insignificant. Several parts of the peninsula were under the sway of one or other of these neighbouring kingdoms. Persia controlled a vast tract to the east, whereas the northern part was under the domination of Rome. Then there was a huge force at the disposal of each, equipped with all weapons of offence and defence, with all the resources of organisation and a rich treasury at its back. Arabia, on the other hand, had neither men nor money to cope with an expedition so stupendous. It had just emerged from most terrible internecine warfare. The erstwhile rebel population could hardly be trusted to stand loyal and steadfast by their country in its hour of need. There was no regular army worth the name, no money, no munitions. Is it conceivable that, situated as the government of Islām was, it could have wantonly set out on a campaign of aggression against two such formidable foes at one and the same time? Here is food for thought for all impartial students of the history of Islām. Another equally baseless accusation against Abū Bakr is that in undertaking the campaigns against Persia and Syria he was inspired by a fanatic fervour for proselytism. The Arabs were too weak to think of subduing two such mighty empires and imposing their faith on them. On the other hand, they themselves were in danger of being crushed any moment by these powerful neighbours.

Aggression on the enemy's part

What after all, then was the motive that urged Abū Bakr to resort to a course fraught with such danger? The foremost thing to receive his attention after having quelled the insurrection should have been to address himself to internal management and the organization of administration. Rather than set his own house in order, what made him rush to the frontiers? As already stated, it was the peril of utter extermination of the power of Islām, standing out so prominently in those quarters. The neighbouring empires were fast fomenting trouble on the frontiers which might any day have enveloped the whole of the peninsula in a conflagration far more serious than the one just subdued. The Caliph's discerning eye perceived the danger and having perceived it, met it with the quickness and courage characteristic of Islām in its palmy days. To strengthen and fortify the frontier, whether in the physical or spiritual sense, is a most important part of the teachings of Islām. This was the guiding principle of the life of the Prophet as well as of his immediate disciples, who had imbibed the spirit of the message of Islām from the Messenger direct. As a matter of fact it is due, among other causes, mainly to the neglect of this golden rule of national security that the various Muslim powers of this age have fallen prey to foreign machinations and greed. A strong frontier is the very first requisite of stable and secure government. Consequently, no sooner was the insurrection put down that Abū Bakr concentrated his attention on this most vital problem. Notwithstanding his realization of the great risk he was running in venturing upon an undertaking so hazardous, notwithstanding the fact that he had no well-organized regular army, notwithstanding all the difficulties and dangers with which this enterprise was beset, he cared not a bit when the clear and imperative call of duty came and, with fearless pluck, threw his ill-equipped, ill-disciplined scanty forces against a mighty foe. How characteristically Islamic! Whereas, on the one hand, Muslims were scrupulous to a degree never to encroach upon others' rights, they were, on the other, possessed of a sense of duty so high as to face, if need be, the whole world single-handed. They would as readily plunge into flames of fire as dash to a pleasant green meadow, should that be the dictate of duty. They rushed to where the swords and spears fell thick and fast as they would to a regal throne. True, they never took the initiative but, when once the enemy transgressed upon their rights or violated their honour, they were not slow to take up the gauntlet, even though they had to oppose the whole world. So it was that, notwithstanding their own weakness and the enormous strength of Persia and Rome, they promptly and simultaneously took up arms against both when they perceived that they were bent on mischief. Sir William Muir's words in this connection are noteworthy: "No sooner was apostasy put down than, first in Chaldea and then in Syria, collision with wild border tribes kindled the fire of foreign war."[11]

Let it be remembered, therefore, that in the Persian and Syrian wars, Muslims were by no means the aggressors. All they wanted was to fortify their own frontiers and, when they did so, Persia and the Roman Empire jumped in. To quote the same historian again:

"Chaldea and southern Syria belong properly to Arabia. The tribes inhabiting this region, partly heathen but chiefly (at least in name) Christian, formed an integral part of the Arab race and as such fell within the immediate scope of the New Dispensation. When, however, these came into collision with the Muslim columns on the frontier, they were supported by their respective

---

11. The Caliphate p. 42.

sovereigns, — the western by the Kaisar, and the eastern by the Chosroes. Thus the struggle widened, and Islām was brought presently face to face in mortal conflict with the two great powers of the East and of the West."[12]

It is thus obvious that the Caliphate of Islām acted up to the true spirit of Islamic teachings. It did not take the initiative in these hostilities. When, however, it took in hand certain defensive measures and mobilized forces such as they had on their own frontiers, the neighbouring powers of Persia and Rome, in the intoxication of their military strength, made it a pretext and rushed to grapple with the Muslims.

Trouble in Arabia was fomented by Persia and Rome

History has not preserved details of the origin of these wars, but there are on record events which throw light on the question. When Baḥrain rose in revolt against the central authority of Islām, Persia openly sent reinforcements to help the insurgents. A Christian woman, Sajāḥ, at the head of Christian tribes, marched from her home on the frontier of Persia against Madīnah, the capital of Islām, and traversed the country right up to the central part. Towards the north, in the territory under the influence of the Christian empire of Rome, Ṭulaiḥah raised his standard of revolt. These are some clear indications that the insurrection in the several parts of the peninsula was inspired and fanned by both Persia and Rome. These parts were either immediately on the borders adjoining these two powers or under their direct influence. Again, Persia exercised a very wide influence over the Province of Yaman, another area affected by the general revolt. It is thus likely that over and above the open assistance which Persia and the Roman Empire rendered to the insurgents, the insurrection itself was due to their secret machinations. The Roman Empire, like some modern

12. Ibid., p. 46.

states, was particularly a past-master in the art of wire-pulling from behind the scenes. It seems, therefore, that these two neighbours did all they could to foment trouble in the various provinces of Arabia that were in any way in contact with them. To safeguard against a repetition of the mischief, the Muslim Government was constrained to resort to military operations on the frontiers. And when it did this, the Persian and Roman empires committed open acts of hostility under the impression that they would thus inspire awe in the hearts of the Arabs. But Islām had brought about a change over Arabia, and the two empires had to answer for the aggression.

It is from such stray events met with in the pages of history that we can trace the causes of these wars. Early historians were not particular about going into the why and wherefore of things. They were just chroniclers of events, beyond which they worried little to go. To ascertain the underlying causes, we must piece together those various events and draw our own conclusions. This is exactly how we are able to tell the causes of the various wars during the Prophet's lifetime, the only advantage in the latter case being that these events have been recorded and handed down to us in greater detail. The period of the early Caliphate, considered comparatively far less important, is not characterised by the same profusion of narration, and most important episodes have often received but a brief reference, — a fact admitted by recent historians. Nevertheless, the guiding rule as to the root causes of things is the same, viz., reading between the apparently scattered events and discovering the common thread running through all. The accuracy or otherwise of the conclusion must obviously depend on that of the events selected as data for investigation. And with this rule in view, we can safely vouch for the accuracy of the conclusions drawn above as regards the causes of the Persian and Syrian campaigns of the Muslims. The events that we have drawn upon are all events of unimpeachable historic authenticity.

Mut͟hannā's Expedition, 12 A.H. (633 A.D.)

We will now take up the course of the expedition which brought about a clash with Persia. In the suppression of insurrection in the province of Baḥrain, Muthannā ibn Ḥārith Shaibānī had rendered much assistance. The next that we hear of him is that he advanced northward along the coast of the Persian Gulf. These are apparently two disconnected events. To find the connecting link we must call in the aid of a third event. Elsewhere we have been told that the Persians had sent reinforcements to the tribe of Banī Bakr during the Baḥrain insurrection. Hence it seems most likely that this expedition by Muthannā towards the north was undertaken to clear that territory of the insurgents and their allies, the Persians. This was the territory where, besides several other tribes, dwelt Muthannā's own tribe. All these tribes were smarting under the constant high-handedness and oppression of the Persians. Consequently, Muthannā, entering into alliance with the rest of the aggrieved tribes, raised an army of 8,000 strong. This, however, was only too small a force as compared with the hosts of the Persian Empire.

Khālid reinforces Muthannā and assumes command

Thus it was that Abū Bakr ordered his famous general Khālid, who had by now suppressed the revolt of Musailimah to proceed immediately to Ubullah, a place somewhere near modern Baṣrah, to reinforce Muthannā, sending instructions at the same time to the latter to entrust the chief command to Khālid. The first encounter between Muslim and Persian forces took place at Ḥafīr, some fifty miles to the south of Ubullah, almost on the border of Persia. The Persians were routed. This battle is known as *Dhāt al-salāsil*, i.e., the battle of the chains, from the fact that the Persian soldiers fastened themselves together by chains.

Ḥīrah taken

Giving the enemy no respite, Khālid defeated them in another pitched battle at Ullais, and marched on along the western bank of the Euphrates right up to Ḥīrah, near modern Kūfah. All territory to the west of the river which, though usurped by the Persians, was inhabited by purely Arab tribes was subjugated and annexed to the mother country. The Persian forces were driven to Mesopotamia to the east of the river. Ḥīrah, the capital of a tributary state of that name under Persia, was also besieged, and the Christian government of the place soon surrendered entering into a treaty with the Muslims by which they agreed to pay tribute to Arabia.

Jizyah and charge of loot

The tribute taken from the Christians of Ḥīrah was termed *jizyah*[13] and this was the first *jizyah* levied in the history of Islām. In addition to the fixed amount of tribute agreed upon, the Hirites also offered presents. These the Caliph accepted, but deducted their value from the amount of jizyah. How presumptuous in the face of such noble instances to impute to the Muslims such base motives as the lust of loot! No doubt, when an army was defeated in open battle, their stocks of provisions and other belongings fell into the hands of the victorious Muslims. But this is not loot. Such spoils of war are considered in this twentieth century of civilization as a perfectly lawful prize for the victors. The Muslims did no more

---

13. The word *jizyah* is derived from *Jazā'* which means *compensation*. This was a tax levied on non-Muslim subjects under the rule of Islām, so called because it was a tax for the protection of life and property which that rule guaranteed them. Muslim subjects were exempt from this tax in consideration of military service, which for them was compulsory. As a matter of fact, they too were made to pay for that protection, but in different form. They bore the hardships of a military life, they fought the country's battles, they laid down their lives in defence of the country. Non-Muslims were exempt from all this, and in lieu of this they contributed their share in the shape of money. It is obvious which of the two alternatives is the easier. In countries where conscription is the law to-day, there would certainly be many who would be glad to buy their exemption from military service so cheaply, paying a small amount as tax. It must be remembered, furthermore, that the tax was not indiscriminately charged to every non-Muslim subject. Males under twenty and above fifty, all females, those suffering from some chronic disease, the blind and the poor were all exempt. As a matter of fact, the Muslims had also to pay a tax in addition under the name of zakāt, and this was much heavier than jizyah as it was levied at the rate of 2½ per cent, on all savings annually.

than avail themselves of such prizes of war, a thing sanctioned by all ancient and modern canons of civilised warfare. The question, however, remains whether the prospects of these spoils, perfectly legitimate in themselves, were in any way a factor in impelling Muslims to undertake these wars. Nothing could be further from their hearts. Who, after all, were the men responsible for launching the wars? Why, men like Abū Bakr and 'Umar. Now if they were really actuated by the motives ascribed to them, they should have taken the lion's share of the spoils for themselves. But it is a fact of history that they never utilized such acquisitions for personal aggrandizement. Nay, more. When during the reign of 'Umar Persia and Syria fell before Muslim arms and large quantities of such spoils — money, goods, precious stones — came pouring into the Muslims' hands, the noble Caliph could not restrain his tears. "I fear," said he, actually weeping, "lest these appurtenances of an ease-loving life may bring ruin." A man with a heart so free of all love of filthy lucre could not enter upon even a day's fighting for such a sordid thing as loot. If Muslims were out for loot, as alleged, they should have behaved as despoilers in the lands they conquered. But history tells a different tale. Their treatment was marked by exemplary moderation and magnanimity, so much so that in Syria the Christian population preferred Muslim rule to that of their own co-religionists while the fire-worshipping population of Persia looked upon the Muslims as their deliverers from the yoke of their own kith and kin. Even Sir William Muir has been constrained to admit this:

"The people of Syria, too, apart from the religious persecution to which they had been subjected, suffered from increased taxation, and in consequence remained passive spectators of the invasion of their country, hoping more, indeed, from an occupation by the Arabs, who abstained from pillage, and whose rule was mild and tolerant, than from the continuance of status quo."[14]

---

14. The Caliphate, p. 65.

What is more, side by side with the Muslim soldiers and under the flag of Islām could also be seen many Christian soldiers fighting against Persia. No writer has ever made the suggestion that they also were out for loot.

Conquest of Anbār and 'Ain Al-Tamr

From Ḥīrah, Khālid advanced northward till he reached Anbār, a place on the bank of the Euphrates, some eight miles from Babel. There he laid siege to the fort and captured it. Some three stages further on was 'Ain al-Tamr, the centre of the mischief of Banī Taghlib. It was from here that Sajāḥ, the female pretender to prophethood, had set out at the head of the Banī Taghlib to attack Madīnah. It was only natural that Khālid should have turned to such a stronghold. This he did and in no time captured the place. Khālid was quite justified in pushing his campaign so far and clearing the whole of the territory to the west of the Euphrates. With anything short of this, a half-measure, Arabia could not be secure from danger in that quarter. And, considering that hostilities against Arabia had actually been hatched and launched from there under the leadership of Sajāḥ, it was necessary that the enemy should be subjugated there. The battle of 'Ain al-Tamr was also won by the Muslims, and Khālid encamped there for some time.

Expedition on the Northern Frontier

Let us now turn to the Syrian frontier. Danger from the Persian frontier had arisen after the Prophet's death, but on the frontier of Syria a skirmish between Muslims and the Chief of Buṣrā had taken place much earlier, in the year 8 A.H., in the Prophet's lifetime. Again, when intelligence was brought to the Prophet concerning the military preparation of the northern tribes, he had in person led an expedition 30,000 strong and marched as far as Tabūk. Finding no enemy troops, however, the Prophet had returned without striking a blow. This was in the year 9 A.H. Yet again, only a couple of days before his death, the Prophet had ordered another expedition towards the Syrian frontier under the command of Usāmah. These events show that the Christian tribes on the Syrian frontier and Heraclius himself were far more inimically disposed towards Arabia than the Persians were; and an invasion of Arabia from this quarter was much easier than from the Persian frontier. Madīnah was comparatively far nearer the Syrian frontier and, besides, the route was easy. There are many reasons to believe that the Muslims apprehended far more danger from the Syrian frontier. Thus 'Umar on one occasion in the Holy Prophet's life, when a certain man said that a great calamity had happened, inquired anxiously: "Have the Ghassanides come?" The Ghassanides were a Christian tribe in the north of Arabia on the Syrian border. The Prophet, therefore, was ever on his guard against that quarter and thrice in his own lifetime had taken or ordered expedition thither.

After the Prophet's death the whole of Arabia was plunged into anarchy and the crisis called for the strongest military force. Nevertheless, the army of 'Usāmah was not detained for a day and was ordered to proceed to the Syrian frontier. This also throws light on the great danger that threatened Arabia from that quarter, danger far greater than the widespread insurrection at home. On 'Usāmah's return, when expeditions were despatched to various parts of Arabia, one was again sent to the Syrian frontier under the command of Khālid ibn Sa'īd. Abū Bakr's instructions to this general are particularly noteworthy. He was ordered not to attack the enemy but to repulse any attacks made on him. It had already been discussed at length that the petty power of Arabia could not think of invading the mighty Roman Empire, especially at a time when it was itself hemmed in with difficulties on all sides. It was only a defensive campaign, the commander having strict orders under no circumstances to strike the first blow. The government of Heraclius, however, was on the look-out for an opportunity and the crisis created by the general revolt afforded it. Now, thought the enemy, was the time to strike and strike hard. Notwithstanding the fact that Khālid ibn Sa'īd was quietly encamped and had not unsheathed his sword, the Romans roused a Beduin tribe against the Muslims, at the same time starting their own manoeuvres for an attack. The hands of Abū Bakr were thus forced by the aggressiveness of the adversary to declare war against the Roman Empire, and further reinforcements were consequently forthwith hurried to the Syrian frontiers.

The Battle of Ajnādain, 13 A.H. (634 A.D.)

There prevails some confusion as to the exact year of the Syrian war. It seems that the final decision to declare war was taken about the beginning of 13 A.H. The Muslim army advanced on Palestine in three or four divisions. Instructions were also issued to Khālid ibn Walīd, who was at the time lying encamped at 'Ain al-Tamr on the Persian frontier, at once to proceed to the help of Khālid ibn Sa'īd. Leaving Muthannā in charge of the Persian frontier with half the army, Khālid accordingly marched to Syria with the other half. The total strength of the Muslim army was forty thousand while the host of the Roman Empire numbered two hundred and forty thousand. The two armies met at Ajnādain. Three thousand Muslims fell on the field but they won the day. This was on the 28th Jumāda I, 13 A.H.. Routed here, Heraclius fled to Anṭāqiyah (Antioch), whereas the Muslim General, Khālid, having won the battle marched straight on to Damascus and laid siege to that historic town. But this episode we must leave to the Caliphate of 'Umar, to which period it properly belongs. The news of the victory of Ajnādain reached Madīnah just at the time when Abū Bakr was in the last agonies of death.

Abū Bakr's illness and death, Jumāda II, 13 A.H. (Aug. 634 A.D.)

It was on the 7th Jumāda II, 13 A.H., that Abū Bakr fell ill. When the disease took a serious turn, he sent for prominent Muslims and consulted them as to a suitable successor. All eyes turned to 'Umar, just as at the Prophet's death all had turned to Abū Bakr. Every one considered him to be the right man for the exalted office. Throughout his reign, Abū Bakr had been conducting state affairs in consultation with 'Umar. He consulted first 'Abd al-Raḥmān ibn 'Auf, then 'Uthmān. Both favoured 'Umar. Thereafter he asked the opinions of Sa'īd ibn Zaid, Usaid ibn Ḥuḍair and other Muhājirīn (Emigrants) and Anṣār (Helpers). The choice of all fell on 'Umar. There were some who feared that by temperament 'Umar was somewhat harsh. Responsibility of office, reassured the dying Caliph, would soften him. Thus with the consultation of Muslims, Abū Bakr nominated 'Umar as his successor, and passed away on Tuesday 22nd Jumāda II, 13 A.H. (23rd August, 634 A.D.) after a fortnight's illness, and was buried beside the Holy Prophet. Reposing side by side with his beloved Master the devoted companionship which he so pre-eminently bore the Prophet in lifetime was now continued after death. The period of his Caliphate was a little over two years, but immense work had been done during this short time.

Simplicity of his life

Abū Bakr was an embodiment of simplicity. Raised to kingship, he retained the same simplicity of life, the same simple dress, the same simple house, the same simple food. To him no work, however humble, was beneath his dignity. He did his own work when Caliph just as before holding that high position. Nay, he even did all sorts of little offices to others. Like his great Master, the Prophet, earthly kingship had wrought not the slightest change in him. If the Prophet set the high example of combining the life of a hermit with the position of a king, even so did he, the greatest of his disciples and the dearest of his companions, faithfully walk in his footsteps. When elected Caliph, the very next day he was seen wending his way to the market with his merchandise. 'Umar chanced to meet him on the way and reminded him that on his shoulders lay the onerous burden of kingship, and as such it was not possible for him to to carry on business pursuits together with state affairs. To maintain his family, replied the Caliph, he must work. The companions held a consultation and calculating his usual domestic expenses settled an annual allowance of 2,500 dirhams on him, which was subsequently raised to about 500 dirhams a month. At the time of death, he had in his possession an old sheet of cloth and a camel, the property of the public treasury. These he returned to his successor, 'Umar. As regards the winding sheet to cover his corpse, he advised that an old piece of cloth, duly washed, would do. The living, he said, stood in greater need of a new piece than the dead. As regards his sincerity of conviction and faith in the Prophet, a historian like Sir William Muir advances this as an argument in support of the Prophet's sincerity: "Had Muḥammad begun his career as a conscious imposter, he never could have won the faith and friendship of a man who was not only sagacious and wise, but throughout his life simple, consistent and sincere."[15] This testimony of a historian who makes no secret of his bias against Islām, with regard to the sincerity and devotion of Abū Bakr should suffice to seal the lips of all detractors. The hand of God manifested itself in the Caliph's support just as it had been manifested in the case of the Holy Prophet, and through his instrumentality Islām, after it seemed to have become submerged under the terrible upheaval on the Prophet's death, was brought back to full life and vigour. As Muir says: "After Muḥammad himself, there is no one to whom the faith is more beholden."[16] Abū Bakr's love of God and his Prophet was the deepest ever cherished by a disciple towards his Master. Consumed as his whole being was in Divine love, worldly power and pelf had not the least charm or attraction for him. His piety and devotion, his simplicity of life, his sublimity of morals, his iron determination, his unflagging perseverance and, above all, his unshakable faith were the many qualities that have won him a place in Islām second only to that of the Holy Prophet.

The collection of the Qur'ān

During the two years and a quarter of Abū Bakr's reign, Islām was once more restored to life. The fire of insurrection all over

---

15. The Caliphate p. 81.
16. Ibid.,

Arabia was extinguished and the power of Islām firmly re-established. Nay, a new vigour was instilled into it; so that when the time came, it was able to overthrow at one blow two of the mightiest empires of the day. But this is only one side of the picture, one phase of the great achievements of the Caliph. He did immense service to the great cause in several other directions. It was in his short reign that the collection of the Holy Qur'ān was brought about. This expression — the collection of the Qur'ān — is often misunderstood. It signifies no more than that all those manuscripts which during the lifetime of the Holy Prophet had been dictated to amanuenses from time to time, as the verses were revealed, were brought together into one volume in the order in which the Holy Prophet had personally directed them to be inserted. The practice with the Prophet was that whenever a verse or a chapter was revealed, a double process was employed to preserve it. There were amanuenses always at hand who committed it to writing; there were also those who committed it to memory. Now it must be noted that the revelation of certain chapters extended over many years, as they were revealed piecemeal. Thus, whenever a fresh revelation came which was to form part of a previously revealed chapter, the Prophet, while directing its commitment to writing and memory, would there and then also point out in what chapter and in what context of that chapter it was to be inserted. Thus the whole of the Qur'ān was arranged and recited in the very order in which we find it in our hands. In this very order the Prophet recited the various chapters in his daily prayers. In this very order were they preserved in human memory. The order and arrangement were done under the Prophet's own decisions. The only thing left undone was that the various manuscripts were not put into one volume. Nor could they be so put during the lifetime of the Prophet, when at any time a fresh piece might be revealed and a rearrangement of the written pieces accordingly become necessary. These pieces were taken down on palm leaves, on paper, or on leather. The work of collection could only be done after the Prophet's death when the Qur'ān had been revealed in its entirety. Consequently, when in the battle of Yamāmah, many of those Muslims who had the Qur'ān by heart met martyrdom, 'Umar reminded Abū Bakr that the time for such collection had come, so that if even all those who had committed the Qur'ān to memory should fall in battle, the Qur'ān might still remain intact and in the same order. This important work was at once taken in hand and entrusted to Zaid ibn Thābit, the scribe who had taken down most of the Madīnah chapters, and he collected all the material bearing these manuscripts and made them into one volume. This is all the term "collection of the Qur'ān" implies, and this is what was done in the reign of Abū Bakr. Later, during the time of 'Uthmān, when the empire of Islām spread far and wide, several authentic copies of this volume were made and sent out to the various centres of the empire, so that each might in that part serve as a standard version and as a reference for all subsequent copies that might be made, thus avoiding all chances of discrepancies in text or in writing creeping in. This was undoubtedly one of the greatest services to the cause of Islām, and will ever be the basis of its unity — one book, without the least variation, for the whole Muslim world.

The collection of Zakāt

The other most important achievement of Abū Bakr was the system of collecting zakāt in the central national treasury. During the stormy days when pretenders had arisen in several parts of Arabia, some of the newly converted tribes took it into their heads to take advantage of the general disorder and refused payment of zakāt. They demanded, as the price of their keeping quiet, that they should be exempted from this compulsory tax. Even a strict and stern man like 'Umar counselled Abū Bakr to show leniency in view of the crisis. Refusal meant the estrangement of these tribes and throwing them into the arms of the rebels. The Caliph, however, resolutely rejected the proposal. It was a system of vital importance to both the solidarity and the stability of the power of Islām, and a compromise therefore was out of question. The slightest relaxation of this public duty would have meant, at that early stage, disintegration of the power of Islām. Shorn of this central national fund, the Caliphate would have been reduced to a mere skeleton without either vitality or vigour, and a few more days would have seen the end of it. Abū Bakr saved the situation. Should so much as a single seed of grain be left unpaid, he replied, he would wage war against the defaulters and carry it on till it had been paid. How many Muslims today ever reflect that much of their present national disintegration is due to lack of this central zakāt fund? With a strong national fund kept continuously replenished by zakāt from the pocket of every Muslim man and woman of means, wonders could be achieved in a short time in the way of nation building, such as the opening of schools, establishment of orphanages, poor houses, missions for the propagation of the faith, and so forth.

Government by counsel

The third most conspicuous service of Abū Bakr was the introduction, in all affairs of state, of the democratic system of taking counsel and arriving at decisions by the majority of votes. The procedure followed was that, first of all, reference was made to the Qur'ān for light and guidance for the matter in hand. If no explicit ruling on the question was found there, reference was next made to what the Prophet had said or done. Failing to find light through that source as well, recourse was finally made to counsel to which all the prominent Companions were invited. The matter was thoroughly discussed and the line of action favoured by the majority of those present was ultimately adopted. This exactly was the principle according to which the Government of the country was conducted during the reign of 'Umar. Nevertheless, where a clear instruction could be had either on the authority of the Qur'ān or the Sunnah, the matter was considered above dispute and settled accordingly even against popular opinion. The despatch of the expedition to Syria under the command of 'Usāmah is a case in point. Though most of the important Companions, in view of the threatening conditions at home, opposed this bold step, Abū Bakr over-ruled the opposition on the authority of the Prophet. An army, he argued, directed by the Prophet himself to proceed to Syria could on no account be kept back. On the same principle, he refused to put a more experienced man in command; for 'Usāmah had been appointed by the Prophet himself. In the absence of any clear light, however, all affairs were decided by the majority of votes, and when once a decision was thus arrived at, the minority cheerfully submitted to it.

Position of the ruler

Another equally momentous reform that gives to Abū Bakr an eminent position in history was the subordination of the status of kingship to the will of the people. The king was to be considered a member of society just as a commoner. There were no privileges attached to that exalted position. For instance, the king was not the master but only the custodian of the public treasury. A civil list was fixed for him beyond which he could not draw a single penny for his personal use. The king was thus the servant of the people. This was a reform introduced centuries ago when the standard of world civilization was very low — a reform of which the most civilized nation of this twentieth century could justly be proud. Then again, Abū Bakr did not convert kingship into a personal property to descend in his own line. At the time of his death, he had sons in every way capable of occupying his position, but he selected 'Umar, as the worthiest of all, to fill that office, and did not consider his choice as final until he had consulted the Companions and obtained their confirmation. Yet again, the king was just as much under the law of the land as the man in the street. "The king can do no wrong" was not to be the Islamic law. The king was as much accountable for his deeds at the bar of the law of the land as a drawer of water or a hewer of wood. When on a visit to Makkah, the Caliph took a seat near the town hall and asked the people if any of them had any grievance against him or if he owed anyone anything. Furthermore, legislation was not placed in the hands of the king. First of all the Qur'ān, then the Prophet's precept or practice, then the will of the people, such was the machinery that framed the law; and the law, not the king, was the supreme authority. In subordinating kingship to the law of the land and the law of the land to the will of the people, Abū Bakr laid the foundations of a truly democratic government as also of liberty and equality in the truest sense of these words. To the misfortune of the community of Islām, however, this golden rule of government was abandoned after the reign of 'Alī, the fourth Caliph. Kingship again became private property, as also did the public treasury. Democracy gave way to despotism, and thus began the disintegration and decay of the power of Islām.

Treatment of enemies

The list of Abū Bakr's multifarious reforms would be incomplete without mentioning those most humane rules which he laid down for the guidance of his army in its behaviour towards the enemy. Here are some specially emphasized:

1. No old man, no child, no woman shall be slain.

2. No hermit shall be molested, nor his place of workshop damaged.

3. Corpses of the fallen shall not be mutilated or disfigured.

4. No fruit-bearing tree shall be cut down, no crops burned, no habitation devastated.

5. Treaty obligations with other faiths shall under all circumstances be honoured and fulfilled.

6. Those who surrender shall be entitled to all the rights and privileges of a Muslim subject.

Strength of character

Unique power of decision was another most brilliant trait in Abū Bakr's versatile personality, and his strength of character was most strikingly displayed in what is known in the history of Islām as the dispute of Fadak. When the Prophet passed away, his daughter

Fāṭimah sent word to Abū Bakr that the property known as Fadak and other property on which the Prophet in his lifetime maintained himself must be divided among his heirs in accordance with Islamic law and that her share must be made over to her. To this the Caliph replied, quoting the Prophet's well-known saying that "Prophets do not leave anything to be inherited and that what they leave behind must go to charity." Such a blunt refusal to the Prophet's dearest daughter, for whom Abū Bakr cherished the deepest regard, was no easy task. In fact, he had the courage to address this disappointing reply to all the Prophet's legal heirs including his own daughter 'Ā'ishah. He displayed the same strength of character at his own death with regard to the allowance he used to draw from the public treasury. "If there is any surplus out of that money left unexpended," he said, "it must be refunded to the public treasury." In this respect as well, Abū Bakr appears as the beacon light to the posterity of Islām, giving the message to all coming generations that nothing should be allowed to dissuade a Muslim from the path of duty — not even the strongest ties of affection.

Appearance and character

Abū Bakr was a man of fair complexion, lean in body and with emaciated cheeks, deep-set eyes and up-drawn forehead. He had a slight stoop. He dyed his hair red and wore a ring on his finger with the inscription *ni'm al-Qādiru Allāhu,* i.e., "How good is God, the Almighty." Amongst his numerous virtues, generosity was conspicuous. It was an instinct with him to help the poor and the needy. As king he did not let money accumulate in the treasury. Whatever came in was distributed amongst the deserving. Man and woman, slave and free, young and old, all got equal shares in the distribution. At his death, the State treasury contained not more than a single dirham. He was humble in disposition and very hospitable. He was so tender-hearted that when he recited the Qur'ān, tears overwhelmed him. Nevertheless he combined with this a high order of bravery. At the most critical junctures he stood by the side of the Prophet, such as on the occasion of the flight, and at the battles of Badr, Uḥud, and Ḥunain. His piety was equally great. For a great part of the night he kept awake praying to God while in the day-time he would fast. For all this, in time of war he was never behind others. When Madīnah had no garrison left and was attacked by rebels, he took all the available men and himself marched out in pursuit of them. Whenever he sent out an expedition, he would in person give it a send-off. Notwithstanding his old age, he accompanied Usāmah on his Syrian expedition a long way on foot, advising him on various matters. Even in the days of his Caliphate he came to Madīnah and went back to his country-house on foot, though he was above sixty years of age. He had three sons, 'Abd Allāh, 'Abd al-Raḥmān, and Muḥammad; and three daughters, Asmā', 'Ā'ishah and Umm Kulthūm.

Chapter 2
‘Umar

Early Life

‘Umar was the second Caliph of Islām. He is also known by his surname Abū Ḥafṣ, while he received the title of Fārūq, (i.e., one who separated truth from falsehood) after embracing Islām. He was the son of Khaṭṭāb. His mother's name was Ḥantamah. His ancestral lineage joins that of the Prophet with the eighth ancestor. In age, he was thirteen years junior to the Prophet. He came of the clan ‘Adiyy which occupied a position of distinction among the Quraish. To this clan was entrusted the important function of providing envoys and arbitrators in cases of dispute. While still young, ‘Umar was an expert in the science of genealogy, a highly skilled soldier and wrestler and a great orator. At the famous fair of ‘Ukāz, where people came from far and wide to display whatever of art or skill they possessed, ‘Umar took part in the wrestling. He had also received education and was one of the few people who at the advent of Islām could read and write. His father had for some time put him to the work of a camel-herdsman. Business, however, was his chief occupation. He had a unique understanding of men and matters which won him a great reputation and he was appointed as an envoy. Thus, before his acceptance of Islām, he enjoyed a position of marked distinction and esteem.

Conversion to Islām

Zaid, a cousin of ‘Umar, was one of the few men who had renounced idolatry before the advent of Islām and who were known as *Ḥanīf.*[1] When the message of Islām came, Sa‘īd, son of Zaid,

1. *Ḥanīf* lit. means *one who inclines to a right state.*

embraced Islām together with his wife, Fāṭimah. A maidservant of 'Umar also joined the fold, for which she received much beating at the hands of her master. 'Umar was bitterly opposed to the Prophet, and one day, under the impulse of this hostility, he took his sword and went out with the resolve to kill him. On the way, he met a man Na'īm ibn 'Abd Allāh who asked him whither he was going. "To kill Muḥammad," came the sharp reply. Na'īm asked him if he was not afraid of the Banī Hāshim and the Banī Zuhrah, who would certainly avenge the murder of their kinsman. "It seems you, too, have renounced your religion and embraced Islām," retorted 'Umar. Thereupon Na'īm said: "Let me tell you something stranger still. Your own sister and your brother-in-law have become Muslims." Hearing this, 'Umar went straight to his brother-in-law's house. At the time a man named Khabbāb was giving a lesson in the Qur'ān in the house. When he came to know of 'Umar's arrival, he hid himself in a corner. 'Umar grew suspicious and enquired of his sister and brother-in-law what sort of recitation was going on there which he had just overheard. "It seems you have become Muslims," said 'Umar angrily. "What then?" replied Sa'īd, "shall we not accept truth if it is somewhere else than in your religion"? At this 'Umar flew into a fit of rage, and fell upon Sa'īd, beating him till he was covered with blood. His sister, Fāṭimah, stepped forward to the rescue of her husband. She also was wounded but loudly recited the *kalimah*,[2] the Islamic declaration of faith. Her steadfast devotion could not but impress 'Umar. Besides, he was also touched at the sight of his own sister bleeding. He asked what they were reciting from. The leaves were produced on which was written the chapter known as *Ṭā ḥā*. 'Umar began to read it. He had not read very far when the truth sank into his heart. He would go to the Prophet, he said, and embrace

---

2. *Kalimah* lit. means a word, but technically it is applied to the well-known declaration *lā ilāha ill-Allāh Muḥammad-un Rasūl-Allāh*, i.e., there is no god but Allāh and Muḥammad is the Messenger of Allāh. It is by this declaration alone that a man enters the fold of Islam.

Islām. K͟habbāb also came out. The Prophet had prayed the previous Thursday night, he said, that God might strengthen Islām either with the conversion of 'Umar ibn K͟haṭṭāb or 'Umar ibn His͟hām, better known as Abū Jahl. That prayer had been granted in favour of the former. 'Umar went straightway to the Prophet who, in those days, used to live in the house of Arqam at the foot of Mount Ṣafā. There the Muslims used to meet together and say their prayers. At the door the Prophet's companions would not allow him to enter, as he had a sword in his hand. Ḥamzah, however, said that if God wished him well, he would accept Islām that day. In case he was out with evil intent, it would not be hard for them to deal with him as he deserved.

The Prophet was as yet inside the house. Coming out he accosted 'Umar, saying, "Wouldst thou not desist, 'Umar? I am afraid thou mayest be visited with degradation." 'Umar stepped forward and, reciting the *kalimah*, declared himself for Islām. The small brotherhood was filled with joy and raised a shout of *Allāh-u-Akbar* (i.e., God is Great) till the surrounding hills resounded with the echo. 'Umar requested the Prophet to come out into the open and thenceforward publicly preach his faith. This took place in the month of D͟hu-l-Ḥajj in the 6th year of the Call. 'Umar was at the time 26 years old.

The Flight

'Umar's conversion no doubt added to the strength of Islām. The Muslims now said their prayers in the sacred House of Ka'bah. But it also added to the fury of the opposition, which at length assumed unbearable proportions. After years of suffering, the Muslims were at length forced to seek refuge in emigration. The first emigration, which had taken place before 'Umar's conversion to Islām, was to Abyssinia, and now it was the emigration to Madīnah. This time the watch on Muslims was very strict and they slipped out in small groups. The Makkans would not let them emigrate. Nevertheless 'Umar refused to be daunted. He openly started for Madīnah with a band of twenty and halted some two or three miles outside Madīnah at the quarter known as *Qubā* or

'Awālī. About two or three months later when the Prophet arrived in Madīnah and founded a fraternity amongst the emigrants and the Madīnah Muslims, 'Umar was made the god-brother of 'Utbān ibn Mālik. They lived at a distance from the Prophet's mosque and therefore arranged to come to the Prophet by turns on alternate days. Each would one day visit the Prophet and the other day attend to his work. When a consultation was held as to the best method to call people to prayer, 'Umar had a vision in which he saw a man reciting the *adhān*, the Muslim call to prayers. While others mentioned bells and horns in this connection, 'Umar suggested that a man should be appointed to do it. The Holy Prophet ultimately adopted the form under guidance of Divine revelation. On several other occasions, too, Divine revelation concurred with 'Umar's judgment.

Help rendered to the cause of Islām

The Muslims fled to Madīnah in the hope that there they would be safe from persecution. The Quraish, however, did not let them alone in this distant asylum. In order to put an end to the movement of Islām, they made repeated incursions on Madīnah. The first of these was made in the second year of the Hijrah in the month of Ramaḍān, and the encounter took place at Badr, which is situated at a distance of three days' journey from Madīnah and ten days' from Makkah. 'Umar took part in this battle. Seventy prisoners of war fell into Muslim hands. 'Umar was of opinion that they should be all put to the sword, because they were the relentless enemies of Islām, bent upon the annihilation of the Muslims. The Prophet, however, did not approve of his proposal and ransomed the prisoners. A year later, the Makkans once more marched against the Muslims and this time they came with thrice their previous strength. The Muslims met them at the foot of the hill of Uḥud, at a distance of three miles from Madīnah. 'Umar stood by the Prophet to the last, and when Abū Sufyān, the commander of the enemy army, asked derisively whether Muhammad was alive, whether Abū Bakr was alive, whether 'Umar was alive, the last-named could not remain silent and shouted back saying, "Thou enemy of God, we are all alive." In the battle of the Ditch in the fifth year of the Hijrah, when the Muslims were besieged within the town of Madīnah, 'Umar on several occasions displayed feats of bravery. In the sixth year of the Hijrah, the Prophet went on a pilgrimage (*'umrah*) to Makkah. But he was yet nine miles away from the sacred town when at Ḥudaibiyah he had to sign a truce, the terms of which were apparently humiliating to the Muslims. 'Umar felt the humiliation most of all, and remonstrated with the Prophet. "Why should we submit to conditions so humiliating," he submitted, "when we are in the right." The Prophet consoled him. On the way back, the Prophet received the Divine revelation known as the chapter of *Victory*. This gave to the Muslims the happy news that the truce of Ḥudaibiyah was the harbinger of a great triumph for Islām. The Prophet forthwith sent for 'Umar and gave him the happy news. 'Umar also participated in the battle of Khaibar which was fought against the Jews in the seventh year of the Hijrah. In the eighth year he participated in the march on Makkah. At the battle of Ḥunain, when the greater part of the Muslim army fled before the enemy archers, 'Umar was amongst the handful who stuck to their ground. The Prophet himself advanced and the enemy was routed. On the occasion of the Tabūk expedition, 'Umar presented half of his life-long savings to the Prophet as a contribution towards the war fund.

The Prophet's death and after

When the Prophet was seized with his last illness, he directed Abū Bakr to act as Imām in his stead and conduct prayers. Twice 'A'ishah pleaded that her father was too tender-hearted and could not conduct prayers without weeping. She implored that 'Umar might be appointed Imām. The Prophet, however, insisted that Abū Bakr must lead the prayers. To these very days of the Prophet's illness relates an incident which has been very much misconstrued. Four days before his death, when the attack of illness was severe, the Prophet asked for writing material. "Let me give you a writing," he said, "so that you may not go astray after me." On this 'Umar said that the Prophet was overwhelmed by a severe attack of illness and that the Book of God was enough of guidance for the Muslims. From this some have drawn the wrong conclusion that ‘Umar prevented the Prophet from writing. They forget that after this incident the Prophet remained alive for four days and could have dictated his wish at any other time if he had so desired. The truth of the matter seems to be that whatever the Prophet wanted to leave behind in writing was just what ‘Umar had said — viz., that Muslims should hold fast to the Book of God. When ‘Umar gave expression to what was in the Prophet’s own mind, he did not feel any further necessity of committing the same to writing. At the Prophet’s death ‘Umar came to the mosque and, thinking that the hypocrites had, out of mischievous motives, spread false news, declined to believe that the Prophet had actually died. Presently, however, Abū Bakr arrived, and, on going inside the house, found out that the news was only too true. When he came out and announced the fact, ‘Umar was silenced. After the Prophet’s death, ‘Umar came to know that the Anṣār had assembled in the Thaqīfah Banī Sā‘idah, and were holding a consultation as to the election of a Caliph. Forthwith, taking Abū Bakr with him, he hastened towards the meeting and put a stop to the mischief in time. And when the decision was arrived at, he was the first formally to swear allegiance to Abū Bakr. In all the important events that took place during the regime of Abū Bakr, ‘Umar’s opinion played a special part. Before his death, Abū Bakr appointed ‘Umar as his successor, after due consultation with prominent Muslims. And the magnificent work of the consolidation of the power of Islām, of which the foundation-stone was laid by Abū Bakr, was carried to completion by ‘Umar.

‘Umar pursues the frontier policy of Abū Bakr

It has already been shown that the campaign undertaken under the orders of the first Caliph of Islām against the Persian and Syrian frontiers were merely defensive measures, inspired neither by ambition for territorial aggrandizement nor by zeal for conversion. They were meant only to suppress the elements of disorder in those quarters which were disturbing the internal peace of Arabia.

These campaigns were confined to territories with an exclusive Arab population. On taking the reins of government in hand, 'Umar pursued the frontier policy of his predecessor with his characteristic zeal and vigour, with the result that in the course of a few years, both the mighty neighbouring empires of Persia and Rome crumbled before the armies of Islām.

Objection against early Muslim conquests

The question arises: How did such an eventuality become possible, if the policy was to fortify the frontiers? Why was not war restricted to exclusively Arab-populated parts; why the conquest of foreign lands? Why were Persia and Syria, nay, even Egypt, subjugated and annexed to the empire of Islām? Was it not clearly the passion of conquest that carried the Crescent far and wide? Non-Muslim historians have made much of this circumstance and, without giving a thought to the real cause, have put these expeditions down to the territorial lust of Muslims, supplemented by a fanatic zeal for proselytism. The objection, as we will presently show, is due to ignorance of real facts. It will be seen, on the other hand, that the Muslims did all they could to avert war, and were driven to it only by the repeated attacks of the Persians and the Romans.

To begin with, we must repeat what we pointed out before, that early historians of Islām do not record anything like a detailed narrative of an episode. These works are mostly the productions of a later period, when the empire of Islām had already spread over many countries. Brought up in the lap of national prosperity and splendour, these historians seem to have been engrossed by the dazzling splendour all around. The question of what troubles their forefathers, builders of that empire, experienced at the hands of neighbouring countries was simply barred out of their mental camera by this all-comprehensive national grandeur. Perhaps their mental vision, being the product of the most glorious of environments, was incapable of turning to the other side of the picture. That their forefathers could have been despised and constantly worried by Persians and Syrians they simply could not imagine in the midst of changed conditions when the banner of the Crescent proudly waved over a vast portion of the globe. Hence it is that these historians are silent on the causes that prompted the early Muslims to these wars. All they tell us is that such and such a battle was fought with such and such a result, without saying why and how were these hostilities started. If details of these events had been preserved, they might have helped modern critics in unravelling the mass of narration and tracing the root causes. Nevertheless, here and there, one does come across just a stray clue which serves as a ray of light in an otherwise dark situation. Take, for instance, the words of 'Umar spoken after the conquest of Mesopotamia and recorded by all historians: "I wish between ourselves and Persia there were a mountain of fire." Muir records in *The Caliphate* that when a certain general, Ziyād, after the conquest of Mesopotamia, asked 'Umar's permission to advance to Khurāsān in pursuit of the Persian forces, 'Umar forbade him, saying: "I desire that between Mesopotamia and the countries beyond, the hills shall be a barrier so that the Persians shall not be able to get at us, nor we at them. The plan of al-Irāq sufficeth for our wants. I would prefer the safety of my people to thousands of spoils and further conquest," Commenting on this, the Christian historian observes: "The thought of a world-wide mission was yet in embryo; obligation to enforce Islām by a universal crusade had not yet dawned upon the Muslim mind." This is a clear admission that Islām is free of the charge of being spread at the point of sword till at least the time of 'Umar.

The safety of Arabia was the sole motive of the Early Caliphate wars

It is noteworthy that the words of 'Umar quoted above pertain to the year 16 A.H. when Syria and Mesopotamia had both been conquered. Thus, at least till the conquest of 'Iraq and Syria, the alleged passion of converting people at the point of the sword had not seized the Muslim mind. This should conclusively establish at least this much, that during the reign of Abū Bakr when these expeditions were launched, and subsequently, for three years during 'Umar's reign, when these countries were subjugated, the causes of warfare were not religious but political. The words of 'Umar leave no room for doubt that national defence was the only motive underlying these conquests. "I would prefer the safety of my people to thousands of spoils and further conquests," he said. Thus the idea was neither the propagation of Islām nor territorial conquest, nor the lust of spoils. "Safety of my people" was the sole motive. 'Umar's words exonerate not only 'Umar himself from the baseless charge, but they also clear Abū Bakr of all base motives that spite has imputed to him. For 'Umar was the chief adviser of Abū Bakr, and nothing of importance was done without his consultation. It is thus obvious that from the very day that these campaigns were started, Muslims were prompted by no other consideration than their own safety.

That the safety of Arabia was the sole consideration of 'Umar is also known by the words which he uttered after the conquest of Persia. Announcing the happy news of the Persian conquest, the Caliph made an impressive speech in the course of which he observed: "Now the Persians will not be able to injure Islām." Thus the only idea was to protect the infant State of Islām from injury by the neighbouring empires, and this, in fact, furnishes the master-key to find out the causes of all the battles. Self-defence had driven Muslims now as in the lifetime of the Prophet to unsheath the sword. With this object alone were these wars undertaken by Abū Bakr and with the same purpose were they continued by 'Umar, and no sooner was that object realised than the sword was sheathed. If, as alleged, territorial extension were the end, why did they stop short at Persia? The campaign should rather have been carried on with greater zeal now that the Muslims commanded far greater strength and resources. But that was never the goal. Self-preservation was the only motive and as soon as the forces which wanted to annihilate Islām were crushed, there was an end to these wars.

Defeat enhanced Persia & Rome's passion for revenge

Such relics of those times preserved in the pages of history, though stray and scanty, furnish proof positive of the accuracy of our contention. Even in the absence of these, a mere commonsense view of the working of human nature should have led to the same conclusion. There is no doubt that at the very outset when Islām took a firm footing in the soil of Arabia, Persia and Rome viewed this rising power in their neighbourhood with jealousy and alarm. From that very time, these powers were anxious to crush the young power and subjugate Arabia. Persia openly sent reinforcements to the rebels of Baḥrain. From 'Irāq, the country under the sway of Persia, Sajāḥ arose with pretensions to prophethood and marched to attack the capital of Islām. This could not have been done without the instigation of Persia, the ruling power of 'Irāq. These were small beginnings but, later on, when in direct hostilities Persia met with reverses at the hands of the Muslims, it was but natural that there should have been imported into the conflict all the fury of a wounded pride. It was the depth of ignominy for a mighty power, as Persia undoubtedly was, to be defeated by an upstart power on which it looked with contempt. Passion of conquest was thus supplemented by the passion of revenge, and this gained in fury with every fresh defeat the Muslims inflicted. If in the beginning there was any wavering in the mind of Persia as regards the conquest of Arabia, its own successive defeats and the loss of territory now made it a matter of necessity and the whole country was now burning with this one passion — viz., to crush Islām. This is ordinary psychology. In the beginning, Persians and Romans considered it beneath their dignity to come out seriously in battle array against Muslims. They only instigated and helped the border tribes against them, or sent a battalion just to teach the naughty youngster a lesson. With every fresh defeat, however, their passion for revenge grew in intensity and, in proportion as this passion gained in fury, they put greater numbers into the field. Now they were out in all earnest to turn the Muslims out of their land and to conquer Arabia and crush Islām. And they made no secret of it. In the year 14 A.H., when Rustam, the famous Persian general, came out for battle on the field of Qādisiyah, this is how he loudly swaggered: "The whole of Arabia will I smash." It shows what the ambition of Persia was. Not the expulsion of Muslims from Persia, but the destruction of Arabia — this was the passion that kindled their bosoms. This exactly was the case with the Roman Empire of Syria. As further events will show, a number of times the Muslims sent envoys to the enemy, expressing their anxiety for the cessation of hostilities, the adjustment of frontiers and the restoration of peace. But every time they met with contemptuous refusal. War was thus actually forced on them and there was no running away from it.

A necessity of war

There is yet another consideration that can rightly be urged in justification of subjugating Persia and Syria. When one nation makes an unprovoked attack on another, it at once becomes the latter's duty not merely to repulse the attack, but also to carry the fight to the finish till one of the combatants should surrender. The Persians, as already shown, struck the first blow. They violated the independence of Arabia by encroaching upon its soil. They made common cause with the rebels and sent troops for the destruction of the power of Islām. Likewise, towards the north, the Romans stirred up Christian tribes against Islām. Consequently, when hostilities formally started and troops met on the battlefield, no canons of warfare bound the Arabs to restrict their operations only to their own territory and content themselves with merely expelling the enemy. Had they been guilty of this blunder, the enemy would certainly have reappeared soon after in greater force. It would have been sheer stupidity to have stopped at that. In all civilized warfare, when once the die is cast, it is open to either party to continue the fight to a finish. Either one of the contending parties must surrender or it must be thoroughly crushed. Such are the rules of the game, and if the Muslims played that game to an issue, where lay the harm? In prosecuting war till Persia and Syria were completely broken down, Muslims had behind them all the sanction of civilized warfare, ancient as well as modern.

Islām, Jizyah or the sword

In this connection we must remove another most gross misunderstanding. The envoys, it is alleged, that were sent during these wars to negotiate with the enemy, were sent with no better terms than the offer of three courses: "Islām, *jizyah* or the sword." This message is apparently worded so as to imply that the Muslims offered their religion at the point of the sword. Now this was never the idea during these Persian and Syrian wars, when this message is said to have been first delivered. One thing that is certain beyond the faintest shadow of doubt is that never was Islām presented in accompaniment to the sword nor thrust upon anyone at the point of the sword. Sir William Muir, as already quoted, admits that at least till the year 16 A.H., when Syria and 'Irāq had already been conquered, no such idea of forcing religion on others had taken birth in the hearts of Muslims. How could they then have given a message the very idea of which had not yet entered their minds? And then, there is another equally well-established fact that shoulder to shoulder with the Muslims and under the standard of Islām there were also Christian soldiers fighting against their common foe and in defence of their common motherland, Arabia. If conversion by force formed any part of the purpose of these wars, it is inconceivable either that Muslims would have invited their Christian fellow-countrymen to make common cause with them or that the latter would have come forward to do so. What is more significant still, there were non-Muslim tribes with whom Muslims concluded peace without either converting them or demanding *jizyah*. The only condition of peace was that they would fight side by side with Muslims in case of a war. The people of Jarjoma, for instance, during the Syrian conquests, when Antioch was captured and payment of *jizyah* was commonly accepted by the populace, refused to pay on the plea that they were prepared to fight the Muslims' battles against their enemy. The condition was accepted and peace concluded accordingly. They did not embrace Islām, nor did they pay *jizyah*. During the Persian conquests as well, twice was peace made on this very condition, once with the Chief of Jurjān and again with that of Bāb. At these two places also military service was accepted in lieu of *jizyah*. These are all clear facts recorded by every historian. Possibly there were others of the kind that were never recorded. Now, on the one hand, the presence of Christian soldiers side by side with

Muslims shows beyond all doubt that the wars could not have been religious but were merely in defence of the country; and, on the other hand, the same conclusion is borne out by the fact that peace was concluded with several of the Christian and Magian tribes without either their accepting Islām or paying *jizyah*. These are all events of authentic history, admitted on all hands, and give the lie direct to the so-called story of "Islām, *jizyah* or the sword."

Significance of the alleged message

Two things are now clear. In the first place, war with Persia and the Roman Empire was forced upon Muslims, and the two great powers sought to crush the rising power of Islām. And secondly, that the alleged message "Islām, *jizyah* or the sword" could never have been conveyed in the form which later writers have given to it because Muslims throughout these wars accepted the alliance of Christian and other non-Muslim tribes, and these tribes fought side by side with them against a non-Muslim foe. What actually happened was, clearly, that the Muslims, finding the Roman Empire and Persia bent upon the subjugation of Arabia and the extirpation of Islām, refused to accept terms of peace which contained no safeguards against a repetition of the aggression. This safeguard was demanded in the form of *jizyah* or a tribute which would be an admission of defeat on their part. How could a war be terminated without bringing it to a successful issue? If the enemy had been victorious, it would have overrun the peninsula of Arabia. The Muslims were willing to avoid further bloodshed after inflicting defeat on the enemy only if the enemy admitted defeat and agreed to pay a tribute which was at any rate not as excessive as the crushing war indemnities of modern days. The offer of terminating hostilities simply on payment of *jizyah* was thus an act of merciful dealing with a vanquished foe, and for this it would be senseless to blame the Muslims. If the payment of tribute was unacceptable to the vanquished power, the Muslims could do nothing but push the victory further until the enemy was completely vanquished. This very natural situation that the Caliph 'Umar had to face is generally described as the offering of two alternatives by the Muslim forces, *jizyah* or the sword.

The third alternative, i.e., the offering of Islām, was not really connected with war. Islām was a missionary religion from its very inception, and it had a world-wide message. The Holy Prophet himself invited, besides the idolaters of Arabia, Jews, Christians, Magians and the followers of other religions to accept the religion of Islām, and many of these people who lived in the peninsula and whom the message had reached had become Muslims. He had even written letters to all the great potentates living on the borders of Arabia, including Heraclius and the Ruler of Persia, urging acceptance of Islām. This was long before the actual commencement of hostilities with these two powers. And the envoys of Islām, wherever they went, looked upon it as their first duty to offer the message of Islām to every people because they felt that Islām imparted new life and vigour to mankind and lifted humanity from the depths of degradation to the height of civilization. The Arabs themselves experienced the great transformation and, out of sympathy for others, invited them to avail themselves of the wonderful change which Islām worked in man. In writing down the history of the Muslim wars, Muslim chroniclers did not care much for the missionary activities of Muslims and hence it is generally without giving any details that they simply refer to the fact that Islām was offered by such and such an envoy. Occasionally, however, when details are referred to, they show that the Arab envoys always related their own experience, stating how Islām had brought about a wonderful transformation in the Arab nation and that it would work the same transformation in any other nation that accepted it. It is a gross distortion of facts to say that Islām was offered at the point of the sword when there is not a single instance in which Islām was forced upon even one prisoner of war, whether he came from Persia or Syria. Islām was offered no doubt, but never at the point of the sword either to an individual or to a nation. Just as there is not a single instance on record in which an individual was told that he should accept Islām or be killed, there is no instance on record in which a tribe or a nation was told that the Muslims would carry sword and fire into its territory if it did not accept Islām. Muslims had to fight their wars as the most civilized nations of today have to fight theirs, but these wars arose out of other causes, and the one thing beyond the faintest shadow of doubt is that Muslims in their struggle with Persia and the Roman Empire were not the aggressors.

There is one more consideration. Never was Islām offered at the commencement of hostilities, so not even a doubt should arise that it was offered as an alternative to the opening of hostilities. It was in the later stages of a war which had been carried on for a sufficiently long time that we find that the envoys of peace offered Islām. The war was already there, and every war has to be carried on to the bitter end until one party is completely crushed. Muslims had to carry on their war until either the enemy admitted defeat and agreed to pay tribute or his power was finally crushed. In the middle of the war, Islām was offered only as a message of mercy, for the one peculiarity of Islām was its unrivalled brotherhood. The different tribes of Arabia which had for centuries been the implacable foes of, and carried on war with, each other, had been converted into one solid nation by their acceptance of Islām. The new religion had therefore the miraculous effect of turning inveterate foes into loving brethren who forgot all their rancours. If, therefore, the enemy nation that had sought to crush Islām came to the conclusion that as a religion Islām was acceptable, Persian and Arab would become brethren and fighting would *ipso facto* cease. No other nation would show such magnanimity to a deadly foe in a deadly fight. As a rule, if one nation makes a wanton attack on another with a view to crushing it, the latter will not rest content until it has inflicted a crushing defeat upon the aggressor. But Islām came as a message of mercy, and that mercy was imported even into the bitter sphere of warfare. As human beings Arabs might be burning with a spirit of vengeance for the wrong done to them by Persians, but the brotherhood of Islām insisted that all ideas of revenge must be given up. Nay, more, erstwhile enemies become as the Qur'ān puts it, brethen in faith. It was in this sense, in this spirit, as a message of goodwill and mercy, that Islām was offered to the enemy as one and the best safeguard against the recrudescence of national rancour and bitterness.

Persian force under Hurmuz, A.H. 13 (A.D. 634)

After these introductory remarks to show how Muslims were driven into these wars, we would now resume the thread of the story where we left it. On the Persian frontier, it will be recollected, Khālid left his headquarters at Ḥīrah, leaving Muthannā in charge, and at the head of half the army marched towards Syria, under the orders of Abū Bakr. Mesopotamia was yet in the possession of Persia. Khālid had with the help of Muthannā cleared only the strip of territory to the west of the Euphrates, which formed part of Arabia. Between Muslims and Persians now lay the strong barrier of the river, and if the Persians had only stopped further molestation, the two countries, divided as they were by water, could have remained at peace, confined to their own positions. But Persia, notwithstanding its domestic disputes, was seized with one mania, viz., the smashing of Arabia. After the departure of Khālid, a force of 10,000 strong was despatched under the command of Hurmuz, to fall upon Muthannā. The Muslim army was comparatively very small but the deficiency in numbers was made up by its unflinching intrepidity. It was decided that, rather than wait for the advancing troops, it would be better to take them by surprise. The morale of Muslim soldiers was such that nothing was impossible. The manoeuvre was at once made. The river was crossed and an attack delivered. The Persian army was overawed by this sudden move of the Muslim forces and took to flight in utter confusion. Having thus routed the foe, the Muslims retraced their steps to their original position on the western bank and encamped there.

Muslim General's appeal to Caliph

Every disaster on the battlefield only added to the flame of Persian fury. Theirs was a vast empire, and great were their resources. Muthannā had grave apprehensions that the Persians, freed from their domestic dispute, would invade Arabia again and in far greater force. His own men, a mere handful as they were, would hardly be able to resist the coming attack. He communicated these reasonable fears to Abū Bakr, stating that without fresh troops, he would not be able to maintain that position. He also suggested that to meet this exigency the ban on rebel tribes might be removed and permission given to enlist them in the army. Many days passed but he received no reply from the Capital. In view of the critical situation, therefore, he set out for Madīnah in person. On arriving there, he found the Caliph on his death-bed. Nevertheless, the dying Caliph, on seeing Muthannā, sent for ‘Umar, and told him not to worry about his own illness or death but to give immediate attention to the Persian frontier and send reinforcements there. Abū Bakr passed away the same day, and the following day the new Caliph made an appeal for volunteers; but at first, owing to the awe in which the Arabs held the Persians, the appeal met with no reply. In the midst of profound silence ‘Umar rose and gave a soul-stirring address. Muthannā also encouraged the people by assuring them that the Persian could not withstand them. There was at the time a considerable gathering of people who had come from various parts to take the usual oath of allegiance to the new Caliph. Quite a respectable army was at once raised. Abū ‘Ubaid, though he did not possess the distinction of being one of the Prophet’s companions, was put in chief command.

Hīrah lost and regained. Battle at Namāraq

Meanwhile, the Persians were busy making preparations for a fresh attack. They sank their domestic differences and sent out the famous Rustam at the head of a large army. Rustam’s first move was to send emissaries to stir up revolt in the Arabian territory captured by the Muslims. The plan succeeded, and the Muslims lost all their possessions. Muthannā was forced to retreat to Ḥirāh, where he waited for Abū ‘Ubaid. In the meantime, one division of Rustam’s army crossed the river and fell upon the Muslims. A battle thus took place at a place called Namāraq, in which the Persians were defeated. The other division of Rustam’s army was yet on the Persian side of the river. Abū ‘Ubaid made haste to cross to that side and defeated the division also. Thus did the Muslims regain possession of Ḥīrah.

Battle of Jasr

Rustam was much infuriated at the news of the crushing defeat. He despatched a fresh army under the command of Bahman which encamped on the eastern side of the river, somewhere near Babel. The Muslims, after defeating the Persians, had returned to their old position at Ḥirāh on the western bank. Thus the river divided the two hostile armies. Bahman sent word to Abū 'Ubaid, suggesting that one of the armies should cross the river in order to be able to engage in battle. Abū 'Ubaid held a council to decide which course to adopt. His officers were of opinion that the enemy should be left to cross the river. At this the Persian reproached the Muslims for becoming cowardly. Abū 'Ubaid's keen sense of honour could not bear this taunt and he ordered his men to cross the river to meet the Persians on their own ground. The river was crossed, but the space on the other bank was too narrow for action. Besides, there were many elephants in the Persian army. The Arab steeds, unaccustomed to the sight of such huge creatures, took fright and would not face them. The Muslim soldiers jumped down from their horses, and made a dash against the elephants — men against elephants! This was a most reckless, though a most heroic, attempt. Abū 'Ubaid perished in the struggle, being trampled by an elephant. The tide of elephants could not be checked, and the Muslim army in utter consternation beat a retreat to the riverside. Someone had in the meantime broken the bridge in the hope that the absence of means of escape would infuse the retreating Muslims with the courage of despair. But this only added to the consternation and many threw themselves into the river. When Mu<u>th</u>annā beheld this alarming scene he at once had the bridge constructed again and himself rushed to check the enemy. He effected a successful retreat of the whole army over the bridge. But many veterans perished in this heroic struggle, while those recently recruited took to flight. Out of an army of 9,000, only 3,000 remained under the standard of Mu<u>th</u>annā. Those, however, who fled were so overwhelmed with shame that for a long time they did not go back to their homes. The history of Islām at this period presents no other event so disastrous. The battle is known as the battle of Jasr or the battle of the Bridge.

Persia again defeated at Buwaib

When the news of this disaster reached Madīnah, 'Umar immediately despatched couriers in all directions calling for fresh volunteers. It was now a question of the defence of the homeland all over Arabia, and the chiefs of the Christian tribes also came to Madīnah with thousands of men as their quota towards the cause of national defence. Had it not been a question purely of the preservation of national independence, there is no reason why thousands of Christians should have so enthusiastically flocked to the standard of Islām to fight the battles of Muslims against non-Muslims. A considerable army was thus raised and despatched to the help of Muthannā under the command of Jarīr. After the battle of Jasr, Bahman, the Persian general, had hastened back to the capital as he had been apprised of an insurrection there. At that time the capital of Persia was Madā'in, situated on the Tigris, some fifteen miles from modern Baghdād and some fifty from the battlefield. The insurrection having been suppressed, the Persians again despatched a large army under Mahrān. The two armies met at a place called Buwaib, somewhere near Kūfah. The Persians were on the eastern bank of the Euphrates and the Muslims on the western. This time it was the Persians who crossed the river, and they were defeated after a hard and bloody contest. Mahrān himself was slain by a Christian soldier of the army of Islām. The Persians fled in utter confusion. But, finding the way to the bridge already blocked, they returned to the charge and perished on the field in large numbers.

Sa'd appointed generalissimo A.H. 14 (A.D. 635)

The fire of revenge once more blazed up in Persia. There was at the time a woman on the throne. She was dethroned and Yazdejird, a young prince of 16, was made king. Domestic feuds were all forgotten. Secret machinations were as usual employed to spread anarchy in Muslim possessions. Once more Muthannā had to retreat, this time far back to the old frontier of Arabia. Arabia was also astir as never before. Proclamation of *jihād* was made all over the land. The Caliph was anxious in person to take the command, but the council of advisers did not approve. Sa'd ibn Abī-Waqqās was chosen for the chief command and given a detailed plan of battle. At the head of a large army he marched to the frontier. At a distance of three days' journey from Kūfah, he encamped, surveyed the situation and wrote a detailed account to the Caliph. Muthannā had already succumbed to the wounds he had received at the battle of Jasr before the arrival of Sa'd. Before his death, however, he had left detailed instructions for Sa'd, which his brother now communicated to the general. The total strength of the Muslim army stood at 30,000. The Caliph sent instructions to encamp at Qādisiyah, and there, with the mountain in the rear, to draw up the army in regular martial array. The Caliph also desired that, before opening hostilities, envoys should be sent over to the Court of Persia with the message of Islām. So confident was he of the intrinsic beauties of the teachings of Islām and of its peaceful principles that he did not consider it impossible to vanquish the foe with the sword of truth rather than that of steel even when passions were running high. Madā'in, the capital of Persia, was forty miles from the Muslim encampment. Forthwith envoys galloped on horse-back, obtained audience of the king and conveyed to him the message of Islām. They were laughed at, ridiculed and scorned. "You are a contemptible people," retorted Yazdejird. "Undoubtedly we were so," replied the Muslim spokesman, "we were a people of no consequence. But God raised a Prophet in our midst who purged us of all those low and base things and put us on the path of virtue. Should you also accept this message, we are all brothers; otherwise it is not possible for us at this stage to give up hostilities without your agreeing to pay us tribute." Hearing this Yazdejird could not control himself and very harshly turned the envoys out. One of them was even made to bear a basket full of earth, to impress upon them that they were a mean people and would be made thus to work as slaves for the Persians. The Muslim deputies, however, were not so easily depressed. They took it as a happy augury and brought away the basket with the earth to their own camp, saying that with their own hands the Persians had made over their land to them. What unshakable faith!

Battle of Qādisiyah 14 A.H. (635 A.D.)

Persia mustered all its strength this time for a decisive blow. An army of one hundred and twenty thousand was raised, and put under the command of their greatest war hero, Rustam. Though this was four times the Muslim numbers, yet there was hesitation in the Persian ranks to take the field against a foe of whom they had by this time had sufficient experience. But an army so stupendous could not long be kept unoccupied without much damage to the country-side where it was encamped. At length, Rustam had to come out. Once more the Muslims tried for peace, the envoy offering Rustam the same terms as were offered to the youthful king. Rustam was much infuriated and boasted that he would smash the whole of Arabia to pieces. The following day, they filled up the canal that separated the two armies, thus preparing a way to cross the enemy's side. The Persian army advanced. Sa'd was feeling unwell and was unable to move about. He directed operations from his sick bed. This was a most bloody battle, lasting for three whole days. The first day's battle is known as *Yaum al-Armāth* or the day of confusion; the second day's as *Yaum al-Aghwāth* or the day of succour; and the third day's as *Yaum al-'Imās* or the day of distress. On the very first day arrived the Syrian division, originally stationed in Mesopotamia, to reinforce the Muslim army. On the first two days fortune fluctuated, but both sides kept their respective grounds. Losses on the Persian side were heavier. The third day also presented the same appearance. The wall of Persian elephants would not let the Muslim horsemen advance. At length Qa'qā' managed to pull down two of the beasts and as a result all the rest fled in terror. The fury of the battle was, however, unabated and it continued throughout the night. When day broke, Qa'qā' took a handful of the most daring soldiers and rushed upon Rustam. This was a signal for the whole army to turn that way. Rustam, seeing this jumped down from his high seat, was wounded and, while running away, was recognised and killed by a Muslim solider. With the death of the commander-in-chief, the Persian troops took to flight. Thus this most terrible battle of Qādisiyah came to a close. A large quantity of spoil fell into the hands of the Muslims. Casualties on the Muslim side during all three days numbered 8,500, but the Persians suffered a much heavier loss. This took place in the month of Ramaḍān, 14 A.H., corresponding to October, 635 A.D.

Sa'd's advance on Madā'in. The Western part evacuated by Persians, 15 A.H. (636 A.D.)

The battle of Qādisiyah was a decisive one in the campaign of Mesopotamia. It completely broke the strength of Persia. The defeated army took refuge in Babel. After a short stay at Qādisiyah, Sa'd advanced on Babel and, driving the enemy out, took possession of the whole of that strip of territory. The Persians took shelter within the walls of Bahrasher, the part of the capital on the western bank of the Tigris, the real capital being on the eastern bank. With the sanction of the Caliph, after a few months, in the year 15 A.H., Sa'd marched against the capital. Several skirmishes took place on the way. At some distance from Madā'in, the queen-mother in person came out at the head of the army to stem the Muslim advance but was defeated. The victorious army pushed forward to the capital and, on beholding the palaces of the Chosroes, Sa'd burst out into an exclamation of joy: "Allāh-u-Akbar," he shouted, "this day the Prophet's prophecy has been fulfilled," referring to the incident when the Prophet, while engaged in digging a ditch around Madīnah before the battle of Aḥzāb, observed that he had just then been shown in a spiritual phenomenon known as *kashf* — the palaces of the Chosroes and that the angel Gabriel had informed him that his followers would possess them. At length, Sa'd laid siege to the western part of the capital. The siege lasted for months and at last the Persians could no longer hold out. They evacuated this part of the town, taking refuge in the eastern part. Thus the whole of the territory between the Euphrates and the Tigris, which is Mesopotamia proper, came into the possession of the Muslims.

Fall of Madā'in, 16 A.H. (637 A.D.)

Now the situation was that on the western bank of the Tigris were encamped the Muslim troops, whereas the eastern was occupied by the Persians. This state continued for some time when, at last, Sa'd explained to his soldiers the danger of their position. All boats, he said, were in the possession of the enemy who might swoop down on them any time they chose, whereas the Persians were immune from attack. Their own situation was, therefore, unsafe until the enemy were ejected from their stronghold on the eastern bank. There was only one way open to them; somehow they must screw up courage and cross the river. Now the Tigris is a stream of great depth and velocity. The Muslims had no boats. But they possessed one thing — indomitable pluck before which could stand neither mountains nor rivers. Six hundred of the bravest men were picked out and divided into ten detachments of sixty each. The first sixty threw their horses into the river and in the teeth of the swift current gained the opposite bank. Their example was followed by the other detachments. This feat of rare valour was displayed under the very eyes of the Persians, who, beholding this wonderful performance, were seized with unspeakable terror and fled in utter consternation, crying, "Genii! genii have come!" Yazdejird had already removed his treasures and the ladies of his household to Hulwān. Now that he heard this terrible news, he also took to flight. In the month of Safar, 16 A.H., corresponding to March, 637 A.D., Sa'd entered Madā'in and, while thus marching through the town in triumph, he had on his lips that prophetic verse of the Qur'ān: "How many the gardens they left, and springs and crops and magnificent mansions and luxuries in which they lived! Even so; and We gave them as a heritage to another people" (44: 25–28).

It was without doubt a clear sign of Divine might that a small nation, looked upon with contempt and whose envoy was sent back with a basket of dust on his head — that such an insignificant nation overthrew a most mighty empire with no more than 30,000 men. Silver, gold and diamonds, the spoils of war, when collected, made a considerable heap. One-fifth, including the Chosroes' robes and ornaments and a highly precious carpet inlaid with diamonds, was sent to Madīnah. Fifteen years before, when the Prophet was running away for his life from Makkah to Madīnah and a price was set on his head, dead or alive, a certain man named Surāqah had gone out in search of the precious fugitive. It so happened, however, that every time Surāqah came within reach of the Prophet his horse stumbled and fell. Seeing that some hidden Power protected the Prophet, the pursuer repented of his conduct and on bended knees asked for pardon. But he had more than a pardon. "Surāqah," said the Prophet, "I see the gold bracelets of the Chosroes on thy wrists." And lo! the spoils that came to Madīnah actually included a pair of the Persian king's gold bracelets. Surāqah was immediately sent for and made to wear them, and the joy of the faithful knew no bounds when they saw the prophecy of their beloved Master come out so literally true. When 'Umar beheld the enormous riches brought as spoils, tears came to his eyes. On being asked what made him weep at that moment of joy, the Caliph said: "I fear lest this wealth and comfort should ultimately cause the ruin of my people." And when Ziyād, who had escorted the soils to the capital, asked the Caliph's permission for the army to extend its conquests towards Khurasān, he positively forbade him: "I would much rather see an insurmountable mountain between Mesopotamia and those lands, so that neither they should be able to approach us nor we should be able to approach them".

Persians' advance on and defeat at Jalūlā A.H. 16 (A.D. 637)

The eastern part of Madā'in fell in the year 16 A.H. Sa'd encamped here for the summer months which passed off peacefully. Yazdejird took refuge in Ḥulwān, about a hundred miles to the north of Madā'in. Once more he ordered the Persian forces to advance and a part of his army occupied Jalūlā, a very strongly fortified place with a rampart and a deep trench around it. Sa'd sent for the Caliph's permission to adopt counter-measures, on receipt of which he despatched a division 12,000 strong under Qā'qā' to meet the Persians. Siege was laid to Jalūlā but the besieged were in unbroken communication with Ḥulwān, from where they regularly received all help. The siege dragged on for eighty days, before the Persians were again defeated. Yazdejird shifted his headquarters along the residue of his forces to Ray. Qā'qā' proceeded to Ḥulwān, took possession of it and left a garrison there.

Battle of Takrīt 16 A.H. 637 A.D. Christian tribes embrace Islām. Mosul occupied

For the moment all was quiet so far as Persia was concerned. There was no apprehension of another attack. But in the meanwhile war clouds were gathering in the north. At Takrīt, about a hundred miles from Madā'in, Roman forces were mustering strong. They had also won over some Christian Beduin tribes. To meet this new danger, the Muslim army marched northward. The two armies met at Takrīt. As usual, the Muslims sent envoys to the Christian tribes with the message of Islām with the result that these tribes embraced the faith and joined hands with the Muslim forces. These were the three tribes of Ayād, Taghlib and Naınar. The Roman army sustained a crushing defeat. The Muslims advanced further and took possession of Mosul. Takrīt and Mosul were both parts of Jazīrah, a province of Mesopotamia. It was the concourse of the Roman forces that compelled Muslims to attack these places. They never invaded Jazīrah until the people of that part had, with the help of Roman forces, first attacked them. But more of this later on in the course of discussion on the Syrian wars.

Baṣrah and Kūfah founded, 17 A.H.

While Sa'd was busy fighting in upper Mesopotamia, 'Umar was not unmindful of the southern part, to strengthen which he directed 'Utbah to take possession of Ubullāh, a sea-port on the Persian Gulf. This 'Utbah did in the year 14 A.H. with the help of a battalion which he took with him from Baḥrain. In the vicinity of the place three years later, in the year 17 A.H., was founded the town of Baṣrah. Towards the north sprang up the town of Kūfah. Thus both these towns, which ultimately developed into big centres, were founded during the reign of 'Umar.

Damascus conquered, 14 A.H. (635 A.D.)

To turn to the Syrian theatre of war. It will be recollected that in a pitched battle at Ajnādain the Muslims had defeated the Roman force, about 250,000 strong, and that news of this brilliant victory arrived at Madīnah just at the time when Abū Bakr was on his deathbed. After this disaster, Heraclius took refuge in Antioch, whereas the Muslim general, Khālid, marched on Damascus in the year 14 A.H. Damascus, capital of Syria from ancient days, is situated in a most fertile valley known for the charm of its natural scenery as the paradise of the world. It is also a flourishing centre of commerce. Khālid, keeping in view the importance of the town, laid siege to it after great preparation. The siege lasted for six full months. Heraclius sent reinforcements to the besieged from Ḥimṣ but Khālid despatched a detachment to block their way. The cold of Damascus was very trying for the dwellers of the desert but rather than give up the siege, they put up with this hardship. One night on the occasion of a festival, intelligence was brought to Khālid that the whole town had given itself up to drinking and merry-making. Taking advantage of the situation, he took a handful of his bravest men scaled the rampart, jumped down and, killing the guard, flung the gate open. The Muslims rushed in. The besieged saw that resistance was of no avail and they themselves opened the gate at the other end of the town to the division under Abū 'Ubaidah. For this reason the whole town was granted immunity. Neither prisoners nor spoils were taken. The conquest of Damascus took place in the year 14 A.H., corresponding to 635 A.D.

Battle of Fiḥl

It has been noticed above that Heraclius sent reinforcements for the relief of the Roman garrison at Damascus which however, could not find their way to their destination. These forces together with others were therefore directed towards Ardan as the next rallying point. Khālid advanced that way and encamped at Fiḥl. Impressed by the determination and perseverance of the Muslims, the Christians made advances for peace. Khālid deputed Mu'ādh to discuss peace terms. During the discussion, the Christians, trying to overawe the Muslim envoy, referred to their large army and abundance of supplies. Mu'adh in reply quoted the Quranic verse: "How often has a small party vanquished a numerous host by Allāh's permission" (2: 249). No agreement could be arrived at with regard to the peace terms. The Muslims' demand was the same as in the case of Persia, whereas the Christians were only trying to buy them off. The following day, a Christian envoy came to the Muslim camp with the offer of two dinars per head to the whole army, provided it departed. The matter was at length referred to arbitration by the sword. A bloody battle was fought in which the Romans, 50,000 strong, were defeated. (Muir places this battle before the capture of Damascus). The victory brought the whole of the territory of Ardan into the possession of Muslims. Wherever the people surrendered, the Muslims guaranteed them, as some of the terms of peace, perfect protection of their lives and property and of their churches. The only condition on the Muslim side was that some pieces of land should be utilized for the erection of mosques.

Battle of Ḥimṣ

After the capture of Ardan, the Muslim army advanced towards Ḥimṣ, and after some feeble resistance this town also surrendered. From here Khālid proceeded further but instructions from the Caliph stooped him from pushing on. This also shows that all that the Muslims wanted was to take possession of places which originally formed part of Arabia, and with that to bring warfare to a close. Consequently, the whole army retraced its steps. Abū 'Ubaidah encamped at Ḥimṣ and 'Amr ibn 'Āṣ at Ardan, while Khālid returned to Damascus.

Battle of Yarmūk, A.H. 15 (A.D. 636)

The Caesar felt greatly crest-fallen at the fall of three important centres like Damascus, Ardan and Ḥimṣ and with full enthusiasm began to raise a large army. Couriers rushed to all parts of the empire with orders that all available men must at once be sent. A huge army gathered at Antioch. When news of this came to the Muslim camp, Abū 'Ubaidah forthwith held council with his officers. It was unanimously agreed that the situation was extremely critical and that a small army like theirs could not withstand the daily swelling tide of the enemy's ranks. Nor was there any near prospect of reinforcements arriving from Madīnah. The territory occupied, it was decided, must be evacuated. This was accordingly done. Abū 'Ubadiah gave up his position at Ḥimṣ and returned towards Damascus. On leaving Ḥimṣ, however, he ordered that the whole amount of *jizyah* realised from the people of Ḥimṣ should be returned to them. *Jizyah*, he said, was a tax in return for protection. When they could no longer give that protection, they had no right to keep the money. The whole amount was consequently withdrawn from the treasury and made over to the people who were thus being left to the mercy of the enemy and who were all either Christians or Jews. In vain will the critic ransack the dusty pages of history for another such brilliant spot, such scrupulous regard for the rights of citizenship in time of war. The treatment by Muslims of the inhabitants was such that, at their departure, Christians as well as Jews actually shed tears and prayed God to bring them back. Muir, after admiring the leniency of the Arab conquerors towards the conquered and their justice and integrity, quotes a Nestorian Bishop of the time: "These Arabs to whom God has accorded in our days the dominion are become our masters; but they do not combat the Christian religion; much rather they protect our faith; they respect our priests and our holy men, and make gifts to our churches and our convents" (p. 128).

The retreat from Ḥimṣ had its repercussion in other parts. Some parts of Ardan had also to be evacuated. The armies of Abū 'Ubaidah and 'Amr ibn 'Āṣ rallied at Yarmūk, where reinforcement previously despatched from Madīnah also arrived. The total strength of the Muslim army was between thirty to forty thousand. The Romans marched down on them with a large force of two hundred thousand. Before the commencement of hostilities, there were negotiations for peace. The Romans again tried to buy off the Muslims who demanded payment of tribute as recognition of defeat. What unwavering fortitude! Two hundred thousand were ready to fall upon them but their faith was unshaken. Truth, they said, must triumph. At length a bloody battle ensued in which even Muslim women participated. The Muslims were repulsed several times, and once they were thrust back to their encampment from where the women-folk reproached them and urged them on once more against the foe. They fought desperately, none caring for his life, each trying to excel in valour and rushing into the very thick of the enemy. The Romans lost their footing and took to their heels. Three thousand Muslim martyrs fell on the field and the number of Christian casualties was very large. When Heraclius heard of the defeat, he left for Constantinople.

The battle of Yarmūk occupies the same position in the Syrian campaign as that of Qādisiyah in the Persian. Like Qādisiyah it was a decisive battle. Thereafter, all the Syrian towns surrendered one by one — Qinnasrīn, Ḥalb, Antioch and so forth. Some of the people joined the faith of Islām but the bulk of the population stuck to Christianity and paid *jizyah*. The people of one place Jarjoma, neither embraced Islām nor paid *jizyah*. Peace was concluded with them on the condition that, if needed, they would fight on the Muslim side. This treaty shows that the Muslims wanted nothing but peace and tranquility; and it was only to establish permanent peace that they were fighting.

Jerusalem capitulates, 15 A.H. (Jan. 637 A.D.)

When Abū Bakr first sent an expedition to Syria, he divided the army into three or four divisions, each to advance to a particular part of the country. The division under the command of 'Amr ibn 'Āṣ was detailed for the province of Palestine, but he was repeatedly required to leave his own front and go over to Damascus to reinforce the small Muslim force engaged there. Jerusalem, therefore, had not so far been captured. After the fall of Yarmūk, the Muslim forces were not much in requisition in that area and siege was therefore, laid to Jerusalem. In addition to these forces, Abū 'Ubaidah also, relieved of his campaign in the north, turned to the help of the besiegers. When Arṭabūn (Aretion) heard of this, he slunk off to Egypt with his army. This incident, by the way, is worth noting in connection with the later conquest of Egypt. The inhabitants of Jerusalem offered to capitulate on condition that the Caliph in person came over and signed the treaty. The holy temple at Jerusalem being the sanctuary of the Israelite prophets, the Muslims respected it as they respected those prophets. 'Umar, therefore, held a consultation and it was decided that the condition should be accepted. Consequently, 'Umar left Madīnah for Jerusalem. This journey of one who was the King not only of Arabia but also of Mesopotamia and Syria is unique for its simplicity. In the same simple coarse dress as he usually wore, with no large retinue, 'Umar set out with just a few men, entrusting affairs of state to the care of 'Alī. Khālid and other officers received him at Jābiyah. He was, however, much displeased at the rich costumes they were wearing, and when one was brought for him, he refused to put it on, retaining his usual simple dress. The treaty was drawn up and signed, and it is produced below to show the treatment of Muslims towards people of other persuasions:

Treaty of Jerusalem

"This is the covenant of peace which 'Umar, the servant of God and the commander of the faithful, has made with the people of Jerusalem. This peace which is vouchsafed to them guarantees them protection of life, of property, of churches, of crosses, of those who set up, display and honour these crosses. Their churches shall not be used as dwelling houses, nor shall they be dismantled, nor shall they or their compounds, their crosses and their belongings be in any way damaged. They shall be subjected to no compulsion in matters of faith, nor shall they be in any way molested. No Jews shall reside with them in Jerusalem. It is incumbent on the people of Jerusalem that they should pay the *jizyah* as people of other towns do. They must also turn out Greeks and robbers. Whoever of the Greeks leaves the town, his life and property shall be protected till he should reach a place of safety, and whoever should stay in Jerusalem, he shall be protected and he must pay *jizyah* like the rest of the inhabitants. And whoever should wish to go away with the Greeks and leaves behind their churches and crucifixes, there is protection for them as well. Their lives, properties, churches and crosses shall be protected till they reach a place of safety. Whatever is contained in this deed is under the covenant of God and His Messenger and under the guarantee of his successors and the faithful, as long as the inhabitants pay the *jizyah*."

This treaty was drawn up in the year 15 A.H., and was signed by <u>Kh</u>ālid ibn Walīd, 'Amr ibn 'Āṣ, 'Abd al-Raḥmān ibn 'Auf and Mu'āwiyah as witnesses. The signature of <u>Kh</u>ālid on this document may, by the way, be helpful in removing a doubtful point of chronology as to when this renowned general was recalled by 'Umar. This evidence establishes for certain that till the year 15 A.H., at least, he was still holding his exalted position; otherwise, in his stead there should have been the signature of Abū 'Ubaidah. Christian historians have recorded that when the Christian Patriarch was showing the Caliph round the antiquities of the town, the hour for Muslim prayers arrived. At that time they were within a most ancient church, the church of the Resurrection. The Patriarch suggested that the Caliph should say his prayers there. He refused the kindly offer with thanks, saying his prayers neither there nor in the famous church of Constantine, where prayer-carpets had already been spread out. "Should we say our prayers here," he observed, "Muslims might some day claim the right to erect a mosque in this place." With such scrupulousness he protected the sanctity of Christian places of worship from violation even at some future time. This is the example of toleration, it must be remembered, set by the immediate disciples of the Prophet. If during the long history of Islām, any Muslim conqueror may have transgressed the limit, Islām cannot justly be held responsible.

Greek efforts to expel Muslims from Syria, 17 A.H. (638 A.D.)

In the year 17 A.H., the Caesar, at the instigation of the people of Jazīrah made another attempt to regain possession of Syria. Jazīrah is the territory situated to the north of Mesopotamia. The Muslim armies, after the subjugation of Mesopotamia, never advanced beyond, either to the north or to the east. The Caliph did not want to take one step beyond what was indispensable in the interest of the defence of Arabia. Syria was conquered; but not a soldier was marched into the neighbouring province of Asia Minor — a country in no way inferior to Syria in point of natural wealth and beauty. And, what is more, the power of Islām had by now immensely increased and money was abundant. But territorial extension was never the object of Muslims. They were fighting for the protection of their homeland and, now that this object was achieved and the dismembered Arab tribes were re-amalgamated with the motherland, all warfare was stopped. But their enemies would not let them rest. After every defeat, they at once set to planning another attack. Consequently at the invitation of the people of Jazīrah, the Caesar once more landed his troops on the soil of Syria by the sea-route. Anṭākiyah (Antioch) opened its gates to the invaders. Qinnasrīn, Ḥalb and other northern towns also rose in open revolt. The people of Jazīrah advanced with an army 30,000 strong. It was a critical situation. Abū 'Ubaidah rallied whatever troops he could at Ḥimṣ, at the same time sending urgent word to the Caliph. Couriers were hurried in all directions with instructions that all available forces must at once proceed to the help of Abū 'Ubaidah. The situation was so serious that the Caliph in person set out for Syria. In the meantime, however, the tables were turned. Under orders from Madīnah, a division of the Muslim army advanced on Jazīrah. These people were now alarmed at the safety of their own home. The Arab tribes that had mustered to the help of the Greeks also repented and secretly sent word to Khālid, promising to withdraw their forces. The Muslims wasted no time in taking advantage of the weakened position of the foe. Without waiting for reinforcements from Mesopotamia or Madīnah, Abū 'Ubaidah led the attack. The enemy forces were once more routed.

Conquest of Jazīrah

It was necessary to punish this transgression on the part of the people of Jazīrah. 'Umar consequently ordered Sa'd to invade that territory. The Muslim army was small but the people of Jazīrah having suffered a reverse with Caesar's army, did not consider it worth while to offer serious resistance. A few skirmishes here and there were all that took place and thus in the year 17 A.H. Jazīrah was added to the territory of Islām.

Removal of Khālid, 17 A.H.

It is not out of place, while narrating the events of the year 17 A.H., to touch upon two other important incidents of the same year. One of these is the removal of Khālid from command. There is no doubt about the fact that 'Umar did not like the war policy of Khālid. As early as the Arab rising after the Prophet's death, Khālid's treatment of Mālik ibn Nuwairah had given cause for offence, and though Khālid's explanation was accepted by Abū Bakr, 'Umar was not satisfied. Oftentimes Khālid was unduly severe on the field of battle, which 'Umar positively disliked. Nevertheless, on assuming the reins of government, he adopted as mild an attitude towards that general as possible and did not in any way interfere with him. His signature as witness to the treaty of Jerusalem shows that up to the conquest of that town, Khālid was in chief command of the Syrian army. It was after this that, in consequence of his refusal to render account for an item of expenditure, he was removed from command and put under Abū 'Ubaidah. In the year 17 A.H., Khālid gave an award of a thousand dinārs to a certain poet. 'Umar disliked this extravagance and called for an explanation. At first, Khālid refused to give it, on which the Caliph ordered Bilal to handcuff him with his own turban — a mark that he was adjudged guilty. Then Khālid explained that he had given the money out of his private purse and, as a mark of acquittal, his hands were untied. Such strong handling of a renowned general whose exploits were the wonder of the world shows what spirit Islām had breathed into it votaries. The man at the top was as liable to answer for his conduct as the man at the bottom. This spectacle of human equality as displayed by Islām stands unrivalled in the annals of man. Later, Khālid returned to Madīnah and personally pleaded his innocence before 'Umar. The

Caliph assured him that he still loved and respected him, at the same time writing to the officers concerned that Khālid had been removed not in consequence of any displeasure incurred by him or of any misappropriation of funds. The only reason of his removal, 'Umar explained, was that he was afraid lest people should attribute the conquests of Islām to Khālid's skill and prowess; these were all from God.

Plague of 'Amwās, 17–18 A.H.

The other incident worth mentioning is the epidemic of plague which broke out at 'Amwās in Syria in 17 A.H., and infected even Mesopotamia, continuing till 18 A.H. To devise preventive measures, 'Umar again set out for Syria. Abū 'Ubaidah and others came out some distance to receive the Caliph. On hearing details of the epidemic from the commander-in-chief, 'Umar called a council of the companions to consider the situation. A saying of the Prophet was also brought to his notice, forbidding a new-comer to visit a place stricken with plague as well as one already there to leave that place for another. Acting on this the Caliph gave up the idea of proceeding any further. "Art thou running away from the decree of God?" objected Abū 'Ubadiah. "Yes," replied the Caliph, "from one decree I am running away to another decree," meaning that if one place is plague-stricken according to the decree of God, another is safe by the same decree: Abū 'Ubaidah was instructed to shift his troops from the low land where they were encamped and scatter them on the hill tops. He gave immediate effect to the orders, but for himself it was too late. He had already caught the infection to which he succumbed while yet on the way. His death was followed by that of another illustrious companion, Mu'ādh ibn Jabal. At length, 'Amr ibn 'Āṣ had the troops scattered over mountains and thus the epidemic was checked, but only after it had taken a toll of 25,000 lives from among the Muslims. 'Umar's order to remove the troops from the infected area throws light on the true significance of the Prophet's words. All that the Prophet meant was that people in infected area must not carry the infection to other inhabited places. The idea was to check its spread.

It was by no means intended that those infected with plague must perish where they were. To remedy the ravages of plague, 'Umar undertook a journey to Syria for the third time. On the way he stopped at Ayla at the head of the Gulf of 'Aqabah as the guest of the bishop of the place. The Caliph's shirt, torn on the journey, was stitched by the bishop with his own hands. This shows what friendly relations existed at that time between Muslims and Christians. In this very year, i.e. A.H. 18, Arabia was visited with the calamity of a terrible famine, in which the Caliph in person did relief work like a common labourer.

Egypt invaded, 19 A.H. (640 A.D.)

The third time when 'Umar visited Syria in connection with the plague, 'Amr ibn 'Āṣ, who was in command of the army at the time, asked permission to invade Egypt. History does not record the circumstances that called for such an expedition. But the silence of history must by no means be misconstrued to imply that there were no weighty reasons for such a measure, that it was just a passion for territorial extension, or (as some Christian historians have put it) the army's idleness called for some occupation. It has been noticed that a most virulent epidemic had wrought havoc in the Muslim army, having thinned its ranks by no less than 25,000. The danger of an invasion by the Caesar had not as yet disappeared. Under these circumstances, the Muslims could ill-afford to quit Syria. It was, as Sir William Muir puts it, after much hesitation that the Caliph gave his consent. And what was the army with which 'Amr ibn 'Āṣ set out to invade Egypt? Just 5,000 strong! No sane general would, with such a force and under such circumstances venture out on an expedition of such magnitude without urgent reasons. The apprehension, it seems, was that the Caesar was about to march on Syria through Egypt and it was to check this advance that 'Umar permitted his Syrian commander to proceed to Egypt. The last invasion of the Caesar at the invitation of the people of Jazīrah, in which the Muslims lost Antioch, had also been made from Alexandria, the famous sea-port of Egypt. And it is likely that this time invasion was again contemplated by that route. It must be recollected in this connection that while 'Amr was advancing on Jerusalem in the year A.H. 15, Arṭabūn had withdrawn his troops to Egypt. These troops were still there, for the name of this same Arṭabūn is mentioned in connection with the siege of Fusṭāṭ. It is recorded that when Muqauqis concluded a truce for five days, Arṭabūn was against it. Thus the permission of invasion was neither asked for, nor given light-heartedly. Dark clouds of danger were gathering in Egypt. Arṭabūn with his troops was there. The Caesar had previously invaded Syria through Egypt. He might have been planning another invasion from that quarter.

Fall of Fuṣṭāṭ, 19 A.H. (640 A.D.)

In fine, 'Amr marched out against Egypt towards the close of the year 18 A.H. with only 5,000 men under his command. The army being so small, the Caliph contemplated recalling 'Amr, but he had already reached Egypt. Consequently, reinforcements were despatched to his help under the command of Zubair. 'Amr reached the Egyptian frontier by the route of Wādī al-'Arīsh on Dhi-l-Ḥijjah 10, 18 A.H., corresponding to December 12, 639. After encounters at a few towns on the way, such as Faramā and Bilbeis, siege was at last laid to Fusṭāṭ. This was a most strongly fortified fort on the bank of the Nile with the royal army for its garrison. The siege lasted for seven months. At last Zubair with a handful of men scaled the wall of the fort by means of a ladder and fell on the besieged with shouts of *Allāhu-Akbar*. The Christians were seized with terror and laid down their arms. The entire garrison was granted amnesty. Thus in the year 19 A.H., the lower part of Egypt was dismembered from the Roman Empire and came into Muslim possession.

Fall of Alexandria, 20 A.H. (641 A.D.)

Hearing of the fall of Fusṭāṭ, the Caesar landed another division of troops at Alexandria. 'Amr obtained the Caliph's permission to advance on that port. On the way, the combined Roman and

Egyptian forces opposed the Muslim advance but were repulsed. Siege was at length laid to Alexandria. Communication by sea was, however, maintained unbroken by the enemy, and the besieged received regular supplies. The siege consequently dragged on for a considerable length of time. But at last the town was captured in 20 A.H., corresponding to 641 A.D., and the whole of Egypt thus came into the possession of Muslims. On instructions from the Caliph, Fusṭāṭ was made the capital. Alexandria, however, had been left without a strong garrison and, finding it thus exposed, the Caesar, during the reign of 'Uthmān, once more captured it with his fleet. In the year 25 A.H., 'Amr ibn 'Āṣ wrested it from the Romans once more.

Library of Alexandria

In connection with the conquest of Alexandria, one is naturally reminded of its famous library and the common allegation that it was burnt to ashes at the instance of 'Umar. Gibbon's conclusions are positive on the point. This famous historian has proved that the library was burnt long before the Muslim conquest of the town. Muir also exonerates the Muslim conquerors from this charge. "The story of the burning of the library of Alexandria by the Arabs," says he, "is a late invention."

The Suez Canal

Besides his most brilliant exploits in the field of arms, one of the great achievements of 'Amr ibn 'Āṣ was in the field of engineering. At the instance of 'Umar, he had a canal dug, connecting the waters of the Nile with the Red Sea. This canal was very useful in transporting the corn of Egypt to Yanbū', the Arabian seaport on the Red Sea. It remained navigable for eighty years, after which, getting filled up with sand, it became unserviceable.

Campaign in Khūzistān, 16–19 A.H. (637–641 A.D.)

"Turning once more to the eastern provinces of the Caliphate we find the cautious policy of 'Umar still tending to restrain the

Muslim arms within the limits of the Arabian 'Irāq, or the country bounded by the Western slopes of the Persian range. But they were soon, by the force of events, to burst the barrier." In these words does Muir admit that the Muslims were averse to carrying their arms beyond the limits of Arab settlements but were actually dragged out by sheer force of circumstances. This is how a new development took place. The Governor of Baḥrain, who occupied the Western coast of the Persian Gulf, was alarmed at the enemy's movements on the opposite coast. In the face of danger brewing in such proximity, he could not sit still. To nip the hostile movement in the bud, he crossed the Gulf and landed his forces on the opposite coast in the year 16 A.H. He, however, found himself caught in the enemy's snare and was not able even to beat a retreat. The Caliph sent a division of army under 'Utbah to his rescue. The rescue was effected but the moral effect of the retreat on the neighbouring provinces was disastrous. Hurmuzān, the Governor of Ahwāz, a province near Baṣrah, who had fought against the Muslims in the battle of Qādisiyah and fled back to his own place, now began to give fresh trouble. "He began now to make raids upon the Arab outposts, and 'Utbah resolved to attack him," says Muir. This was in the year 17 A.H. With the help of a Beduin tribe, 'Utbah succeeded in ejecting the enemy from Ahwāz. According to the treaty that was concluded, the province was ceded to the Muslims and entrusted by 'Utbah to the same Beduin tribe. Soon after, however, 'Utbah died, and Mug̲h̲īrah was appointed Governor of Baṣrah in his place. Hurmuzān again picked a quarrel with the Beduin tribe on some frontier dispute and, violating the treaty, waged war against the Muslims. He was again defeated and Ahwāz once more fell into Muslim hands. The victorious Muslim army wanted to push their victory forward beyond Ahwāz, but the Caliph again withheld permission.

Hurmuzān had fled eastward but was again granted immunity by the Muslims. This happened in the year 18 A.H. Shortly after this the defeated Persian monarch, Yazdejird, who had taken refuge in Merv, sent his emissaries into Persia, rousing the populace to insurrection. The attitude of Hurmuzān again became dubious and consequently, in the year 19 A.H., the Caliph sent orders to the forces of Kūfah and Baṣrah to march against him under the command of Nu'mān. With large Persian army, Hurmuzān gave battle at Rām Hurmuz but was once again defeated, taking refuge in the castle of Shustar, some fifty miles to the north of Ahwāz. The castle remained besieged for several months. At last, discovering a secret entrance, Muslim soldiers entered the castle and captured it. Hurmuzān gave himself up on condition that he would be guaranteed a safe conduct to the presence of the Caliph, who might deal with him as he pleased.

Hurmuzān becomes a Muslim

When brought before 'Umar, Hurmuzān was dressed in the most gorgeous regal robes, followed by a long train of courtiers and attendants. The triumphant king, on the other hand, was at the time lying stretched on the ground wearing a coarse shirt. Fairly long contact with Muslims had already acquainted Hurmuzān with the virtues of Islām. Now beholding with his own eyes the sublime simplicity of the Caliph, the truth of Islām instantaneously sank into his heart. How wonderful must be the force, he said to himself, which thus makes man indifferent to worldly attractions, which had thus transformed the master of many kingdoms and countless treasures into a hermit to whom gold and diamonds were no more than dust. The wealthiest king, yet leading the life of an indigent recluse! Thus musing within himself his heart had already fallen prey to the fascinating force of Islām but he would not as yet declare his faith, fearing lest this might be suspected as a subterfuge to save his skin. The king seated on the throne of dust was revolving in his mind the repeated treachery of the vanquished foe of the gorgeous costume and he did so in a mood of deep anguish. At last he spoke: "To pardon a man who has been the cause of shredding so much Muslim blood! Impossible!" Hurmuzān thereupon begged for a cup of water, which was given him. He hesitated. "How I can drink this water," he said, "unless I am assured that I will not be slain even before I drink it." "You are safe," rejoined the Caliph, "till you have drunk the cup." Forthwith he let the cup drop to the ground, saying that according to the pledged word of the Caliph, he could not be killed. 'Umar was surprised at the trick. Now that he was safe and his position secure against the suspicion of subterfuge, he recited aloud the *Kalimah*, saying that the was already a Muslim.

Ban against advance on Persia withdrawn, (641 A.D.)

'Umar had issued strict orders to stop all advance towards Persia. A deputation of Muslims waited upon him to implore him to withdraw the prohibition. Thus Muir writes: "The deputation which, along the spoil of Tostar, carried al-Hurmuzān a prisoner to Madīnah, throws light upon reasons that weighed with the Caliph to withdraw his long-standing embargo on a forward movement . . ."

"What is the cause," inquired 'Umar of the deputation, "that these Persian persistently break faith and rebel against us? May be, ye treat them harshly." "Not so," they answered; "but thou hast forbidden us to enlarge our boundary, and the king is in their midst to stir them up. Two kings can in no wise exist together until the one expels the other. It is not our harshness, but their king, that has incited them to rise against us after having made submission. And so it will go on until thou shalt remove the barrier and leave us to go forward and expel their king. Not till then will their hopes and machinations cease." The demand, continues the historian, was supported even by Hurmuzān and at last the Caliph was convinced that the restriction ought to be removed. To quote Muir again:

> "The truth began to dawn on 'Umar that necessity was laid upon him to withdraw the ban against advance. In self-defence, nothing was left but to crush the Chosroes and to take entire possession of his realm."

And yet again:

> "He was compelled at last by the warlike attitude of the Persian court to bid his armies take the field with the avowed object to dealing the empire a final blow."

These last words from the pen of Christian historian are clear and yet, in the face of this positive admission, 'Umar is accused, for his subjugation and annexation of Persia, of lust of loot and territorial extension. He was by no means inclined to resort to such a measure but, if allowed any longer lease, Persia would certainly have gathered strength and crushed Arabia. Circumstances thus forced the Caliph's reluctant hand.

Battle of Nihāwand and conquest of Persia, 22 A.H. (643 A.D.)

As already stated, Yazdejird was fanning, from his refuge at Merv through his agents, the fire of another war against the Muslims over the length and breadth of Persia. He succeeded in enlisting the co-operation even of some independent kingdoms. A huge army, 150,000 strong, was rallied at Hamdān, with Firozān in chief command. Sa'd kept the Caliph informed of this general mobilization. The advance of this army would have been most dangerous to the Muslims. A counter-army was immediately raised and marched to Ḥulwān under the command of Nu'mān. A little ahead at a place called Nihāwand, the two armies met in the year 22 A.H. Nu'mān was killed in the action but the laurels of victory fell to the Muslims. Most of the enemy's army perished. From Nihāwand, the Muslim army advanced on Ray. In the meanwhile, Yazdejird fled to Ispahān and thence on to Kirmān, finally taking refuge in Balkh. At Ray, the Persian army gave another battle under Isfandyār but was as usual defeated. Yazdejird was still active. With the help of Tartars and Chinese he kept up some show of fighting, but all to no purpose. In the meantime, Muslim forces had spread over the whole of Persia. Fāris, Makrān, Sajistān, Khurāsān, Āzarbaijān, all of these provinces were one by one occupied. Thus the whole of Persia came completely under the rule of Islām. It is worthy of note that on this occasion while the tax known as *jizyah* was imposed in some parts, there were other adjacent parts where the people neither embraced Islām nor paid *jizyah*. They only agreed to render military assistance in time of need. The peace with Jurjān, for instance, was concluded on this very condition, viz., that the people who agreed to assist the

Muslims in withstanding a foreign invasion would be exempt from *jizyah*. Likewise Shahr Barāz, an Armenian chief, concluded peace on the condition of military assistance and exemption from *jizyah*. Kirmān and Sīstān were conquered in the year 23 A.H.

Death of 'Umar, 23 A.H. (644 A.D.)

'Umar met his death at the hands of a Persian slave, Abū Lu'lu' (Firoz) by name, who had, under the influence of his Roman masters, turned Christian. He fell into the hands of Mughīrah in Mesopotamia who, on his return home, took him along. Here he one day came with a complaint to the Caliph that his master realized from him two dirhams a day. He was told that this was not too much for a carpenter, which greatly incensed him. The following day at early dawn when the Caliph was conducting prayers, Abū Lu'lu' slipped forward and stabbed him. With unruffled composure 'Umar made 'Abd al-Raḥmān ibn 'Auf the Imām in his own place and went on with his prayers. The assassin, after stabbing some other persons, committed suicide. When after prayers the Caliph was informed that the assailant was a Christian, he thanked God that he had not met his death at the hands of a Muslim. The wound was deep and the bowels had been cut. There was no hope of recovery. The first thing he did was to ask 'Ā'ishah's permission to be buried by the Prophet's side. Then for the election of his successor, he selected six most prominent men — 'Uthmān, 'Alī, Zubair, Ṭalḥah, Sa'd ibn Abī Waqqās, and 'Abd al-Raḥmān ibn 'Auf, and left the decision in their hands. Whoever from among themselves, he said, these six men, elected by a majority of votes should be made Caliph. Then he had the account of his debts brought to him. This, he said, should be paid out of his legacy. Wounded on Dhi-l-Hijjah 26, 23 A.H., he passed away four days later on Muharram 1, 24 A.H.

Reasons underlying the great conquests of 'Umar's reign

Of the glorious achievements of 'Umar, what strikes one as the most conspicuous, is the great conquests of Islām. That such vast territory should have been subjugated within the brief space of ten years is by itself a wonderful phenomenon, the more so when it is borne in mind that hostilities were started at one and the same time against two most mighty empires, each apparently possessed of power enough to trample Arabia under foot in days. But one's wonder knows no bounds when one beholds that on no field did the Muslim army exceed 40,000 whereas the enemy at times put into the field as large an army as 250,000. Of equipment, the Arabs had not a hundredth part of that possessed by those empires. The enemy, long used to warfare, had a good military organization, whereas the Arabs had never before seen rallies so vast nor had they ever experienced warfare abroad. In military training, the Arabs were as deficient as their opponents were skilled. Then the battles were fought not in Arabia but on the enemy's ground, where they had, besides abundant supplies, well-fortified strongholds. Notwithstanding all the odds favouring the enemy, what a wonder that, except at Jasr, not once were the Muslims defeated! European historians have assigned only two reasons for this: firstly, that the Persian and Roman Empires had considerably degenerated; and, secondly, that the prospect of spoils, rather of loot as they put it, had roused the martial spirit of the Muslims.

Weakening of the Roman and Persian Empires

That the empires of Persia and Rome were at the time undergoing a process of decay, though true to a certain extent, does in no way explain the conquests of Islām. They had undoubtedly lost much of their original power and glory. Their civilizations were things of the past and by mutual warfare they had greatly undermined each other's power. But when all this has been said, the question still remains: Were they too weak for Arabia? Certainly not. The Arabs were utterly insignificant compared to them even in this fallen state. Parts of Arabia were actually under their sway — the northern part under the Caesar and the eastern under the Chosroes. The Arabs had such terror of them that even in parts other than their possessions, they did just as they pleased. Furthermore, the war was caused by the transgression of these two powers on the frontier. They were obviously conscious of their strength. If they had really been weak, as is alleged, their weakness should have manifested itself in some outward sign. They should have been unable to put enough forces into the field or the soldiers should have been ill-equipped. But history tells a different tale. They brought twice, thrice, nay even five times as large armies as the Muslims did. Of equipment too, their soldiers had abundance, offensive as well as defensive. Their common soldiers were from head to foot clad in iron. Thus, notwithstanding their comparative downfall from their original glory, either of these two empires was still far too formidable for Arabia, and before their combined forces Arabia was absolutely insignificant. The hostilities were, in a way, against their combined forces, inasmuch as they were carried on simultaneously against both.

False charge of love of loot

In their second explanation of these conquests of Islām, European historians seem to reflect the modern mentality of their own lands but they have overlooked one most important factor in all expeditions for purposes of loot. Such expeditions are invariably undertaken by the strong against the weak, and not vice versa. It is a law of physical nature and as such insusceptible of change. Does it not work just the same in this twentieth century? Do not the strong nations of Europe dominate the weaker nations of the world under our own eyes, exploiting all the resources of their soil for their own aggrandizement? What is this but a more refined and, hence, less palpable form of loot? Such is this immutable law of physical nature. But, on the contrary, the history of mankind presents not one instance where a weak nation has assailed a strong one with a view to robbing it. All robbers take good care to see that their victim is not their superior in strength. No robbers would run the risk of waylaying a well-equipped army, knowing it to be so. There is yet another consideration which makes this explanation untenable. Love of money invariably begets love of life. People out for loot are incapable of feats of valour such as were displayed by the Muslims. Their foremost consideration is their own safety. The reckless courage with which Muslims fought the foe in these wars, regardless of life and death, should convince any fair-minded man that sordid love of loot could not inspire such invincible bravery. These men must have been inspired by a far nobler passion which made them oblivious of all personal considerations. To take up arms against Persia and Rome was, humanly speaking, to run into the very jaws of death, and no band of mere robbers could possibly think of doing so. It must have been something far higher that banished all fear of death from the hearts of Muslims. It was their high sense of duty.

Glorious deeds of Muslim soldiers

A brief summary such as this is hardly the place to sketch in any great detail the most remarkable feats of valour, determination and self-sacrifice that Muslim soldiers displayed in these battles. The chapter they added to the history of warfare is resplendent with the most glorious deeds. To point to just a few, let us take the reader to the field of Jasr, where the Muslims suffered a defeat. Crossing the bridge, they find the enemy in battle array in a narrow space. In the forefront is the wall of elephants wearing loudly ringing bells. The Arab steeds take fright at so strange a scene and wheel round. Forthwith Abū 'Ubaidah, the commander, leaps to the ground sabre in hand. His example is followed by others. But for poor mortals to push back this moving wall is no easy task. Nevertheless the reckless daring with which they charged these giants is a sight for the gods to behold and admire. Sword in hand, Abū 'Ubaidah dashes against this wall and grapples with one of the beasts. The elephant pulls him down and with his stupendous weight crushes his body to pulp. A sight that would have umanned even the strongest nerve only inspires greater courage in his followers. The dead commander's brother rushes to the scene, takes hold of the standard and dashes against the same animal. He meets with the same fate. Another follows and likewise falls. Another and yet another till seven most valiant men were crushed underneath that one beast.

At the battle of Qādisiyah, Ṭulaiḥah rushed single-handed into the ranks of enemy, 60,000 strong, in the dark of the night and, dealing death right and left, came back with a prisoner of war. At this very field, Abū Miḥjan, the famous poet and a brave man, was one day found drunk and consequently put in the camp prison. As the battle raged hot, he saw from his dungeon that the Persians by numerical superiority were pushing the Muslims back. He could not bear the sight. His blood boiled within him and he implored Salmā, the commander's wife, to unfetter him, promising to be back and put the same fetters on if he survived. No sooner was he released than, like a lion uncaged, he rushed upon the foe, sweeping rank after rank before him. In the evening when the battle stopped, he returned to the camp and with his own hands put on his fetters. When Sa'd, the commander, who had seen his daring deeds, came to know of it, he at once ordered his fetters to be taken off. A man of such daring and such spirit of self-sacrifice, he observed, could not be kept a prisoner. Abū Miḥjan's response was equally noble; he took an oath that never again would he touch a drop of wine.

Madā'in was the scene of similar feats of fearless valour. The first man to throw his horse into the deep and rapid stream of the Tigris was the commander, Sa'd himself. Others followed, one by one, as if it were no more than a gallop on a level race-course, and this under the very eyes of the enemy watching from the opposite bank. At Fiḥl, in one of the Syrian battles, the centre of the enemy's army was repeatedly attacked by the Muslims but would not budge an inch from its position. Hishām Ibn 'Utbah, commander of a detachment, jumped from his horse and darted into the centre, swearing that he would either fix the standard of Islām there or perish in the attempt. At Ḥimṣ, Shuraḥbīl advanced alone towards the town. He was attacked by a troop of cavalry but he fought stubbornly, killed eleven men and put the whole troop to flight. At Yarmūk, when 'Ikrimah ibn Abī Jahl saw the Muslims hard-pressed, his spirits were aroused. In his former days, he said, he had been fighting even against the Prophet. How could that day his steps recede before the infidels? Four hundred men fired with his enthusiasm also pledged their lives to repulse the foe. They dashed against the enemy and it was the fiercest dash ever made. They fought a desperate fight and fell to the last man, but the enemy was repulsed. On another occasion Shurahbīl, while surrounded by the enemy and fighting single-handed, was heard, while thus fighting, reciting the Quranic verse: "Allāh has purchased of the faithful their lives and their property in return for this that they shall have paradise." And while thus reciting the verse he was calling aloud: "Let those who will have this Divine bargain come forward!" The Muslims had been pressed as far back as the female camp, but this supernatural call rallied them once more to the onslaught and the advancing enemy was hurled back. Too numerous to mention are the deeds of daring and devotion to duty shown by Muslim soldiers in these wars; the few examples quoted above will suffice to show that the Prophet had breathed an invincible spirit into them.

Muslims' sense of duty

The rank and file of Muslims, as these few events illustrate, were imbued with a feeling which made them accomplish such prodigies of valour and which removed from their hearts all fear of the overwhelming odds against them, the feeling of confidence that in the eye of God it was their foremost duty to fight. They were swayed by one passion to do what God wanted them to do. Called upon in the name of God, they cared not for their lives nor could love for wives and children swerve them from the path of duty. Worldly riches were insignificant in their eyes. At that moment they were under the spell of one all-consuming passion — the love of God. Every other consideration sank into insignificance. The Nation brought into being by the master-hand of the Prophet was characterised by two outstanding qualities. He had firmly implanted into their hearts faith in the existence of God and he had infused into them a sense of duty, which to them, meant no more nor less than obedience to the will of the Lord. Their faith in God, deep-rooted as it was, served as a never-failing battery of power which electrified the whole of their beings. They were certainly not a nation who would cause so much as a pinprick to another for nothing. Far from it. They even put up with much at the hands of others with forgiving generosity. When, however, things were carried to an extreme and attempts were made to wipe truth out of existence, they behaved as lions. This exactly was the life drama of the Prophet himself. Personal persecution, ridicule, molestation, hardship — he submitted to all with patience and fortitude without ever thinking of striking back. But when the enemy, not content with that, actually unsheathed the sword to extirpate Islām, he was not the man to stand aside. With might and main — limited though it was — he came out to defend the Truth. Three hundred against 1,000, 700 against 3,000, 1,500 against 15,000, — in spite of such disparity in numerical strength, it was not for him to shirk or shrink. These two words had no place in Islām. A tower of moral strength, though physically weak, he triumphed in spite of the odds against him.

In the early Caliphate wars the same drama was being re-enacted. Muslims never offered molestation to their powerful neighbours. When, however, these neighbours, puffed up with the pride of their vast physical resources, rose to destroy the independence of Arabia, the Muslims, undaunted by either their numbers or their resources, made short work of them, and in the course of a few years the whole face of the map was changed. Their lives were a practical commentary on the Quranic verse: "How often has a small party vanquished a numerous host by Allāh permission" (2: 249). They demonstrated that success depends neither on numbers nor on armaments, but on the strength of heart born of a firm faith in God. As a matter of fact, they were a living proof of His existence. Humanity refuses to believe what a tremendous force is true faith in God. It is generally dismissed as superstition. These early sons of Islām, however, demonstrated for all the world to see that, though God is invisible, the great miracles that were wrought through connection with Him revealed Him too obviously for denial. Thus the true secret of the success of Muslims during the reigns of Abū Bakr and 'Umar lay in their force of conviction. It is true they had, in this respect, a great advantage over later generations of Islām. They had with their own eyes seen the whole drama of the Prophet's life. They had seen how one lone man arose to proclaim the name of the Lord, how not only his immediate relations but the whole of the country — idolaters, Jews and Christians — made common cause against him, how all their opposition melted away, how all that had been said in a state of helplessness ultimately proved true. They had watched this drama with their own eyes, and small wonder that a spark of the same faith kindled their own hearts. Moreover, through the same prophetic lips, they had also heard that, just as the opposition of the Arabs had, rather than injure Islām, served to help forward its growth and development, in like manner, the aggressions of the Caesar and the Chosroes would only bring about the downfall of their own empires. They had this happy prophecy from the Prophet's own lips and, filled with the conviction of its truth, what did they care for the vast numbers of the Persians and the Romans or their abundance of material strength?

Strength of character of the Muslim soldiers

It is undoubtedly true that those conquests brought Muslims immense wealth; and of this wealth they gladly availed themselves. But the act remains that their hearts were free of attachment to riches. The one dominating passion of the love of God had elevated them far above worldly attractions. Not that they were a race of hermits who would have nothing to do with the world and all the good things of this life. They lived this life and lived it in the fullest measure. They looked upon wealth as one of the gifts of God and appreciated it. But they never allowed it to capture their hearts. They knew too well that a nation devoted to worship of Mammon in the long run becomes bankrupt of high morals. Many a time the Caliph 'Umar, when war-spoils were brought before him, expressed sorrow. In the wake of these worldly riches, he was afraid, might come their concomitants, ease and jealousy. Neither the fabulous wealth of the two richest empires nor the heaps of other things that fell into the hands of Muslims as fair spoil of war made the faintest impression on 'Umar. In the midst of all these appurtenances of luxury, dazzling to mortal eyes, he had within his bosom the same heart which the Prophet had filled with the love of God; even as on his person he had the same coarse patched costume of the days of need and poverty. Such was this Caliph, Emperor of Islām, 'Umar the Great, conqueror of three kingdoms.

In fact, this rigid simplicity and detachment from worldly splendour characterised all those who had sat at the feet of the Prophet and learnt the true meaning of life from his lips. When these pupils of the Prophet found themselves transplanted, on diplomatic missions as ambassadors or envoys, from the stark simplicity of Arabia to the gorgeous splendours of the courts of the Caesar and the Chosroes, their equanimity was not disturbed by the faintest ripple. To them it was no more than a huge farce, dazzling yet hollow. Clad in garments worn and torn and with swords having no better scabbards than a few rags slung across their shoulders, they would walk across these magnificent halls as calm and composed as if moving about in one of the dusty streets of Madīnah. Far from their being in any way impressed with the imposing spectacles of the courts of the Caesar and the Chosroes, it was the gay courtiers of those emperors who were struck, as these Muslims entered, with awe at their sublime simplicity. Before the battle of Qādisiyah, a Muslim deputation waited on Yazdejird, King of Persia. The King in a contemptuous tone reminded them that they were a low race and that, whenever they gave any trouble, a handful of border peasants were sent to put them right. On this Mug̲h̲īrah ibn Zarārah sprang to his feet and replied that the King was right, that they had indeed been a fallen and misguided people, ever quarrelling among themselves and plunged in vice, but since God had raised a Prophet in their midst they were purged of all those evils and elevated to high position.

Rabī ibn 'Āmir was sent to negotiate with Rustam, the Persian Commander-in-Chief. And what was the uniform of this Muslim envoy? For a belt he had a common rope of camel's hair tied around his waist, and from this belt hung his sabre, the scabbard of which was bandaged in rags. And an attendant? What need had he of any such luxury? All alone he entered the court, leading the steed that had brought him and as he entered the slung the bridle of the animal across a gorgeous reclining pillow and walked straight to the throne at the other end, without heeding in the least all the splendour around him. Again, when Mughīrah was deputed on the same mission he found the court in perfect array. He walked straight on and took his seat by the side of Rustam himself. When the courtiers objected, he administered a sound rebuke. "It is not the custom among us," he said, "that one man should be seated on a throne as if he were an object of worship while all the rest should sit below with their heads bowed down."

Mu'ādh was sent to the court of Syria. When shown to a seat on the magnificent carpet, he bluntly refused to sit there. "I do not want to sit on a carpet," he said, "that has been prepared by robbing the poor." Thus saying, the envoy seated himself on the bare ground. The Romans remonstrated saying that they wanted to do him honour and that that was the place for slaves, "If it is a sign of slavery," he replied, "to sit on the ground, who can be a greater slave of God than myself?" Surprised at this, the courtiers asked him if amongst the Muslims there was anyone superior to him. "Is it not enough for me," replied, "that I am not the worst of them all?" The Romans reminded him of their numerical superiority and he replied: "Our God says: "How often has a small party vanquished a numerous host with Allāh's permission."

Such were these disciples of the Prophet, far above terrestrial pomp and glory. Likewise, when foreign ambassadors came to the Muslims they were wonder-struck at their austere simplicity. When the Roman envoy was ushered into the presence of Abū 'Ubaidah, the Muslim Commander-in-Chief was seated on the ground, examining some specimens of arrows. The officer was dumbfounded when told that the man who was the terror of the Roman army was no other than the one seated before him on the ground. There are hundreds of such incidents recorded which show that, from the Commander of the Faithful down to the common solider, every Muslim was imbued with this humility of spirit, this indifference to worldly pomp. Their sole greatness lay in their firm faith and high character. Apparently, they were busy wielding the sword; but within their bosoms were hearts met with not even in the solitude of hermitages. They were saints in communion with God, though with swords and spears in hand. They knew how to bow to the glory of God and to the right of man.

On one occasion the women-folk accompanying the Muslim army were in danger of being attacked by the Christian population, the army itself being engaged with enemy troops. Abū 'Ubaidah, the Commander, suggested that to meet the exigency the Christian population should be driven out of the town. A subordinate officer objected, saying they had no right to do so for they had once pledged them safe residence within the town. Heraclius himself once asked his Christian advisers the reason why Muslims had the upper hand in spite of the fact that they were inferior to the Romans in numbers, in strength and in equipment. After many explanations, a hoary-headed man spoke out: "The Muslims," he said, "are superior to us in morals. They worship God by night and keep fast by day. They do not oppress anyone and consider themselves equals. We, on the other hand, are given to drinking and to sexual corruption. We care not for our word and we oppress others. The Muslims possess great pluck and perseverance which they bring to bear upon anything they undertake." Even in the estimation of the enemy it was the strength of character of the Muslim that brought about his triumph on the battlefield.

Solidarity of Islām

One more characteristic of these pioneer Muslims which needs to be mentioned is the unique unity and solidarity of Islām. Only a few years earlier, Arabia was the battle ground of internecine feuds. A house so divided hardly existed on the face of the earth. Tribe against tribe, clan against clan, rushing at one another's throat on mere trifles and continuing the blood feuds for generations. The most sanguine optimist saw no prospect of any interfusion between these warring and jarring elements. It was, indeed, nothing short of a miracle that the Prophet out of such discordant and chaotic conditions evolved, in the course of a few years, a well-knit and well-organised society. Deadly enemies were transformed into close friends and centuries-old grudges were transmuted into mutual affection — one of the greatest miracles of the world, admitted by historians, Muslims and non-Muslims, alike. The same tribes and clans that had sought the lives of one another now sacrificed their lives for one another. If the life of one was in danger, another came forward to save him at the sacrifice of his own. If one tribe was in straits, another extricated it by involving itself. The blow aimed at one head was received by another. Soldiers laid down their lives for officers and officers for soldiers. There was no such thing as jealously between two officers or two soldiers over the laurels of victory. Even if a subordinate officer pledged his word with the enemy it was considered a national pledge and as such inviolate. Nay, the obligations accepted by a common solider were redeemed by all Muslims. This high sense of national solidarity was one of the chief factors contributing to the triumph of the Muslim army against overwhelming odds.

Democratic spirit

The democracy of Islām, first planted when Abū Bakr took the reins of government into his hands, found growth and development during the caliphate of ‘Umar. The seed of democracy lay, of course, in the very principles and teachings of Islām. The Qur’ān had explicitly laid it down as the fundamental law of Muslim polity that affairs of state should be conducted by consultation and counsel.[3] The Prophet himself decided momentous affairs by conferring with his followers. Abū Bakr’s very election was the result of a deliberative council of Muslims, and this was throughout the principle also of his rule. During the reign of ‘Umar there were two such consultative bodies. One was a general assembly which was convened by making a general announcement; and in this only affairs of special national importance were discussed. For the conduct of daily business there was a separate committee on a smaller scale. Even matters pertaining to the appointment and dismissal of public servants were brought before this working committee. In addition to the deputies from the capital, there were

3. “And their government is by counsel among themselves” (43: 38).

also invited to these deliberations representatives from outlying parts of the empire. Non-Muslims were also invited to take part in these consultations. For instance, in connection with the management of Mesopotamia, the native Parsi chiefs were consulted; the Muqauqis was consulted on the administration of Egypt, and a Copt was invited to the Capital as a deputy to represent that country. This principle was extended down to the masses, who were consulted on certain state matters. As a rule, provincial governors were appointed after consulting the population. In case of a complaint against a governor by the public, an inquiry commission was duly appointed and the governor dismissed if found guilty. Among those thus removed were some most prominent companions, Sa'd, the conqueror of Persia, was recalled from the governorship of Kūfah on one such complaint from the people, although there was no serious charge against him. The Caliph's principle was that the governor was the servant of the people and as such he must have the confidence of those he governed. It seems that civilisation, at least in this respect, is yet to reach the high mark attained in that golden age thirteen centuries ago. On occasion the Caliph would even write to the people to choose their own governor and intimate their choice to him. The people of Kūfah, Syria and Baṣrah, for instance were given this high privilege. Every individual citizen of the state of Islām enjoyed the right to give his opinion and was perfectly free to do so. From the districts came deputations to enlighten the Caliph on local conditions. In his lectures and sermons, the Caliph laid special emphasis on the point that the people must avail themselves of the right of free expression of opinion. This was considered the birthright not only of a Muslim, but of every human being. Every possible measure available under existing conditions was adopted to ascertain public opinion. Above all, the position of the Caliph, or the King, was exactly that of a common subject. The emoluments granted to the Caliph were on the same scale with others. If sued, the Caliph appeared to defend himself in the public court of justice just as any other defendant. Once in a dispute with Ubayy ibn Ka'b, the Caliph appeared as a defendant in the court of Zaid ibn Thābit. Zaid wanted to show him respect but

'Umar was displeased, saying this amounted to partiality. Thus under 'Umar the principle of democracy was carried to a point to which it will yet take the world time to attain.

Simple life and concern for the ruled

To the early Caliphs of Islām, their kingly position was not an opportunity to have a good time to eat, drink and be merry. To them it was an office of service to the people, involving great sacrifice of personal comfort. In the discharge of his duties as king or, more appropriately, as the greatest servant of the people, 'Umar displayed extraordinary devotion. It may be said that in this respect as well 'Umar was a mirror reflecting the high sense of duty of his illustrious Master. Just as the Prophet considered no piece of work too low for him or beneath his dignity, even so did his most devoted disciple attend in person to the meanest offices of the state. If camels belonging to the state were sick, there was the Caliph with his own hands applying treatment. If one such camel was lost, there was the Caliph again searching for it in person. During the Persian wars, when times were critical and news from the theatre of war was anxiously looked forward to, he would in person go out for miles to see if a courier was coming. On one occasion when one such courier came with the news of victory, the venerable old Caliph came running back to the capital, keeping pace with the courier's camel and asking him all sorts of questions. It was only when he arrived at his destination that the perplexed courier came to know that the man running on foot by the side of his camel was no other than the Caliph himself. Hurmuzān, a Persian chief, when brought as a captive, was wonder-struck on finding the great Caliph stretched in the mosque on bare ground. On the important occasion of signing the treaty of Jerusalem, he was clad in his usual coarse and patched clothes and officers who implored him to put on a stately costume met with a sound rebuff. The Muslim's dignity, he told them, lay elsewhere than in his dress.

When Arabia was stricken by famine, on his own back the Caliph carried sacks of corn to distribute among the famishing people. At night he visited the dwellings of the famine-stricken, brought them flour and even helped them in preparing food. On one such nocturnal visit, he found a woman with nothing to eat. Her children were crying for bread but she had nothing to give them. Just to console them, she had put a kettle on the fire with nothing but water in it. Touched to the quick, the Caliph ran back to Madīnah, some three miles away and shortly after returned with a sack of flour on his back. When some one offered to carry the load for him, he simply replied: "In this life you might carry my burden for me, but who will carry my burden on the day of Judgement?" He was ever accessible to the public and in person listened to the meanest troubles of the people. His door was ever open for such complainants. Even the governors had instructions to have no guard at their gates, lest people coming with their complaints should be kept back. For such people they must be at all times accessible. Many a time 'Umar was harshly treated by others but he kept quiet. When a certain man repeatedly said to him, "Fear God, O 'Umar," some people wanted to stop him. "Let him say so," said the Caliph, "of what use are these people if they should not tell me such things?" At the dismissal of Khālid, some one stood up and thus addressed him: "O 'Umar! Thou hast not done justice. Thou hast removed a worker of the Prophet and sheathed the sword which the Prophet himself had unsheathed. Thou hast cut asunder the tie of relationship and hast acted jealously towards the son of they uncle." In reply the Caliph simply said: "Thou hast been carried away by passion in support of thy brother."

Treatment of non-Muslims

The human sympathies of 'Umar were not confined to Muslims. He showed just the same charity of heart to Christians and other non-Muslims that came in contact with him. On his death-bed, he enjoined his successor to take particular care of the rights of non-Muslim subjects and not to burden them beyond their capacity. The life and property of a non-Muslim were made as inviolate as those of a Muslim. A Muslim assassin of a Christian was condemned to capital punishment. In affairs of state, non-Muslims were duly consulted. On one occasion while on a journey, the Caliph saw that some non-Muslims were worried for non-payment of *jizyah*. On enquiry they were found to be indigent. The Caliph ordered them to be let off. Non-Muslims enjoyed perfect freedom of religion. Even on grave charges of conspiracy and sedition he gave them but light punishment. When the Jews of Khaibar and the Christians of Najrān were, on some such charges, ordered to settle elsewhere, they were at the same time paid the full value of their properties from the public treasury. Orders were also issued to allow them special concessions on the journey as well as to exempt them from *jizyah* for some time. Out of the *zakāt* money raised from Muslims, the Caliph also helped poor Christians. Once, the Caliph saw an old Christian begging for alms. He was not only exempted from *jizyah* but was also awarded a subsistence allowance from the public treasury. General orders were then issued that old age pensions must be granted to all the old people among non-Muslim subjects, who must also be exempt from *jizyah*. Poor-houses for the weak and the disabled were open to Christians just as to Muslims. To consider *jizyah* a hardship is to betray ignorance. The Muslim subjects had to pay a higher rate of tax, *zakāt*, and at the same time they were required to render military service, from which non-Muslims were exempt. Is there a government anywhere today in this twentieth century that levies no taxes on its subjects for the maintenance of peace and order? Notwithstanding their being a ruling race, Muslims put up with grave insults from Christians. Once a Christian openly used a foul word of the Prophet in the face of Muslims. A Muslim merely gave him a slap on the face. The case was brought before 'Amr ibn 'Āṣ, the Governor. The Muslim pleaded that in their own churches they might say whatever they liked, but in public they had no right to use such harsh words about the Prophet. This shows the extent of Muslim toleration at the time. Of course, things that were likely to disturb public tranquillity were forbidden. For instance, it was forbidden to carry the cross in procession through Muslim crowds, to blow the church bugle at Muslim prayer hours, to carry pigs towards Muslim quarters and so forth. Those who have generalized these prohibitions to mean that the Christians were absolutely forbidden these things are mistaken. Once such prohibition was that the children of Christians who embraced Islām must not be baptized until they attained the age of puberty. To generalize this to mean that baptism as such was absolutely forbidden is wrong.

Condition of Women in the time of 'Umar

Women in Arabia were the subject of much harsh treatment, and 'Umar had a special reputation for this failing of his race. Long before the revelation of the Quranic verse enjoining the seclusion of women, he urged that the females of the Prophet's household must observe seclusion. But it was not the seclusion that is in vogue now. 'Umar's own example shows that women did all necessary work. Once, it is recorded, a certain friend was putting up as a guest at his house and 'Umar's wife in person served the food. It was 'Umar again who placed the supervision of the market in the hands of a woman. Nay, during his reign, women actually enlisted and went to the theatre of war to tend the wounded, dress their wounds and do similar relief work. Some even participated in fighting. Women were also free to attend lectures, sermons and similar functions. Once when 'Umar delivered a sermon against the practice of settling large sums as dower-money, it was a woman who stood up and objected, saying: O son of Khaṭṭāb! How dare thou deprive us when God says in the Qur'ān that even a heap of gold may be settled on the wife as dower?" Far from resenting this, 'Umar appreciated this courage of conviction and complimented the objector, saying: "The women of Madīnah have more understanding than 'Umar." When as Caliph he made education compulsory in Arabia, it was made so for both boys and girls. In short, consistently with the requirements of their household functions, women were seen side by side with men in almost every walk of life.

Gradual abolition of slavery

It must be recorded as one of the greatest achievements of the Caliph that he took a very long step towards the abolition of slavery. With regard to Arabia, a definite order was issued that no Arab should be made a slave. This, in fact, was the first step towards total abolition. If later generations of Muslim kings had carried on this gradual reform, as originally intended in the Qur'ān itself the institution would have been eradicated from among the Muslims twelve centuries ago. As a rule, only prisoners of war[4] were considered slaves, and the civil population was in no way interfered with. But the Caliph granted a great deal of freedom even to prisoners of war. For instance, the war prisoners of Egypt were all restored to their homeland and those of Manādhir were also set at large. In various treaties, whenever mention was made of security of life and property, it implied that the vanquished foe would not be converted into slaves. Notwithstanding these reforms, whatever number of slaves still existed, they were treated by Muslim soldiers as brothers.

Equality of man

Equality of man was another great virtue of Islām which stands out conspicuously in the caliphate of 'Umar. He himself was a living example of this principle, and through him his spirit was diffused among the rank and file of state officials and down into the general public. Elected a king, he yet gave no preference to himself over others. When subsistence allowances were fixed, he refused to accept more than was allowed to all those who had taken part in the battle of Badr. This was five thousand dirhams a year. When 'Abd Allāh, the Caliph's son, grumbled that he had

4. It must be borne in mind that prisoners of war were distributed among the soldiers as there were no other arrangements for keeping them. But they were set free either as a matter of favour or on receipt of ransom. To this effect there is a plain injunction in the Holy Qur'an: "When you have overcome them make them prisoners and afterwards (set them free) as a favour or ransom" (47: 4).

got a smaller allowance than Usāmah, the son of Zaid, he was curtly told that Usāmah's father was much dearer to the Prophet than his own. Bilāl, 'Ammār, and others who were, originally slaves but were among the first to embrace Islām, were shown preference over the great chiefs of the Quraish. In the appointment of governors, the Caliph never showed partiality in favour of his own or of the Prophet's tribe. High officials, if guilty of transgressing upon others' rights, were called to account and subjected to similar treatment at the hands of the aggrieved. Jabalah, a Syrian chief, when performing *ṭawāf*, i.e., circumambulation around the Ka'bah, dealt a slap to a man whose foot had chanced to touch his flowing robe. The man returned the blow. Complaint was brought to the Caliph, who ruled that all Muslims were equal and difference in social status made no difference in rights as citizens. Offended at this, Jabalah recanted the faith, 'Amr ibn 'Āṣ, governor of Egypt, had a pulpit set up in the mosque. The Caliph disallowed it, saying it was not Islamic for one man to sit above the rest. The Caliph's own son, Abū Shaḥmah, was found guilty of drinking and was given the usual punishment of eighty stripes. All distinctions of heredity were abolished and society was ordered on the Quranic principle: "The most honourable among you is the one who has the greatest regard for his duty." What could show a greater sense of human equality than pledges taken from high state officials that they would not wear fine clothes, that they would not use sieved flour, that they would ever keep their doors open to the needy, that they would never keep any guard at their doors? When such behaviour was demanded from governors and high state dignitaries, the equality pervading the general public may well be imagined.

Works of public good

Works of public good and charity received special attention at the hands of 'Umar. The weak and disabled were granted allowances from the public treasury, and in this there was no discrimination between Muslim and non-Muslim. The system of old-age pensions now prevailing in many countries in Europe was first introduced by 'Umar. For wayfarers, large caravansarais were erected in all big centres. Children without guardians were brought up at the expense of the state. During famine the Caliph worked day and night to render succour to the starving and even gave up the luxury of meat. He never squandered public money on poets. When in the great plague of Syria, thousands of Muslims died, in person did he attend to the needs of bereaved families, making every arrangement as regards their property and children. To ascertain the weal and woe of his subjects, he would go out at night on tours of investigation. On one such round, he came upon a solitary tent. As he was seated there on the ground with the Beduin, from inside the tent were heard the cries of a woman. On inquiring, he was informed that the Beduin's wife was all alone and these cries were the travails of child-birth. Forthwith the Caliph hurried back to his house and took his wife, Umm Kulthūm, to the tent to nurse the lonely woman.

Spreading of Islām and the knowledge of Qur'ān

During the reign of 'Umar there was no separate organization to push forward the propagation of Islām. Nevertheless, on unorganized lines, every opportunity was availed of for its spread. Generally speaking, the commanders of the army were selected from among the learned so that they might, in addition to their military duties, disseminate the light of Islām, wherever they went. Every Muslim solider was also supposed to be a preacher of Islām, which fact has given rise to the common misunderstanding that a Muslim carried his sword in one hand and the Qur'ān in the other. This they did, but not in the sense implied. They were there to fight in defence of their liberties. It was zeal for their faith that would not let opportunity slip, and they availed themselves of it for the promulgation of truth. It was thus that the sword and the faith appeared side by side — not in the sense that the Muslims were out to spread their faith by the sword, and offered the choice between the sword and the faith; but in the sense that even the soldier who had to fight the battles of the nation was animated with a zeal for spreading the truth. Side by side with preaching, the practical example of Muslim was a great force to attract the hearts of others. The northern part of Arabia, and most of the Arab tribes of Syria that had embraced Christianity under the influence of Christian rule, were soon attracted by the beauties of Islām. Likewise Mesopotamia also joined the faith. In Persia, the great Magian chiefs were the first to join and through their example created an inclination for the acceptance of Islām among the masses as well. In Egypt, too, Islām spread by leaps and bounds. The simplicity, sincerity and righteousness of each individual worked as a charm as no sermon could do and, as a result, group after group came pouring into the fold. In certain places, two to four thousand came in together. In the army of Islām there was quite a large proportion of these new converts. In the city of Fusṭāṭ, ward after ward were inhabited by these newcomers. Not only were the people converted but they were also instructed in the faith of their adoption. In the conquered territories teachers were appointed for this purpose and were paid out of state treasury. This system of paid teachers is also one of the noteworthy institutions of 'Umar. Instruction in the Qur'ān was compulsory for all Beduin tribes, and an inspector was appointed to tour round and report those who neglected to avail themselves of these arrangements. Such distinguished companions as Abū Ayyūb, Abū Dardā' and 'Ubādah were deputed to Syria for the purpose of organizing Muslim education in that country. They spent some time in Ḥimṣ, Damascus and Palestine and popularized Quranic instruction in those parts. Soldiers had instructions to learn the Qur'ān, and even while fighting their country's battles, in their leisure hours they acquired knowledge of the Qur'ān. Every division of the army had several hundreds of those who had the Qur'ān by heart.

Soldier and administrator

'Umar was not merely a great soldier. He was an equally great administrator. Side by side with his conquests, he displayed unique genius in organizing the civil administration of subjugated territories. Had he neglected this part of his duties, his conquests would have been but a passing phase, and in a short time those countries would have been lost to Islām. But he did not do things by half-measures. Islām went to these countries and was going to stay there by the beneficent administration and the general good treatment that it extended. With the advent of Islām, people grew in prosperity. Every country was divided into provinces; measurement of land was made; census was taken; offices were established; a police force was organized; jails were built; cantonments were set up; canals were dug; public treasuries were started, and the Muslim eṛa of Hijrah, which has been a great help in the preservation of history, was introduced.

A true successor of the Prophet

'Umar was a great conqueror. He was a great administrator. Yet, it must be remembered, he was in no sense a king. In the truest sense of the word he was the Caliph i.e., a successor of the Prophet. To walk faithfully in his Master's footsteps, was his sole anxiety. Just as in the Prophet, so in his Caliph, worldly power or wealth produced not the slightest change. Just as the Prophet, even so his Caliph, lived the plain simple life of a humble man. At his table there were never any dainty dishes. During famine he gave up even such small luxuries as meat and olive oil. His dress was spotted with many patches. Worldly riches were of little consequence in his sight. He often feared that wealth might become the ruin of Muslims. For his residence he had no palaces built, nor was any magnificent council-hall erected. The business of government was conducted in the same old mosque where the Prophet used to sit and teach and conduct other business. There in the mosque met the councils, there on the floor of the mosque were received the ambassadors and grandees of the Persian and Roman empires. Like the Prophet, he performed all little offices for others, and in person would he carry to the families various letters received from the battlefield. A sense of accountability for the great national trust always caused him anxiety. The most glorious of conquests produced not the faintest air of pride in him. Master of four kingdoms, he walked on God's earth with the meekness of the humblest man. He did not touch a single thing belonging to the *Bait al-Māl* except the fixed amount sanctioned by the council for his subsistence. Once when, as a cure for some ailment he wanted honey, he refused to take it from the *Bait al-Māl* until the council had sanctioned it. Once the Caliph enquired of Salmān, one of the great companions, whether he was Caliph or King. "If you extort money from people," replied the wise man, "If you misappropriate money from the public treasury, then you are a king: otherwise, a Caliph," Thus, most scrupulously fulfilling the trust of the Prophet's successorship, the great Caliph 'Umar showed tḥat, though a king in name, his true office was that of the Caliph of the Prophet.

Chapter 3
'Uthmān

Early Life

'Uthmān was the third Caliph of Islām after the Holy Prophet. Before joining the brotherhood of Islām, 'Uthmān was known by his *kunyah*, Abū 'Amr; later as Abū 'Abd Allāh. Dhu-l-nūrain[1] was his epithet of honour. His father was 'Affān and his mother Arwā. At the fifth place his ancestral pedigree joins that of the Holy Prophet. He belonged to the Banī Umayyah clan of the Quraish. This was the clan which, after the period of the early Caliphate, acquired possession of the empire of Islām and wielded the sceptre of authority for about a century. Abū Sufyān, who had repeatedly led the Quraish and other tribes in war against the Prophet and at length embraced Islām at the fall of Makkah, was a prominent figure of this clan. Even before the advent of Islām, the Banū Umayyah enjoyed a position of distinction being entrusted with the custody of the national flag of the Quraish. 'Uthmān was six years younger than the Holy Prophet. From his childhood he was upright and honest. He had also learnt reading and writing. When he grew up, he took to trade and did a flourishing business. He enjoyed special esteem for his integrity and was on friendly terms with Abū Bakr.

---

1. *Dhu-l-nūrain.* lit. means possessor of two lights 'Uthmān was so called for having married two daughters of the Holy Prophet, one after another. Of these two, Ruqayyah bore him a son called 'Abd Allāh, after whom he adopted the *kunyah* Abū 'Abd Allāh. The child died at the age of six.

Conversion to Islām

When the Holy Prophet proclaimed his mission, 'Uthmān was thirty-four years of age. Abū Bakr was the first man to carry to him the message of Islām. One day 'Uthmān and Ṭalḥah ibn 'Ubaid Allāh came to the Prophet, who explained to them the teachings of Islām and recited a passage from the Qur'ān. He told them of the obligations that Islām imposed as also of the high place to which it wanted to uplift man. Both embraced Islām. This took place before the Prophet had repaired to the house of Arqam. On this occasion 'Uthmān related a personal experience. "I have just come back from Syria," he said. "On the way at one place we were feeling somewhat drowsy when there came a voice: 'Wake up, ye sleeping ones, Aḥmad has appeared in Makkah'. On our arrival back here we came to know about thy mission."[2]

The clan of Banū Umayyah to which 'Uthmān belonged was the only clan among the Quraish which was opposed to the Banū Hāshim, the clan of which the Prophet came. For this reason the leading men of this clan such as 'Aqbah ibn Mu'ait and Abū Sufyān were among the bitterest foes of the Prophet. 'Uthmān, however, was not in the least influenced by these considerations and when Truth dawned on him he did not hesitate to accept it. When his uncle Ḥakam came to know about his conversion, he had 'Uthmān tied down with a rope and said that until he had renounced the new faith, he would never be released. To this 'Uthmān replied that he would never forsake Islām, come what may.

Emigration to Abyssinia

'Uthmān had not been very long in the fold of Islām when Abū Lahab made his son, 'Utbah, divorce the Prophet's daughter,

---

2. *Tabaqāt ibn Sa'd*, Vol. III, p. 37;

Ruqayyah. Thereupon the Holy Prophet gave her in marriage to ‘Uthmān. When the persecutions of Muslims exceeded all bounds and the Prophet counselled them to emigrate to Abyssinia, ‘Uthmān along with Ruqayyah was one of the first batch of emigrants. After remaining there for a number of years, he returned to Makkah, from where he again emigrated to Madīnah with the rest of the companions.

Services rendered to the cause of Islām

After emigration to Madīnah, ‘Uthmān took a most prominent part in serving the cause of Islām. He was a rich man and, in point of financial sacrifices, he was second only to Abū Bakr. Madīnah had only one well of drinking water, called Bi’r Rūmah. When the Muslims settled there it was in the possession of non-Muslims who charged Muslims for the water. The Prophet keenly felt this trouble to which the Muslim brotherhood was put and expressed a wish that a Muslim might purchase it and make it public property. ‘Uthmān was the man who fulfilled this wish of the Prophet and purchased the well for 20,000 Dirhams (according to some for 35,000). When the Prophet’s Mosque appeared too small to accommodate the daily growing congregation of Islām, the Prophet expressed a wish that someone would purchase the adjoining piece of land and add it to the mosque. ‘Uthmān fulfilled this wish too. He purchased the ground and carried out the extension of the mosque from his own pocket. Just before the battle of Tabūk, when the Muslims were passing through a period of extreme difficulty and a huge expedition was to be sent out against the Roman Empire, ‘Uthmān contributed ten thousand Dīnārs in cash and a thousand camels. Thus he bore the expenses of a great part of the army.

‘Uthmān’s part in warfare

Persecuted by the Quraish, the Muslims emigrated to Madīnah. There, too, they were not left in peace and were repeatedly attacked.

The first attack took place at Badr in the second year of the Hijrah. As this battle-field was three days' journey from Madīnah and 'Uthmān's wife, Ruqayyah, the Prophet's daughter, was seriously ill, he could not take part in this battle. He stayed behind with the Prophet's express permission in order to attend to his sick wife. She, however, did not get over the illness and passed away before the news of the victory of Badr reached Madīnah. 'Uthmān's absence from this battle was due to unavoidable circumstances and so, when the war-spoils were distributed, he also was given the due share of a soldier. After the death of Ruqayyah the Prophet gave his second daughter, Umm Kulthūm, in marriage to 'Uthmān.

'Uthmān took part in the battle of Uḥud which came about a year later. The enemy was repulsed. But the Muslim archers blundered. They left their position where the Prophet had posted them and where he had ordered them to remain whatever the issue, victory or defeat. The Quraish were quick to see their opportunity. They took possession of the same strong point and fell upon the Muslims from the rear. The scales were thus turned and the victorious but scattered force of Islām was in dire straits. A portion of the army cut off from the main body, fled back to Madīnah. Another, though it kept the field, lost its foothold and drew aside. Among these latter was 'Uthmān, and for this some people subsequently reproached him. As a matter of fact, it was no occasion for reproach. The Holy Qur'ān itself considers this fault to be pardonable (3:154). No one is therefore entitled to blame or criticise him on this account. 'Uthmān took part in all other battles. He was not present at the treaty of Ḥudaibiyah but that was due to the fact that the Prophet himself had deputed him as an emissary to the Quraish who kept him prisoner. News even got abroad that he had been killed. The murder of an envoy was tantamount to a declaration of war, and the Prophet consequently took from his men a fresh pledge of allegiance. The pledge known as *Bai'at al-Riḍwān* was due to this emergency. The Muslims vowed that, however formidable the enemy's onslaught, they would remain in the field and fight till the last man. When all had taken the vow, the Prophet in person took a similar vow on behalf of 'Uthmān, placing one of his hands on the other. This shows the esteem in which he held him. The Quraish were so impressed at the sight of this display of devotion that they concluded a truce, and set 'Uthmān at liberty. The army drawn up for the battle of Tabūk, known as the *Jaish al-'Usrah*[3] owed its formation, in very large measure, to the self-sacrifice of 'Uthmān.

Part played in earlier Caliphate

'Uthmān occupied an important position in the affairs of State during the Caliphate of both Abū Bakr and 'Umar. He was a prominent figure in the Council, and his advice was sought on all important matters. When the end of Abū Bakr drew near, anxious to nominate a fit person to succeed him, he consulted first of all, 'Abd al-Raḥmān ibn 'Auf and 'Uthmān. After he had sounded their views, he consulted others. The same position of trust and confidence was enjoyed by him during the reign of 'Umar.

Elected Caliph

For the appointment of a suitable successor to himself 'Umar made on his death-bed the best arrangement possible under the circumstances. The choice of the first two Caliphs had presented little difficulty. At the Prophet's death, there was amongst his companions a man of Abū Bakr's overtowering personality, a man commanding universal respect both for his piety and his capacity, and all eyes spontaneously turned to him as a fitting successor. Likewise, when the earthly life of Abū Bakr was drawing to a

3. Lit., the army of difficulty. The Tabūk army was so-called because in the first place the journey had to be undertaken in the intense heat of the summer and secondly, it was the time of reaping the harvest and ripening of fruit which made it very difficult to proceed.

close and the question of a Caliph again came up before Muslims, fortunately there yet existed among them a man of 'Umar's conspicuous calibre and on him fell the unanimous choice. After 'Umar, however, there were amongst the companions many on whom the Prophet's mantle could fittingly have fallen, but among them there was none standing out in distinct relief from the rest as did Abū Bakr and 'Umar in their respective times. They were all more or less on the same plane and hence the question of choice out of so many, all fitted for the exalted office, was a matter for some anxiety. During his life-time 'Umar used to say that Abū 'Ubaidah ibn Jarrāh, should he survive him, would make the best Caliph. But Abū 'Ubaidah was already dead. Then there was 'Abd al-Raḥmān ibn 'Auf, who was held in the greatest esteem and whom 'Umar had made imām in his own place when he received the fatal wound. But 'Abd al-Raḥmān was not willing to shoulder the great responsibility. Among others qualified for this great national trust the most prominent were those nominated by the dying Caliph to make the choice from amongst themselves. There was 'Uthmān, a venerable man of 70 who had behind him a proud record of great pecuniary sacrifices in the cause of Islām and who, besides, had the honour of having taken in wedlock two of the Prophet's daughters, one after the other. There was 'Alī, the Prophet's cousin and son-in-law, whose strength of arm was the dread of foes as his erudition and piety were the blessing of friends. Sa'd ibn Abī Waqqāṣ, the conqueror of Persia, was also prominent. Though recalled from the governorship of Kūfah, it was for only a trifling affair. He possessed special administrative capacity. Ṭalḥah and Zubair enjoyed great esteem for their glorious deeds in the service of Islām and the defence of the Prophet and had the additional distinction of being two of the Blessed Ten (*'Ashrah Mubashsharah*). *'Ashrah* means *ten*, and *mubashshar* means *one to whom good news is given*. The ten companions to whom the Prophet gave good news that they will be in paradise are known as *'Ashrah Mubashsharah*. 'Umar charged these six persons with the election of one from their midst as Caliph. A better arrangement and a better set of men could not have been imagined. If left to the masses, the question was sure to give rise to dissension and disturbance. They had further been instructed to make the choice within three days. After the Caliph's death, five of the nominees, Ṭalḥah not being present at the time, conferred and it was unanimously resolved that the choice should be left in the hands of 'Abd al-Raḥmān ibn 'Auf. 'Abd al-Raḥmān consulted each one individually. Sa'd favoured 'Uthmān; Zubair mentioned both 'Uthmān and 'Alī. 'Uthmān voted for 'Alī and 'Alī for 'Uthmān. Thus, barring 'Abd al-Raḥmān himself, the majority of votes were in favour of 'Uthmān. But 'Abd al-Raḥmān went still further and sounded the prominent figures of the nation who had, in connection with the pilgrimage, assembled from all parts of the country. The trend of general opinion was in favour of 'Uthmān. On the fourth day, therefore, early in the morning, 'Abd al-Raḥmān declared 'Uthmān as the duly elected Caliph and everybody, forthwith, took the oath of allegiance. After the oath-taking, Ṭalḥah appeared. 'Uthmān related the whole matter to him and told him that he was prepared to withdraw even at that stage, if he (Ṭalḥah) was against his election. But Ṭalḥah expressed his agreement and took the oath of fealty.

Revolt in Persia leads to extension of Empire

Perfect peace and tranquillity reigned in Persia till the end of the second Caliph's life: but some six months had hardly passed, when to the violation of solemn treaties, the whole country rose in open insurrection against the authority of Islām. The ex-king Yazdejird, though in exile, was still alive, and was at the bottom of this mischief. His agents let loose over the length and breadth of the land, succeeded in rousing sentiments of loyalty to the old ruling dynasty and the eyes of the populace once more turned to their exiled ruler. 'Uthmān met the situation with a firm hand. Troops were promptly hurried to the scene, the insurrection was quelled and treaty relations were established anew. This time, however, the Muslim army had to extend its operations to the Persian frontiers where, in fact, the whole trouble had originated. Thus this second conquest of Persia led to the further extension of the Empire of Islām. On one side, the flag of Islām fluttered over Balkh and Turkistān and on the other was won the homage of the chiefs of Hirāt, Kābul and Ghaznī. Most of Khurāsān, including Nīshāpur, Ṭūs and Merv, fell into Muslim hands in the year 30 A.H. The following year, which was the eighth year of the rule of 'Uthmān, Yazdejird passed away in exile. In 32 A.H., the Muslim army had an encounter with the Turkish forces in the valley of Ādharbaijān. At first, the Muslims suffered a reverse, but on the arrival of reinforcements the reputation of Muslim arms was amply retrieved. Thus during the reign of 'Uthmān not only was peace established in the countries conquered during that of 'Umar, but towards the east and the north the frontiers of the Muslim Empire were considerably pushed forward.

Roman attack on Syria and further conquests

There was also trouble in Syria. 'Umar had appointed Mu'āwiyah to the governorship of Damascus, but gradually the whole of the country came under the sway of that governor. The Caesar of Rome looked quietly on and for a time there was no move on his part. In the second year of 'Uthmān's reign, however, Roman armies poured into Syria by the land route of Asia Minor. The Syrian garrison at the disposal of Mu'āwiyah was not sufficiently strong to withstand the invaders. Fresh troops were consequently sent by the Caliph and the Caesar's forces were defeated. Here as in Persia, the Muslims did not stop with repelling the enemy and carried their arms beyond the Syrian frontiers right into Asia Minor and, having scoured through Armenia, they linked up with the Persian army in Ṭabristān. From there, they pushed straight north, going as far as Tiflis and the Black Sea. Thenceforward, almost every year, the Roman hordes from Constantinople would swoop down on the Muslims and, consequently, the Syrian army was kept busy fortifying the frontiers.

Cyprus occupied

The island of Cyprus was occupied in the year 28 A.H./649 A.D. Even during the reign of 'Umar, Mu'āwiyah had moved the Caliph for permission to capture this small island which, the Governor urged, was in such close proximity to the Syrian frontier that even a dog's bark there could be heard on the Syrian coast. 'Umar, however, was averse to naval warfare. Now, when the Romans made repeated incursions on the Syrian frontier, Mu'āwiyah once more urged the occupation of this important strategic point. Permission being granted, the island was immediately seized. The inhabitants agreed to pay the same tribute to the Muslims as they did to the Romans. Some years later, however, the Cypriots assisted the Roman armies against the Muslims, and Mu'āwiyah had therefore again to invade the island which henceforth became part of the Muslim Empire. This took place in 33 A.H.

Roman invasion of Egypt and further conquests in Africa

The death of 'Umar was, so to speak, a signal for foes on all sides to attempt to overthrow the Empire of Islām. There was insurrection in Persia. The Romans attempted to regain possession of Syria. Egypt, following suit, shared the common fate of its sister-dependencies. In the year 25 A.H./646 A.D., the Romans landed at the port of Alexandria and took possession of the town. Soon after, however, 'Amr ibn 'Āṣ, the Governor, drove the Romans out and recovered that port. Tranquillity was thus restored in Egypt, but towards the west, the Romans still kept up hostilities. And in the meantime the governorship of the country changed hands. There arose a dispute between 'Amr, the Governor, and 'Abd Allāh ibn Sa'd on certain administrative matters. This 'Abd Allāh was the foster-brother of 'Uthmān, and a capable administrator. The Caliph had put him in charge of upper Egypt. The dispute was brought before the Caliph who decided against the Governor, and ultimately recalled him to the capital. His place was occupied by 'Abd Allāh ibn Sa'd. During the reign of 'Umar, territory extending as far as Tripoli and Barqah had come under Muslim sway. The Roman garrisons, nevertheless, held on to their positions, and as yet no decisive battle had been fought on that front. The Caliph sent instructions to the new governor to proceed thither and clear the Romans out. For, so long as Roman forces were on the soil of north Africa, the position of Islām in Egypt could in no way be secure. Gregory, the Roman commander, had a force 120,000 strong, an army too big for the meagre force of 'Abd Allāh. Additional troops were consequently sent to Egypt to enable the Governor to carry out the Caliph's instructions. Among other distinguished soldiers, there were in this army 'Abd Allāh ibn 'Abbas and 'Abd Allāh ibn 'Umar. The Romans offered stubborn resistance and hostilities dragged on. Fortune fluctuated sometimes one way, sometimes the other. At last, Gregory was slain at the hands of 'Abd Allāh ibn Zubair and on the fall of their commander the Roman forces were disheartened and took to flight. This came about in the year 26 A.H. Five years later, in 31 A.H., the Roman Empire made another attempt. A fleet of 500 vessels was prepared to invade Egypt. On the other side, 'Abd Allāh also had a fleet prepared though on a much smaller scale. The two fleets met, vessel was grappled to vessel and a hand-to-hand fight ensued in which the Romans were defeated. Notwithstanding these signal victories, however, the Governor, 'Abd Allāh ibn Sa'd, became unpopular among his fellow-Muslims.

Causes of the discontent in 'Uthmān's Caliphate

As all these events in various parts of the Empire of Islām bear out, the machinery of Government had in no way slackened, as is sometimes supposed, during the reign of 'Uthmān. It worked with its usual smoothness and speed. Wherever, an insurrection cropped up, it was forthwith put down. Frontiers were expanded and fortified and many a new land annexed to the Empire. A successful beginning was made even in naval warfare, of which Muslims had no experience. Thus Muslim society had in no way lost anything of its vigour and vitality. But a subterranean current of mischief was all the while gathering force under this appearance of all-round prosperity and it ultimately burst forth, shaking the whole fabric to its foundations. In the newly-conquered lands, large numbers had joined Islām — Magians, Jews and Christians. This general tide of converts had also brought with it into the fold some men who were by no means fascinated by the beauties of the faith. Their sole game was to use the cloak of Islām in order to undermine it. And that greatest virtue of Islām, its unique spirit of democracy, served as a ready weapon in the hands of this unscrupulous gang. The faith of the Prophet stood for perfect equality of man, irrespective of earthly distinctions. There was no restriction whatever on freedom of opinion or on the expression of that opinion. Governors were made accessible to the public to the extent that they were forbidden to have guards at their doors lest there should be the least hitch for the aggrieved to approach the highest authority at any time. Not only were Governors thus readily accessible to all; they were actually at the mercy of the public. If there were complaints against a Governor, real or imaginary, the Caliph's door at the capital was ever open to receive them. On the smallest trouble at the hands of a Governor, people would approach the Caliph and have another of their own choice appointed in his place. The position of the Caliph himself, in this wonderful democracy, was no higher than that of a commoner. He was considered the servant of the people, not the king, and as such he was open to criticism. Individual expression of opinion is not freer even in this twentieth century of civilization than it was in the galaxy days of Islām, but this very fact endangered the freedom of the state. Though Emperor of four great kingdoms, the Caliph was no more than an individual member of society. It was open to anybody and everybody to pick any amount of holes in him. This unrestricted freedom, in itself the highest virtue, served in the hands of mischief-mongers as the most deadly weapon to undermine the power of Islām. Every Muslim was supposed to be a partner in the government and so were these conspirators. Wearing the badge of Islām, they passed for Muslims and enjoyed Muslim rights — which rights they seized the more easily to wreck the society of which they pretended to be members and which, openly, they could not injure. In the capital itself, there was little danger of the abuse of this privilege of free expression of opinion. Most of the inhabitants were those who had sat at the Prophet's feet and imbibed directly from him the true fraternal spirit of the faith; others were the offspring of such people, and they walked in the footsteps of their elders. But such new colonies as Baṣrah, Kūfah and Fusṭāṭ were inhabited by a medley of all kinds of people, and it was in these centres, therefore, that the germs of mischief found congenial soil. Here brewed that storm which sullied the latter days of the rule of 'Uthmān and ultimately led to his murder.

Appointment and dismissal of governors

The main accusation brought against 'Uthmān appertains to his distribution of the loaves and fishes of government office. During the first six years of his reign, it is admitted, he gave no cause for complaint. Rather, among a particular section of the people, the Quraish, he was considered decidedly a better man than his illustrious predecessor. But the trouble began in the latter half of his rule when, in the appointment of governors, he was, it is alleged, influenced in favour of his own relations, against whom, furthermore, he would not even listen to the grievances of the populace. These were the charges brought against the Caliph by those who rose against him and killed him. Now to weigh these charges, let us turn to the cold facts of history. The charge-sheet consisted of three counts, the distribution of the governorships of Baṣrah, Kūfah and Egypt. The Governor of Syria, Mu'āwiyah, too, was a near relation of 'Uthmān but this appointment had been made by 'Umar and was simply continued under 'Uthmān. To take the dispute about Kūfah, it will be recollected, that Sa'd, conqueror of Persia, was during the reign of 'Umar appointed the Governor of that province, and subsequently on a minor complaint recalled by that Caliph. He was replaced by Mughīrah. On his death-bed, however, the Caliph 'Umar expressed a desire that Sa'd should be reinstated. Accordingly, when 'Uthmān took the reins of Government in hand, he recalled Mughīrah and reappointed Sa'd to the governorship. Now there arose a dispute between Sa'd, the Governor, and Ibn Mas'ūd, the treasury officer of Kūfah. Sa'd had taken a loan from the treasury and after some time, when he was reminded by Ibn Mas'ūd of the debt, there ensued an altercation between the two, and this altercation developed into an open dispute. Such strained relations between two highest dignitaries of the State could not but have repercussions on the general public. The Kufites ranged themselves in support of either side. Such a state of things could not be allowed long to continue without serious danger to public tranquillity. Sa'd was consequently once more recalled from the governorship, and Walīd ibn 'Aqbah appointed in his place. Walīd was no doubt a near kinsman of the Caliph on his mother's side, but the mere fact that the event took place in the year 25 A.H. should suffice to exonerate the Caliph from any suspicion of partiality for relatives. It was yet the beginning of his reign and all critics are agreed that, at least for the first six years, his hands were perfectly clean. This charge must therefore be summarily dismissed on the accusers' own admission. That the Caliph was in no way moved by considerations of relationship is further evident from the fact that when Walīd was accused of drinking liquor he was not only dismissed but actually given the prescribed number of stripes as required by law. What greater proof could there be of his absolute freedom from the weakness imputed to the Caliph — viz., partiality for relations? It is certainly no slight thing to have a provincial Governor flogged in public, and if 'Uthmān had been really actuated by motives of relationship, he could very well have managed to shield him at least against this ignominy. Walīd was succeeded in the year 30 A.H., by Sa'īd ibn 'Āṣ, an inexperienced youth who also happened to be a relation of the Caliph. Under him the rowdy elements of the population of Kūfah secured considerable ascendancy and consequently in the year 34 A.H., he was replaced by Abū Mūsā Ash'arī who had no blood-relationship with the Caliph. This disarmed the mischief-mongers of the only weapon with which they spread discontent against the rule of 'Uthmān.

To turn to affairs at Baṣrah, Abū Mūsā Ash'arī had been appointed Governor of the place by the Caliph 'Umar. In the year 29, when the people of Baṣrah accused him of partiality for the Quraish, 'Uthmān removed him and appointed in his place a man of their own choice. This man, however, could not acquit himself well in that position of responsibility and therefore he was replaced by 'Abd Allāh ibn 'Āmir. Though a relation of 'Uthmān, the achievements of 'Abd Allāh in the re-conquest of Persia and annexation of extensive new territory to the Empire furnish concrete proof that in his selection the Caliph was influenced solely by the considerations of sterling worth. Subsequently events put the seal of confirmation on this choice, as they did in the case of 'Abd Allāh ibn Sa'd who was appointed Governor of Egypt instead of 'Amr ibn 'Āṣ.

As already stated, he was a foster-brother of 'Uthmān, but his African triumphs against vast Roman hordes as well as his breaking absolutely new ground in creating a strong navy for the Muslim Empire show that he was a man of genius and daring; and certainly it was as such, not as a relation, that 'Uthmān chose him to be at the helm of Egyptian affairs in those critical times. Nevertheless, when the insurgents reached Madīnah and demanded his removal, the Caliph readily consented, recalling 'Abd Allāh and appointing their own nominee, Muḥammad ibn Abū Bakr, in his place.

'Uthmān's impartiality in the choice of Governors

From what has been said above, it is evident that among 'Uthmān's choices were some who happened to be somehow related to him. But to jump from such data to a general conclusion and accuse him of partiality is certainly unwarranted. In the first place, relationship is a very comprehensive term, including within its meaning the most distant relations. And the relations chosen by 'Uthmān for these appointments could by no stretch of significance be called near relations. Then comes the still more weighty consideration that, if he appointed his relations, he removed them whenever there were complaints against them. Partiality would have dictated that he turn a deaf ear to the clamour against his relations. Then again, the consideration that these relations of the Caliph distinguished themselves in the Persian and African conquests should go to justify these selections on their own merits and absolve 'Uthmān of any pro-relation proclivities. The assertion that such appointments of relations were made only in the last six years of the Caliph's rule and not in the first six is not borne out by facts. Walīd was made Governor of Kūfah in 25 A.H., the second year of his reign. 'Abd Allāh ibn Sa'd was made Governor of Egypt in

26 A.H., the third year of his reign. And at that period of his rule, when these appointments were actually made, there was, as all critics agree, no complaint against the Caliph on this score. This shows that there was nothing genuine in the charge; that it was a mere pretext, seized on at a much later date and dangled in the public eye with a view to spread dissatisfaction against the rule of the Caliph. The charge was thus absolutely baseless and the character of 'Uthmān perfectly free of the blemish imputed to him by malice as clever propaganda.

Nevertheless, it may be frankly conceded that it would have been more desirable, had 'Uthmān followed the policy of his predecessor and, instead of his relations, made the choice of other capable men to fill the offices of governors — more desirable, we say, because, at least, it would have deprived the mischief-mongers of one means by which to throw dust in the eyes of the public and spread disaffection against the Caliph. But perhaps it is not for us in the twentieth century to sit in judgment on and dictate to those pioneers of Islām, not knowing their difficulties nor their dangers, nor the conditions under which they had to steer the bark of Islām. However sound this counsel of precaution may look at this distance of time, we find that immediately after 'Uthmān, his successor, 'Alī, followed exactly the same policy and gave away most of the high offices of the State to his own kinsmen, the Banī Hāshim. Perhaps the situation then obtaining called for such a course. Perhaps the men they chose were the best available. At any rate, of one thing, on the score of facts already enumerated, we are certain there was no base motive, no partiality for relations.

Ibn Sabā leads agitation against 'Uthmān

The root of the trouble that led to the assassination of 'Uthmān and the general undermining of the fabric of Islām was one Ibn Sabā, a Yamanite Jew. In the eighth year of the reign of 'Uthmān this man came over to Baṣrah, where 'Abd Allāh ibn 'Āmir was Governor, and embraced Islām. As his subsequent conduct shows, this was just a mask that he put on to conceal his dark designs. At the outset he confined his propaganda to creating disaffection against governors appointed by the Caliph. When the Governor of Baṣrah came to know of this, he had him deported. Leaving Baṣrah he visited various centres of the Empire — Kūfah, Syria and Egypt — and, though turned out from every place, he succeeded in injecting some of his venom everywhere. In Baṣrah and Kūfah, there sprang up a sprinkling of people who fell into his trap and kept up his nefarious propaganda. Syria alone was protected from his ominous influence by the prudence of Mu'āwiyah. Arriving in Egypt, he displayed himself in his true colour, openly denouncing the Caliph as a usurper. 'Alī, he began to preach, was the rightful king, being the rightful heir of the Prophet. This seditious teaching he broadcasted from Egyptian headquarters to other places, especially Baṣrah and Kūfah, by means of his agents. And by giving this religious colouring to the campaign, he succeeded in finding many dupes.

Agitation gains strength

This was the main plank of the agitation launched by Ibn Sabā and his gang of agents against 'Uthmān. They denounced his caliphate as a usurpation of what legitimately belonged to 'Alī. The ingenuity of the author, however, was in no way at a loss to discover many others. Any small thing that could in any way be made to add to the flames of disaffection was eagerly seized upon, painted in the most fantastic colours and dangled before the simple, the unsuspecting and the credulous. As already stated, the ranks of Islām were swollen during the reign of 'Umar by a whole flood of converts from among the border tribes, especially in Mesopotamia, where sprang up the two most flourishing settlements of Baṣrah and Kūfah. So far as knowledge of Islām was concerned or the realization of its spirit, these multitudes had little in common with the veterans of the Prophet's days, nevertheless, in the matter of privileges of citizenship, there was no distinction between new and old. The mere badge of the faith was enough to confer Muslim rights. Now equality and freedom of opinion were the two most important rights that Islām conferred on every individual. With the older generation of Muslims, the exercise of these rights was tempered by the sense of duty and honesty they had imbibed from the teachings of Islām and in their use they never overstepped the line of propriety. But not so with these new-comers who had the rights without the sense of duty and honesty, and some of them abused this newly-found liberty and equality. All sorts of imaginary charges were concocted against governors and the Caliph and promulgated without let or hindrance. The masses, with whom listening is believing and who had neither the capacity nor the resources to ascertain the truth of the allegations, fell ready victims to vicious propaganda.

Disaffection spreads among Beduins

The main plank of this propaganda, as already observed, was given a tinge of religion. To the disaffected nucleus were added as many others as the agitators could lay their hands on. To create disaffection among the Beduin tribes, it was dinned into their ears that all the high offices of the State were monopolized by the Quraish. When it was a time of sacrifice, of undergoing the privations of the battlefield and of spilling blood — so preached the agitators — the Beduins were seen in the forefront. To the strength of arm of these brave tribes was due all glorious conquest on many a field. When, however, it came to the distribution of government offices, the Beduin was conspicuous by his absence and the Quraishite was all in all. There was apparently much force in the argument. It was a fact that the Quraish had almost a monopoly of high offices of the State; but it was equally a fact that the Quraish alone had the requisite qualifications properly to fill those offices. The Quraish were admittedly the brain of the nation and, however precious the strong arm of the Beduin might be on the field of the battle, it was a strong head that was needed in an administrator, and this the brave dweller of the desert did not possess. Nevertheless, the Beduin was shown only one side of the picture: that he was exploited by the Quraish and, unaccustomed as he was to any subtle thinking, it was but natural that he should feel this as a personal wrong. The propaganda succeeded. A wave of discontent was set in motion among the Beduins.

Deportation of Abū Dharr

Among the companions of the Prophet there was one, Abū Dharr, a man of retiring temperament and something of a hermit. He was one of the early converts to Islām and it was a hobby with him vehemently to denounce riches as anti-Islamic. In Damascus, where the Muslims possessed abundance of wealth, he was seized with one of these fits and began to preach against it. Worldly wealth, he argued, was meant only to be spent on charitable objects and was in no way to be hoarded. Gradually his views on the point reached the extreme limit and he would denounce all accumulators of wealth as fodder for hell. He based his verdict on the Quranic verse: "Those who hoard up gold and silver and do not spend it in Allāh's way, announce to them a painful chastisement" (9:34). Such unhinged effusions created a stir in society and there was fear of a breach of the peace. Consequently, the Governor, Mu'āwiyah, sent Abū Dharr to Madīnah. The Caliph in vain argued with him that his conclusions from the verse in question were wrong and that, beyond the prescribed tax of *zakāt*, people could not be forced to part with their wealth. He went on proclaiming his own views and, there being apprehension of trouble in the capital itself, the Caliph sent him off to a place called Rabdhah, where he died two years later. This afforded another propaganda-point for the agitators. The removal of Abū Dharr merely in the interest of public peace was depicted as an oppressive deportation of a saintly man by the Caliph.

Burning of unauthentic copies of Holy Qur'ān

Islām had already spread far and wide. People of diverse nationalities and languages had joined the fold. In Arabia, itself, there was a variety of dialects with differences in pronunciation. This had resulted in a corresponding variety of Quranic recitations. In one part, a particular word was pronounced in one way; in another, in a different way. The Prophet had himself permitted these slight variations of pronunciation according to local dialects owing to lack of education among the people. But such freedom in recitation was not necessary for foreigners. Being utter strangers to the language, to them all pronunciations were equal. If they could pick up one, they could pick up another with equal ease. In the interest of uniformity, it was desirable to have the same pronunciation. In Arabia itself, the Prophet's permission was only a temporary measure and was confined only to pronunciation. The script was to be the same everywhere. It seems, however, that people extended the permission originally granted by the Prophet from pronunciation to script as well, and the varieties of pronunciation found their way into writing. Thus there sprang up copies of the Qur'ān with differences in script, and in the academies that were established during the rule of 'Umar a variety of recitations were followed. Then there arose a third necessity In the outlying parts of the empire, there were no standard copies of the Holy Book with which all copies made in those parts could have been compared. Under these circumstances it was desirable that there should be some arrangement to standardize the text of the Qur'ān throughout the world of Islām. Of such a standard text there was but one volume, the one made under the orders of Abū Bakr, as previously discussed. This volume was now in the hands of Ḥafṣah. The Caliph called a council of the most prominent companions, and it was decided with one voice that other copies of the one in Ḥafṣah's possession should be made and placed in the various centres of the empire to serve as standard versions. To carry this out a committee was appointed under whose supervision fresh copies were made and one placed in each one of the big centres of the Muslim world. At the same time, to avoid discrepancies, all the unauthentic copies, the product of individual efforts, were burnt. All this, as already said, was done under the supervision and according to the instructions of a committee duly appointed for the purpose. And as a matter of fact, in thus preparing a standard version, the Prophet's own idea had been carried into effect. The Prophet himself, though he allowed variety in recitation as suited to the convenience of various dialects, maintained strict uniformity so far as the script was concerned. It was indeed a great service to Islām to take measures to preserve the original script used by the Prophet's emanuenses. Several copies were consequently made from the standard volume prepared in Abū Bakr's time but even this would, at best, have been a half measure had not the unauthentic versions been absolutely obliterated for, in the presence of these, confusion must again have arisen. This second measure, the burning of the unauthentic copies, was thus equally a service to Islām. Yet even such a commendable work did not fail to afford the tongue of malice material for pushing forward its own propaganda. The mischief-mongers raised their hands in horror that an act of great sacrilege had been committed. A hue and cry was raised that the Caliph had caused the sacred volume to be burnt and people far removed from the capital, when presented with such half-truths, naturally felt excited. Whatever it was, religious or sacrilegious, it was not the work of 'Uthmān alone. It was the work of the whole body of responsible Muslims duly met in council. But such small scruples did not trouble the agitator, so long as he had something with which to rouse the ignorant masses against the Caliph.

Mischief started

Egypt was the headquarters of this movement aiming at the overthrow of 'Uthmān and thereby causing disruption within the house of Islām. From there, Ibn Sabā carried on his propaganda and gained converts in several other parts, notably in Baṣrah and Kūfah. In Madīnah, the capital, Ibn Sabā found barren soil for his propaganda. He could entice only two men there, Muḥammad ibn Abū Bakr and Muḥammad Ibn Abū Ḥudhaifah. They were both young men who had a personal grudge against 'Uthmān's administration. While in Egypt they had both quarrelled with the Governor, 'Abd Allāh ibn Sa'd, the Caliph's foster-brother. When Ibn Sabā reached Egypt and started his agitation, he found easy victims in these two aggrieved youths. It was thus that they caught the contagion. Things in Kūfah moved fast. The ringleaders now began openly to condemn the Caliph and his officials. On one occasion when the Governor was holding one of his usual social gatherings, a young man in the course of talk expressed the wish that the Governor might come in possession of some lands, hinting thereby that he would then be in a position to patronize his friends. The accomplices of Ibn Sabā who were also present seized this opportunity to kick up a row. "Do you wish to see others take possession of our lands," they exclaimed and fell upon the youth and well-nigh killed him and his father. Such a scene in the Governor's presence amounted to open flouting of his authority. The matter was reported to the Caliph who ordered these men to be deported to Syria where, he expected, Mu'āwiyah might with his usual tact cure them of their seditious tendencies. Ten men were thus exiled, including one Ushtar. Mu'āwiyah tried his best to bring them round but to no purpose. Consequently, he packed them off to another place at a safer distance, where they were kept under surveillance. In the meantime, Sa'īd, the Governor of Kūfah, had come to Madīnah to confer with the Caliph. The seditionists welcomed the opportunity as a god-send, sent back for their exiled comrades and stirred up general opposition. When Sa'īd returned, accompanied by one servant, they barred his entry to the town and killed his attendant. The Governor, consequently, retraced his steps to Madīnah. Now this was open insurrection and called for rigorous measures. 'Uthmān, however, was too meek and, rather than give exemplary punishment to the ringleaders, he conciliated them by appointing another Governor, Abū Mūsā Ash'arī. Arriving at Kūfah, Abū Mūsā made the people renew their oaths of allegiance to the Caliph, but the embers of mischief kept smouldering under this seeming tranquillity.

Enquiry into grievances

The influence of the seditionists was gradually on the increase. The most effective weapon in their hands was to bring the Caliph's governors into disrepute. This was a matter in which the ignorant masses could easily be duped. Even Madīnah was affected by the poison and tongues began to wag freely. Day in and day out, many complaints poured into the capital from Baṣrah, Kūfah and Egypt — of course, all fabricated in pursuance of a widespread conspiracy. This constant influx gave the propaganda some semblance of reality and even some of the companions, having no means to ascertain the truth for themselves, began to entertain a suspicion that there must be something really wrong with the

Governors. They approached the Caliph to remedy the evil, but he said that according to his reports the Governors were working well. A council was consequently held and it was decided that reliable men should be sent to Baṣrah, Kūfah, Damascus and Egypt, who should, after due enquiry there, report on the matter. 'Abd Allāh ibn 'Umar, Usāmah ibn Zaid, Muḥammad ibn Muslim and 'Ammār ibn Yāsir were selected for this mission. Of these 'Ammār, who was deputed to Egypt, was so taken in by the mealy-mouthed propagandists of Ibn Sabā that he himself was caught in their net and never returned to submit his report. The reason seems to be that the Governor of Egypt was not popular with the people and, moreover, the Sabaites were too clever for 'Ammār, who believed everything they told him as gospel truth. The other three deputies, however, were men of position and of independence of character. After thorough enquiry on the spot they reported that the charges were baseless.

Governors' conference

As a further precaution the Caliph sent word to all parts, informing the people that at the following Pilgrimage season, all Governors would be present and whoever had any grievance might put it before the Caliph. This was the utmost that 'Uthmān could do to remove public grievances. Trusted men had made searching enquiries and now by proclamation a general invitation was issued to anybody and everybody to put up complaints during the Pilgrimage. The Pilgrimage came and all the Governors collected. But there was no one with a grievance. The reality of the matter was that, as reported by the enquiry commissioners, there was no oppression by the governors anywhere. At last the Caliph called a Council of all the Governors and other prominent men to devise ways and means to put an end to this mischief. The unanimous counsel offered him was to deal firmly with the ringleaders and to make examples of them. This, however, was the last thing that a man of 'Uthmān's gentle nature would agree to. He would on no account see a Muslim's blood shed or a disturbance caused among Muslims. Therefore nothing came out of the conference to check the tide of sedition. On departure Mu'āwiyah apprized the Caliph that he sensed serious mischief brewing and begged that either he might be permitted to send a detachment to serve as the Caliph's body-guard or that the Caliph might accompany him to Damascus. Both offers were rejected. How could he quit the place, replied the Caliph, where the Prophet's earthly remains lay enshrined? Nor would he, for personal safety, burden the public treasury with the upkeep of a body-guard.

Seditionists gather at Madīnah: Shawwāl 35 A.H. (March 656)

The Caliph had summoned the aggrieved to meet him during the Pilgrimage when Governors would also be present. Taking advantage of this, the seditionists had made a plot of their own. It had been arranged that, when at the appointed time the Governors left their respective provinces for the capital, large bodies of people should in their absence start from Baṣrah, Kūfah and Egypt, and simultaneously reach Madīnah, thus bringing pressure to bear upon the Caliph, either to dismiss his Governors or to abdicate. Should he refuse both, resort was to be had to the sword. Consequently as the Governors under the Caliph's instructions left for Madīnah at the Pilgrimage season, the seditionists, taking advantage of their absence, set about carrying out their own prearranged scheme. But their preparations were still going on when to their dismay the Governors returned to their respective headquarters after having conferred with the Caliph, as described above. Thus was their first attempt baulked. The following year, however, they made the necessary arrangements beforehand. Under the pretence of the Pilgrimage, they formed caravans of their own and left their respective centres, Baṣrah, Kūfah and Egypt. Arriving at Madīnah, they encamped there in separate places. When informed of the arrival of these bands and their designs, the Caliph, in the course of an address from the pulpit, sounded a note of warning to them. "They want to put an end to me," he observed, "but they must remember that if they raise their hands against me it will lead to a conflagration among the Muslims and they will themselves have to repent." The people of the capital consequently took up arms to defend the Caliph. This came as a sore disappointment to the conspirators, who were under the impression that the Madinites were also discontented with the rule of 'Uthmān and expected no opposition from them. The ringleaders, seeing that they could not force their way into the town with the whole population up in arms against them, thought of another stratagem. The idea was somehow to get into the town since, once they were inside, the Madinites would not be in a position to oppose them. They would thus have the town and the Caliph at their mercy. To effect this, therefore, they waited in deputation on the Prophet's widows and told them that they wanted nothing more than the presentation of certain grievances to the Caliph, asking him to recall the Governors. The trick, however, was seen through and they were told that their explanation was not acceptable. And clearly enough, anybody could smell that the mischief was far too serious. If it were a case merely of a few grievances, how was it that bands from three different places in different directions had arrived simultaneously? Obviously, it was according to a pre-arranged programme, a set plot. Disappointed in that quarter, the conspirators turned to another. They approached 'Alī from whom they had every reason to expect a good reception. In his propaganda, Ibn Sabā had been advocating the cause of 'Alī as the rightful heir of the Prophet and they expected, judging human nature from their own point of view, that the Prophet's cousin would accord them, a hearty welcome. They had sadly misjudged him, however, 'Alī was too noble a soul to entertain any such sordid schemes. To their disappointment, they found that 'Alī would be the first to unsheath his sword in the Caliph's defence. There were yet two quarters left to try. Like 'Alī, the conspirators had in their propaganda set up two other candidates to the Caliphate. The Baṣrites were for Ṭalḥah and the Kufites for Zubair. Consequently, in time of need, they turned to their respective candidates for help. There too they met with scornful rebuff. These exalted companions of the Prophet were far too noble for any such meanness. Thus disappointed in every quarter, the conspirators resorted to a more ingenious hoax. Expressing regret at their conduct, they simply requested the recall of the Governor of Egypt and the substitution of Muḥammad ibn Abū Bakr. The Caliph, in his extreme gentleness of nature, rather than call them to account for their seditious activities, acceded to their request and placed the appointment order of their nominee in their hands. Taking this document with them, all three bands left the capital, pretending to be thoroughly satisfied. This was only the first act of the tragedy.

Seditionists' entry into Madīnah

The people of Madīnah breathed a sigh of relief. The conspirators were gone and the crisis, it seemed to them, was over. Normal activities were resumed. But they were soon undeceived. Only a few days had passed when to their bewilderment, all three bands reappeared at one and the same time and took the town by surprise. 'Alī with a few others went to them to find out the reason. They produced a letter under the seal of the Caliph addressed to the Governor of Egypt, containing instructions that as soon as the malcontents reached Egypt, they should be put to death or otherwise punished and also that he should consider his dismissal order as null and void. This letter, they said, they had intercepted, when on its way to Egypt by the hand of a particular servant of the Caliph. 'Alī at once saw through the whole game. How was it, he asked, that the courier with the letter was on his way to Egypt whereas all the three bands were back simultaneously? The roads to Baṣrah, Kūfah and Egypt led in different directions. The return of the Egyptian band could be understood, but how could that of the other two, at one and the same time, be explained? The spot where the letter was said to have been intercepted was far off from Madīnah and in that short interval of time it was an obvious physical impossibility for word to reach the other two bands already at so many days' distance from the capital. The plan in reality was this. The conspirators on their first arrival found all Madīnah ready in arms to oppose them, should they attempt to force their way into the town. To lull them into security, they went back with loud protestations of their entire satisfaction. They only wanted to put the Madinites off their guard, to return under some other pretext and take them by surprise. This other pretext was supplied by this forged letter. If it had been a genuine interception, only the Egyptian band could possibly come back with it. The fact that the other two also reappeared and at the same time clearly shows that the whole thing was prearranged. They had gone in different directions and, if they had wanted to communicate the news to the bands of Baṣrah and Kūfah, the Egyptians could have done it only by way of Madīnah. But by the time they arrived in Madīnah, the other two should have reached their respective destinations. It was thus physically impossible for all the three to reassemble at the same time except by pre-arrangement. The whole thing thus was a huge hoax. The ringleaders forged the letter and it was agreed that at a particular time all three bands would turn on their heels and reach the capital at the same time. The letter, it is contended, bore the Caliph's official seal. There is nothing impossible in this. A counterfeit seal could easily have been made. This exactly was the suspicion expressed by 'Uthmān himself when the matter was put up before him. The allegation that the courier was one of the Caliph's servants was also a fabrication, as the servant was never produced as a witness. The Caliph demanded that to prove the charge they must produce witnesses; but they were not able to present a single one. Another conjecture is that perhaps the letter was written by Marwān without the Caliph's knowledge. If so, at least that servant should have been produced as a witness and the whole thing would have come to light. This was not done. The absence of any witness, even of the alleged courier, is proof positive that neither the letter was genuine, nor the seal, nor the story that it was found on the person of a courier. If circumstantial evidence can be relied upon, surely there is in this case overwhelming evidence to lead to the conclusion that the whole thing was a fabrication, a mere pretext to return and capture the capital unawares. When confronted by 'Alī with the most relevant question as to how it was possible for all the three bands to reach Madīnah simultaneously, the conspirators simply replied: "The Caliph's seal is there and that is enough." 'Alī took the ringleaders to the Caliph but their behaviour towards the venerable companion of the Prophet was most insolent. 'Uthmān affirmed on solemn oath that he had neither written the letter nor knew anything about it. The conspirators pointed to the seal. The Caliph pleaded complete ignorance of how it came to be there. Had there been not a shred of other evidence, the solemn oath of a man of 'Uthmān's righteousness should have sufficed for conviction that in this matter the hands of the Caliph were absolutely clean. In reply to his denial, however, the conspirators resumed their insolence. "Whether you have written this letter or whether someone else has written it, in both cases you are unfit for the office of the Caliph and you must abdicate." "Abdicate I will not," replied the aged Caliph. "How can I throw off the mantle which God has put on me. Tell me where I am wrong and I am open to correction." The conspirators repeated their demand. "It is now too late for correction," they said . "There are only two alternatives now — either you must abdicate or here is the sword to make you abdicate or to finish with you." To this insolent threat the aged Caliph replied with characteristic calmness and gentleness: "As to death, I have no fear of it and consider it the easiest thing. As to fighting, if I wished such a thing, there would today have been thousands here to fight for me. But I cannot find it in my heart to be the cause of shedding a drop of Muslim blood." Thus the curtain dropped on this painful scene of insolence to an old, unprotected monarch of four kingdoms. The seditionists rose and went away with ominous determination in their looks.

The Caliph is maltreated and imprisoned in his house

The town was in the hands of the seditionists. The Caliph and the companions, nevertheless, were so far free to attend the mosque for daily prayers. Once in the mosque, the Caliph rose to address a few words to the people, but he was not allowed to speak. Dust was thrown on his face and his supporters were thrust aside. The ringleaders made it a point not to let the Caliph say a word to the public. They knew fully well that if the whole truth about the forged letter and the plot were disclosed, their own dupes would desert them. Then came Friday and the congregation prayer. The Caliph as usual stood on the pulpit and, addressing the seditionists, reminded them of the Prophet's curses on them and exhorted them to show repentance. The reference was to a prophecy in which the Prophet had mentioned a few places and said that those encamping there would have the curse of God on them. Now these bands of seditionists had on their first unsuccessful incursion on the capital actually encamped at these spots. At the mention of the prophecy they made a disturbance in the mosque. Distinguished companions, such as Zaid ibn Thābit and Muḥammad ibn Muslim, rose to support the Caliph in this view, but the ringleaders caught hold of them and forced them to sit down. Then followed a volley of pelting on the Caliph, the companions and the Madinites. One man snatched the Imām's reclining rod from the Caliph's hand and broke it. Then came stone after stone hailing down on him. His aged limbs gave way and he fell to the ground senseless. He was removed to his house and thenceforward he was prevented from attending the mosque. His house was blockaded. The capital was astir and full of feeling for the Caliph. A handful of men were posted at his door to prevent the seditionists from breaking in. 'Alī, Ṭalḥah and Zubair placed their own sons there fully armed to defend the Caliph with their blood. This spontaneous demonstration of public sympathy, for a while, damped the violent spirits of besiegers. As yet they were afraid of carrying things to the extent of bloodshed. But the blockade was so rigorously maintained that even the supply of water was stopped. 'Alī tried to persuade them that the treatment they were meting out to the Caliph of Islām was sinful even towards the worse enemy of Islām. They were, however, unmoved. At length, Umm Ḥabibah, the Prophet's widow, in person riding on a mule, tried to carry water into the Caliph's house, but in vain. Even she was shown no respect by these insolent upstarts. She was roughly handled and with difficulty escaped a fall.

Madīnah Muslims were averse to shedding Muslim blood

An important question arises here as to the attitude of the people of Madīnah, among whom were such influential men as 'Alī,

Ṭalḥah and Zubair. Why did they keep quiet and let the rebels have their own way with the Caliph? Was it not their duty to defend his person from insult and harm, even at the sacrifice of their own lives? This question has been the puzzle of many historians who, not being able to account for it, have been misled into a great blunder. They believe that though 'Alī, Ṭalḥah and Zubair were not in conspiracy with the rebels, nor did they wish to help them, yet they watched events not without some feeling of gratification. In other words, they were also displeased with 'Uthmān and therefore kept looking on while this infamous persecution and crime was going on without raising so much as a little finger in the defence of the helpless Caliph. They let things have their own course. This is quite a mistaken view. In the first place, the town was entirely under the domination of the rebels, and they, being masters of the situation, were free to do as their sweet will dictated, the people of the town being quite helpless. Then comes the second question that, if the Madinites could not in any way restrain the hands of the rebels, it was open to them at least to strike a blow and honourably fall in the attempt. In fact this was the call of the duty and the call of honour. With regard to this, it must be remembered that the Madinites were in every way prepared to defend the Caliph with the last drop of their blood. An armed posse was posted at his door. The sons of 'Alī, Ṭalḥah and Zubair were also there, ready to lay down their lives in his defence. But they could not, under the law of Islām, strike the first blow. The rebels had not as yet unsheathed the sword. Under these circumstances the Caliph himself was against the use of the sword. In fact, in his official capacity as Caliph he had positively forbidden the people of Madīnah to raise their hands against the rebels. The situation was no doubt critical, but that was no justification for ignoring the Caliph's word. It was the duty of the people to obey his order, and his order emphatically called upon every Muslim not to unsheath his sword against the rebels. What could the Madinites do? Besides the Caliph's imperative order, there was, as they well knew, the clear injunction of the Qur'ān not to be the first in unsheathing the sword even against an enemy of Islām. How could they take the initiative in shedding the blood of fellow-Muslims? Of course, they were ready to draw the sword as soon as the enemy did so and to lay down their lives in the Caliph's defence. They were only waiting for the rebels to draw the sword first. On the other hand, the rebels also were loth to go to that length in the face of the Quranic prohibition. Of course, there were some who had not scruples and were prepared to go to any extremity. But barring these, the ringleaders, the bulk of the rebels were only the dupes of clever propaganda and their leaders could not afford to flout such an important injunction of the Qur'ān. That would have at once alienated from them the sympathies of their dupes. In all this conflict, therefore, they had to keep up appearances and maintain some show of reason and reverence. Hence they hesitated to take an extreme step. Thus there was a state of armed suspense on both sides. Both wanted to avoid bloodshed, at least not to incur the heavy curse of starting it. This was the reason that the rebel leaders were restraining themselves to mere pressure on the Caliph to make him abdicate. The hands of the Madinites were equally bound by the law of Islām. Besides, they never thought that the rebels would have the audacity to transgress those sacred limits and spill the blood of any Muslim, much less of the Caliph.

Annual Pilgrimage

Such was the state of things when there arrived the season of the Pilgrimage to Makkah. Though under a strict blockade, the Caliph was not unmindful of the duties of his office. From the top of his house, he issued instructions to the people and, appointing Ibn 'Abbās head of the pilgrim caravan, bade them set out on the pilgrimage. Ibn 'Abbās was one of those who kept guard at the Caliph's door. He was loth to leave that post of sacred duty, but the Caliph's order had to be obeyed. He went and so did some others, including 'Ā'ishah, the Prophet's widow. She wished to have her brother, Muḥammad Ibn Abū Bakr, for her escort but he was far too busy otherwise. He was one of the ringleaders and could not afford to be away when affairs were about to come to a head. The fact that the people of the capital went on the pilgrimage shows that they had no apprehension that the rebels would resort to bloodshed. The Caliph was pressed hard for abdication. He sent word through the Madīnah pilgrims to the assemblage of pilgrims at Makkah, explaining the situation. He said he had done nothing objectionable and the rebels were bent on mischief, spreading all sorts of calumnies against him and inciting others to disown his authority. He also wrote letters to the Governors telling them that mischief was exceeding all limits and some measures must be taken. The idea was that the arrival of help from outside would in itself serve as pressure on the rebels and mischief would thus come to an end without bloodshed.

The Caliph is slain: 18 Dhu-l-Ḥijjah, 35 A.H. (17 June 656)

But on the other side the rebels could not afford to let things drift. They were well aware that in a few days their schemes would be undone. The general populace assembled at Makkah would come to know of their mischief and flock to the capital. Troops would also arrive to rescue the Caliph. There was thus no time to lose. The capital was almost empty owing to the pilgrimage. The momentous hour had arrived, the hour to strike the blow. It was already the 18th of Dhu-l-Ḥijjah, and in a few more days crowds of pilgrims would be pouring into the streets of Madīnah. Consequently, the rebels made an attempt to force their way into the Caliph's house and finish him. The guard of armed men at the door stuck to the position. They were, however, but a handful and the space was very narrow. After some exchange of blows and thrusts, the guard took up their position on the inside of the door, closing it against the assailants. An attempt to break open the door did not succeed. The ringleaders planned that, while the guard was thus occupied, they should steal in through some other way and quietly commit the black deed. A few of them, consequently, went round to a neighbouring house and from there let themselves down into the inner quarter of the Caliph's house. The Caliph in the midst of his family was at the time reciting the Qur'ān. The venerable hoary-bearded man with his family members around him and with the Book of God open before him made a scene of peace and innocence which, for a moment, held even the callous intruders in awe. They hesitated to shed the blood of a man they knew to be quite innocent and harmless. But this feeble inner whisper was soon hushed. Muḥammad Ibn Abū Bakr stepped forward and held the Caliph by the beard. "O son of my brother," the old Caliph calmly said, "if thy father were alive, he would know better how to treat these grey hairs." Overwhelmed with shame, the son of Abū Bakr shrank back. The more callous then stepped forward and struck their helpless victim with their swords. The Caliph's wife interposed to shield her husband. Her fingers were chopped off. The household servants also offered resistance. One man was killed and the rest were soon overpowered. At last, the Caliph fell dead in a pool of blood. He was then 82 years of age. News of the tragedy reached the unsuspecting guard at the outer door. They all rushed in but it was too late. The rebels, having finished with the Caliph now rushed on the treasury, but found nothing there. Whatever money used to come in was spent on public welfare. News of the murder came as a thunderbolt to the people that were still there in the town. But opposition was now useless. The rebels dominated the whole town. The body of 'Uthmān could with difficulty be interred on the third day.

'Uthmān sacrificed his life for the unity of Islām

There are some who are inclined to attribute these seditious activities culminating in the tragic end of 'Uthmān to the Caliph's own weakness. A more thoughtful critic, however, would hesitate to fling such a charge in the face of one whose glorious career as Caliph was crowned with martyrdom yet more glorious. No man is free from the common frailties of the human race and 'Uthmān was but a man. Flaws and frailties there might have been in him just as in all of us, but to accuse him of weakness of resolution or lack of courage is a gross travesty of facts and a most cruel assault on the memory of one who faced the assassin's sword with calm and dignity. Though old in years, 'Uthmān certainly displayed the energy and courage of youth throughout his Caliphate and even in his death. No sooner had he taken the reins of power in hand than he had to face a general wave of revolt or invasion. There was insurrection in Persia. There was an invasion of Syria and an invasion of Egypt, by land as well as by sea. The question is, how did he bear himself in this most trying situation. Did he play the coward and shrink before this tide of difficulties? Let facts speak for themselves. Not only was the insurrection in Persia thoroughly quelled, but the flag of Islām was carried farther over vast territories, right to the confines of Ghaznī. On the Syrian front, the Romans were driven back, pursued and defeated in their own lands, and the flag of Islām proudly fluttered on the coast of the Black Sea. Rome was proud of being mistress of the seas, yet in her own element she was humbled by the Arab soldiers who had never seen naval warfare before. On the soil of Africa too, the hosts of the Romans were thoroughly defeated. Were all these the achievements of a weak man, of a man who would shrink before difficulties and dangers? In these perilous times, 'Uthmān steered the bark of Islām with a composure of mind and steadiness of hand that should entitle him to a place among the greatest leaders of men. Under him the crescent was carried farther and farther and shone brighter and brighter on land, and, for the first time, on sea. It is thus a great injustice to the memory of this great son and servant of Islām to interpret as pusillanimity what in fact constituted the crowning act of his glory, viz., his martyrdom. It was certainly no weakness that made him so indulgent towards the insurgents. A man who could deal with the hundreds of thousand of the Roman hosts would certainly not cow down before a rowdy rabble. He could smash them with his little finger had he so wished. But he would be the last man on earth, he said, to be the cause of shedding a drop of Muslim blood. That would shatter the solidarity of the house of Islām. Even at the last stage, when the besiegers' swords were at his throat, he stood for the cause of that solidarity and under express orders forbade the townsmen to unsheath their swords. And it may legitimately be said of him that he offered his own life as a sacrifice at the altar of that solidarity, thereby serving as a beacon-light to all coming generations of Islām to keep their ranks closed and never to unsheath the sword against a brother Muslim nor wish him any harm, even at the risk of death.

Prophet's great qualities mirrored forth in the first four Caliphs

The period of the first four Caliphs was in fact a continuation of the Prophet's own life, inasmuch as each of these great luminaries mirrored one particular phase of that life in full resplendence. Abū Bakr was an embodiment of the Prophet's firmness of faith and resolution that knew no wavering under the most trying circumstances. 'Umar reflected in his person the Prophet's domination over the opponents of Islām. And 'Uthmān illustrated in letters of his own blood the Prophet's unbounded affection for his community. In simplicity of life and devotion, 'Uthmān walked in the footsteps of his two illustrious predecessors, Abū Bakr and 'Umar. He never looked at the enormous wealth that came pouring into the public treasury in his reign, spending every penny on public good, and in this respect too he proved himself worthy successor to his great Master.

'Uthmān took nothing from the Public Treasury

The financial services that 'Uthmān rendered to the cause of Islām during the lifetime of the Prophet show that he must have been a big merchant and withal a most generous man. It was a period when Muslims were in very straitened circumstances, yet even then 'Uthmān spent thousands, nay, hundreds of thousands of dirhams in the cause of Islām. This gives some idea of the riches he must have possessed. And when better days came and Muslims became rich, 'Uthmān's wealth must have increased in the same proportion. But money had little value in the eye of the companions of the Prophet. Just as 'Uthmān spent lakhs in the service of the Faith, so he showed great generosity towards his relations. For instance, he gave a lakh of dirhams as dowry to one of his daughters. This, let it be remembered, was his personal property; and there was no harm in a man who could afford to spend lakhs in the cause of the Faith giving away a lakh out of consideration for ties of blood. It is a baseless allegation to say that to satisfy his generosity towards his relations he drew upon the public treasury. His hands are clean of any such stain. Rather than take anything from the treasury, he liberally spent his own wealth for the public good. An amount was duly sanctioned from the treasury to meet the personal needs of the Caliph. But 'Uthmān did not draw even this sum. On one occasion he called a general meeting of Muslims and addressed them to vindicate his position against such allegations. The following is a part of his address, as quoted by Ṭabarī:

"When the reins of Government were entrusted to me, I was the biggest owner of camels and goats in Arabia. Today I possess neither a goat nor a camel, save the two that are meant for the Pilgrimage. Is this true? (The people replied: It is so.) It is alleged that I have given the war spoils to Ibn Abī Sarḥ whereas I have only given him a part of these spoils which comes to a hundred thousand.[4] This was exactly what Abū Bakr and 'Umar used to give. When, however, the people disapproved of it, I took even this much back from him ... It is further alleged that I love my relations and I give them riches. As regards my love for them, it has never induced them to usurp the rights of others. I put upon them the obligations that are due from them. As regards my generosity towards them, I give them whatever I do out of my own property. As regards public property, I consider it lawful neither for myself nor for anyone else. Even during the time of the Prophet, Abū Bakr and 'Umar I used to give large sums out of my own earnings. This I did when I was yet a young man and as such stood in need of money. Now that I have reached the normal limit of my family age and my days are coming to a close and I have made over all my possessions to my family, misguided people say such things for me. By God, I have taxed no city beyond its capacity so that such a thing might be imputed to me. And

4. 'Uthmān gave this sum to the General in fulfilment of a promise that if Tripoli were conquered, he would be entitled to one twenty-fifth of the spoils.

whatever I have taken from the people I have spent on their own welfare. Only a fifth of it comes to me. Out of this too, I consider nothing lawful for my personal use. This is spent on the deserving people, not by me, but by the Muslims themselves, and not a farthing out of public funds is misappropriated. I take nothing out of it so that even what I eat, I eat out of my own earnings."

Every word of this address, delivered before a packed mosque, was corroborated by the audience. This shows that during his Caliphate, 'Uthmān accepted nothing from the public treasury for his personal use, though he had every right to it. He spent the whole of it on the advancement of public welfare and himself did not cast a glance at it. Nay, during his last days, he spent the whole of his wealth — and he was a millionaire — on the public good, thus proving himself a worthy successor to the Holy Prophet.

'Uthmān's reign

The reign of 'Umar stands out so conspicuously in the territorial expansion of the Empire of Islām, and mighty empires fell one after another, before the arms of Islām, in such quick succession that subsequent conquests dwindle into insignificance. But the fact is that the reign of 'Uthmān was to no less degree a period of Islamic strength. No signs of weakness are seen in the power of Islām under him. Suppression of rebellion and anarchy is as important as territorial expansion. And 'Uthmān had only been six months on the throne of the Empire when Persia raised the standard of rebellion. He put it down with a strong hand. Not only was the subject territory cleared of all insurrectionary influences but, as a measure of strategic necessity, further territory was annexed to the Empire of Islām, such as Afghānistan, Turkistān and Khurāsān. This revolt had hardly been suppressed when the Roman Empire invaded Syria. Here too the forces of Islām displayed considerable strength. The Roman hordes were driven off and, over and above this, such territories as Armenia, Āzarbaijān and Asia Minor were added to the Empire of Islām. It was during 'Uthmān's reign that the naval conquests of Islām began and Muslim ships captured the island of Cyprus. The Caesar also invaded Egypt and captured Alexandra. 'Uthmān's army not only recaptured Alexandria but also turned westward to exterminate the Roman army altogether, and the Empire of Islām was largely extended and fortified in that direction. All this should suffice to show that the power of Islām was at the zenith of its glory during the reign of 'Uthmān. Notwithstanding the fact that the Caliph was murdered and there was an insurrection in Madīnah, the very heart of the Empire of Islām, no foreign dependency had the courage to rise in revolt. Such was the prestige the power of Islām had attained during his reign.

Administration

There was absolutely no change in the form of government during the reign of 'Uthmān. The machinery of government worked exactly on the lines that had so far grown up as a peculiar institution of Islām. The same were the powers of the Caliph, the same his rights over the public purse. The *Majlis-i-Shūrā* or Council of Consultation was also maintained and all affairs were settled by the council. The Caliph kept himself fully informed of the state of affairs in the various parts of the Empire. Every Friday, before prayers, he would gather whatever information he could from those in the mosque. There was no obstacle in the way of approaching the Caliph with a complaint or grievance against a Governor or public servant. Every such case received full and prompt attention. All the departments of state worked as during the reign of 'Umar. The Revenue Department was in a much more flourishing condition. The subsidy from Egypt alone went up from twenty to forty lakh dirhams. With the swelling of income, the stipends that were awarded from the public treasury were also increased. Many new buildings were erected. Roads, bridges, mosques and guest-houses were constructed in different towns. Adequate provision was made for the comfort of wayfarers along all the routes leading to Madīnah. Military posts and caravanserais, together with water fountains, sprang up everywhere. To protect Madīnah against floods a huge dam was constructed. The Prophet's Mosque was extended and rebuilt with stone. Farms for the feeding of horses and camels were opened on a large scale and water arrangements were also made.

Standardization of the Qur’ān

In the record of ‘Uthmān’s services in the cause of Islām, one particular service must stand pre-eminent. It was he who had copies made from the only authentic copy of the Qur’ān and had them sent to the big centres of the Empire of Islām. This is an achievement of which Muslims cannot be too proud. If today all over the world of Islām, in east and west, one and the same copy of the Qur’ān is in the hands of the various sects of Islām, it is due to ‘Uthmān. When he came to know that people disputed among themselves regarding the various copies of the Qur’ān then in circulation, he sent for the authentic copy prepared during the reign of Abū Bakr on the advice of ‘Umar. It was in the custody of Ḥafṣah. ‘Uthmān sent for it, had several copies of it made and sent one to each one of the big centres of Islām, so that it might serve as a reference edition and local editions might be corrected accordingly. This was an act of great far-sightedness on the part of ‘Uthmān. In an age when the printing machine had not yet been invented, no better arrangement could have been made to maintain the purity of the text of the Qur’ān. ‘Uthmān was not the collector of the Qur’ān, as is generally thought but, doubtless, he brought the whole of the world of Islām together on one single uniform edition of the Holy Book.

Manners and morals

From his very early life, ‘Uthmān was gifted with a pure nature. Islām brought lustre to this inner gem. In chastity and integrity he was as firm as a mountain. During his reign when worldly wealth found its way to Muslims in great abundance, ‘Uthmān’s integrity, ‘Uthmān’s honesty, ‘Uthmān’s chastity, ‘Uthmān’s piety wavered not thereby so much as an hair’s breadth. Riches had as little fascination for him when he earned lakhs and spent lakhs in the way of God as when he became the master of the richest treasury in the world. He scrupulously followed in the foot-prints of the Prophet. Modesty was the most salient feature of his character. Even the Prophet did not become as free with him as in the company of other companions. For instance, once he was seated while his knee happened to be uncovered. Abū Bakr and 'Umar were also there, but he took no notice of it. As soon, however, as the arrival of 'Uthmān was reported, he covered his knee. During his Caliphate, 'Uthmān in person conducted the five daily prayers and was regular even in his midnight prayers, notwithstanding the fact that he had already attained to the good old age of 80. When, however, he got up for his midnight prayers, he took care not to disturb any of the servants for his own comfort. He was rolling in plenty, yet he contented himself with plain dress and plain food. Even his wife he did not wish to see in expensive clothes. His generosity has already been noted. It went to all alike. His deep love of brother Muslims made him sacrifice his own life rather than wield the sword against them. Not only did he himself refrain from using the sword against Muslims, but he even stayed the hands of his associates.

Chapter 4
'Alī

Early Life

'Alī was the fourth Caliph of Islām after the Holy Prophet, and was also known by his *kunyah*, Abū-l-Ḥasan. He was the son of Abū Ṭālib, the Prophet's uncle, under whose guardianship the Prophet, after the death of his grandfather, 'Abd al-Muṭṭalib, was brought up. His mother's name was Fāṭimah. He came of the clan of Banū Hā<u>sh</u>im which was considered the most respectable among the Quraish. The Prophet also belonged to the same clan. The high function of the custody of the Sacred House of Ka'bah was entrusted to this clan, and on account of this the Banū Hā<u>sh</u>im were held in special esteem all over the peninsula. 'Alī was born in the thirtieth year of the *'Ām al-Fīl* (i.e. the year of the Elephant), ten years before the Call. Abū Ṭālib had a large family, and he had also brought up the Holy Prophet. Now that the Prophet found him in somewhat straitened circumstances he took upon himself the upbringing of 'Alī. Thus, in addition to being a near kinsman of the Prophet, 'Alī was also bound to him by another tie. He had been brought up as a child in the Prophet's household.

Conversion to Islām and determination to help the cause

At the time of the Call, 'Alī was only a boy of ten. From his very childhood, he had been brought up in the house of the Prophet. So he knew all about him and was therefore among the earliest few who embraced Islām. Some are even of opinion that he was the first person to come into the fold, but it is an admitted fact that the honour fell to the lot of <u>Kh</u>adījah. After her came Abū Bakr, Zaid ibn Ḥāri<u>th</u> and 'Alī. It is difficult to tell the exact order among these three. But probably it was Abū Bakr who joined

Islām immediately after Khadījah. Though a mere boy at the time of his conversion, 'Alī showed remarkable enthusiasm in the propagation of the Faith. Once the Prophet invited his kinsmen to a feast. The idea was to give them the message of Islām. When the dinner was over, he addressed the party. "Who of you," said he, "is coming forward to own allegiance to me and thereby become my friend and brother?" All remained silent. 'Alī alone got up and offered himself for the cause of the Faith. Thrice the Prophet repeated his exhortation and thrice 'Alī responded. He was only a boy; yet this youngster was destined one day to become a tower of strength to Islām.

Flight to Madīnah

'Alī had a goodly share of the persecutions to which the Prophet and the rest of the Muslims were put in Makkah. Contemporary accounts take no specific notice of this because of his comparatively tender age. The climax of these persecutions was reached when all the Muslims had to quit Makkah in small batches and take refuge in Madīnah. 'Alī played an important role on this occasion. Like Abū Bakr whom the Prophet detained to be a companion to him on the journey, 'Alī was also kept back. He was to return to the people, after the Prophet had left, whatever money they had deposited with him. It is remarkable that while the Prophet was, on the one hand, the victim of bitter persecution by his people, the same people would, on the other, deposit their valuables with him for safe keeping. So implicit was their confidence in his integrity! 'Alī was at the time twenty-three years old. At night the enemies surrounded the Prophet's house and were waiting to fall on him when he emerged in the morning. The Prophet, however, made 'Alī occupy his bed and unnoticed by the besiegers slipped out and escaped through their midst in the dark of the night. 'Alī remained in the bed. When dawn came the besiegers were surprised to see 'Alī instead of the Prophet. They had no grudge against him, nor could their purpose be served by doing him harm. They were out to take the life of the Prophet and put an end to Islām. As instructed by the Prophet, 'Alī cleared up all accounts on his behalf and immediately this was done, set out for Madīnah. At Madīnah he put up with the Prophet and subsequently, when every emigrant was united in brotherhood with resident of Madīnah, 'Alī enjoyed the honour of being so united with the Holy Prophet. (According to another report, he became brother to Sahl ibn Ḥunaif).

Marriage with Fāṭimah

In the first or second year of the Hijrah, the Holy Prophet gave his daughter, Fāṭimah, in marriage to 'Alī. 'Alī was about twenty-four or twenty-five years of age at the time while Fāṭimah was nineteen or twenty. 'Alī lived a humble life. For the purpose of dowry money and wedding presents, he sold his camel, shield and other articles for 480 dirhams. Three sons, Ḥasan, Ḥusain, and Muḥsin, and two daughters, Zainab and Umm Kul<u>th</u>ūm, were the fruit of this marriage. Of these, Muḥsin died in childhood. The children of no other daughter of the Prophet survived, and the offspring of Ḥasan and Ḥusain is known by the honoured title of Sayyid (lit. Master).

'Alī and Fāṭimah were very fond of each other. Once they fell out over a petty affair. 'Alī left the house and lay down in the mosque in the dust. The Prophet happened to visit the family just then and, not finding 'Alī enquired where he was gone. He was told what had happened and seeing him lie in dust in the mosque, he said: "Get up O Abū Turāb (i.e. *one lying in the dust*). From this Abū Turāb came to be a surname of 'Alī. Fāṭimah died at an early age of twenty-nine, and 'Alī married other wives after her, and other children were born to him of these wives.

Martial exploits

'Alī was a young man when he embraced Islām. So we do not hear of any activities on his part in the way of the propagation of Islām such as those of Abū Bakr, 'Umar and 'U<u>th</u>mān. Nor was he a man of riches. So it was not his lot to render financial services to the cause of Islām as did these three illustrious men. God had, however, gifted him with an extraordinary measure of daring which he devoted to the service of Islām performing wonderful deeds of heroism. At the battle of Badr, as also on other occasions, he was the bearer of the Prophet's standard. On that field of battle, three Quraishite youths came out and, according to the custom in Arabia, challenged the army of Islām to single combat. On this, the Prophet detailed three men, 'Alī, Ḥamzah and 'Ubaidah, and all three overpowered their opponents. After this a general engagement ensued in which, too, 'Alī displayed his valour. In the third year of the Hijrah when Mus'ab ibn 'Umair, the standard-bearer of Islām, fell fighting at Uḥud, 'Alī at once took hold of the standard, rushed forward and killed the standard-bearer of the enemy. For these wonderful exploits a catch-phrase, *lā fatā illā Alī*, i.e., 'Alī is the one youth, gained currency. It is stated that this cry was first raised by someone at the battle of Uḥud. In the fifth year of Hijrah, 'Alī had to meet 'Amr ibn 'Abd Wudd, the famous warrior of Arabia, in a duel. This man was so proud of his bravery that when 'Alī came out to measure swords with him, he said: "I do not wish to slay you." "But I do wish to slay you," retorted 'Alī. After a hard contest 'Amr ibn 'Abd Wudd was killed. At the siege of Banū Quraizah also the standard was in the hands of 'Alī. In the sixth year of Hijrah, he defeated the Banī Sa'd who were rallying to the reinforcement of the Jews of Khaibar. At the truce of Ḥudaibiyah, when terms were drawn up, 'Alī acted as scribe. The Quraishite representative objected to the words "God's Messenger" affixed to the Prophet's name in the treaty. The Prophet agreed to substitute "son of 'Abd Allāh" instead. But 'Alī who had already written the words "God's Messenger," refused to delete them, and the Prophet did it with his own hand.

Of all the martial exploits of 'Alī, the most brilliant was the capture of Qamūs, the famous fort of Khaibar. The Jews had very strongly fortified this fort. The Prophet entrusted the standard first to Abū Bakr. There was a tough fight but the fort did not fall. He then entrusted it to 'Umar. The fight was fiercer than before and yet the fort withstood the onslaught. On this the Prophet said: "Tomorrow the standard will be in the hands of a man who will capture the fort, and who loves God and His Messenger and whom God and His Messenger love." Next morning when the Prophet came, he enquired about 'Alī. He had some eye trouble, he was told. The Prophet sent for him, applied his saliva to his eyes and prayed, and the trouble was no more. The Prophet then put the standard in his hand and the fort was captured.

When at the fall of Makkah the Prophet entered the town at the head of 10,000 strong, the standard was in the hands of Sa'd ibn 'Ubāidah, who in excess of zeal marched on shouting: "Today is the day of bloodshed for Makkah." This was against the wishes of the Prophet, who abhorred bloodshed. So he took the standard from Sa'd's hand and gave it to 'Alī. At the battle of Ḥunain, the main body of the Muslim army, unable to withstand the volleys of the enemy archers, fell back. 'Alī, however, stood firm and wrought deeds of daring. The expedition of Tabūk was the only enterprise in which 'Alī did not take part. He stayed behind at Madīnah under the Prophet's own orders. 'Alī objected but the Prophet pressed him saying, "You stand to me in the relation in which Aaron stood to Moses, except that there is no prophet after me".

As an envoy and preacher of Islām

After his return from Tabūk, the Prophet sent a party of Pilgrims to Makkah with Abū Bakr at their head. Thereafter he received a revelation declaring breach of relations with those Arab tribes that persecuted Muslims and broke their solemn agreements. This is known as the chapter of *Barā'ah* or *Taubah*. It was necessary to communicate this ultimatum to the enemy, who assembled from all over Arabia on the occasion of the Pilgrimage. The choice to discharge this mission fell on 'Alī who, accordingly, made the announcement on the Pilgrimage occasion. In the tenth year of Hirjah, 'Alī was deputed to carry the message of Islām to the people of Yaman. Before departure, the Prophet emphatically warned him against any warfare so long as there was no aggression from the other side. This clearly shows that even after the revelation of the chapter *Barā'ah* the Prophet still acted up to the Quranic verse which permitted the Muslims to fight only against such non-Muslims as fought against them. 'Alī met with great success in this mission. The tribe of Hamdān embraced Islām in one day. 'Alī communicated the happy news to the Prophet who immediately fell to the ground in a thanksgiving prostration. Other people of Yaman also joined Islām gradually.

At the Prophet's death

'Alī returned from Yaman before the Prophet's Farewell Pilgrimage to Makkah and joined the pilgrims. A few days after returning from the Pilgrimage, the Prophet fell ill. 'Alī tended him during this illness. One day during this period, 'Abbās suggested to 'Alī to ask the Prophet to make a will for successorship in his favour. 'Alī, however, rejected the suggestion. At the Prophet's death, when Abū Bakr, 'Umar and other prominent companions were busy managing the affairs of state so as to avert any blow to the power of Islām in consequence of the Prophet's death, to 'Alī fell the privilege of looking to the funeral arrangements.

Oath of allegiance to the Caliph

According to some reports, 'Alī did not take the oath of allegiance to Abū Bakr for six months. If these reports are taken as authentic, perhaps the reason was that 'Alī kept at home to console Fāṭimah who was much shocked at the Prophet's death. Besides this when Fāṭimah demanded a share of the property at Khaibar, from which the Prophet took his maintenance, Abū Bakr replied that prophets left no property to be inherited. This offended Fāṭimah. Possibly it was in sympathy with Fāṭimah on this count that 'Alī refrained from taking oath of allegiance for some time (When Fāṭimah fell ill, Abū Bakr went to enquire after her health, which shows that Fāṭimah's displeasure was only temporary). Or the reason may have been that 'Alī devoted his time to the arranging of the Quranic chapters in chronological order. Whatever the reason for his delay in taking the oath of allegiance, whether out of sympathy with Fāṭimah or owing to being busy with the Qur'ān, 'Alī had no special grudge against Abū Bakr. But there are strong reasons for doubting these reports, as already shown. When the apostates attacked Madīnah, 'Alī took due part in the defence of the capital. After Fāṭimah's death, he participated in all counsels and affairs of state. After Abū Bakr's death he pledged fealty to 'Umar, and was a prominent figure in the counsels of state in his Caliphate. No important affair was settled without his advice. The friendly relations between 'Umar and 'Alī were further strengthened by the marriage of 'Alī's daughter, Umm Kulthūm, to 'Umar. After 'Umar, 'Alī's name was one of the six from among whom the Caliph was to be elected. When the majority went in favour of 'Uthmān, 'Alī forthwith stretched his hand and swore allegiance to the new Caliph. Towards the close of 'Uthmān's caliphate some mischief-mongers tried to make the caliphate a bone of contention and thereby bring about a rupture between 'Uthmān and 'Alī. 'Alī, however, was too shrewd and too noble to fall into their snare. When the insurgents' attitude towards 'Uthmān became threatening, 'Alī ordered his own son, Ḥaṣan to keep guard at the gate of the Caliph's house.

'Alī becomes the Caliph

During the last days of the reign of 'Uthmān, the insurgents, from the very day they effected their entry into Madīnah, were in virtual possession of the town. The Government lost all hold over the capital. At the news of the murder of 'Uthmān, people generally kept within doors and a state of anarachy prevailed. Of the three bands of insurgents, the one from Egypt, which was the centre of Ibn Sabā's machinations, was the most powerful. Their chief acted as the Imām at the daily prayers. This state of confusion lasted for five days. The three bands of insurgents could not come to an agreement regarding a successor to 'Uthmān. The Egyptian band, however, was the most dominant, and Ibn Sabā, their leader regarded 'Alī to be the rightful Caliph, in whose favour it was alleged the Prophet had made a bequest. 'Alī was, therefore, elected as Caliph by the insurgents, and on 24th Dhi-l-Ḥijjah, 35 A.H., people swore allegiance to him. Most of the Madinites took the oath of fealty without hesitation. Notwithstanding this, however, there is no doubt that it could not be called a free election. There was no occasion for any such election, the town being entirely in the hands of the insurgents. Nevertheless, it is equally true that if a free election had been held, the choice would have even then fallen on 'Alī. On the previous occasion, too, when 'Uthmān was elected, the final choice was between 'Uthmān and 'Alī. 'Uthmān had voted in favour of 'Alī and 'Alī in favour of 'Uthmān as the fittest person for the office of the Caliphate. 'Alī was even then given preference over such overtowering personalities as Ṭalḥah and Zubair, both of whom had to their credit a glorious record of service in the cause of Islām. 'Abd al-Raḥmān ibn 'Auf was another great man who was definitely in the public eye as a fit successor to 'Umar. 'Umar himself considered him as the fittest person for the Caliphate. He could have been a possible rival to 'Alī in a free election. But he had already passed away. Another prominent figure, Sa'd, the conqueror of Persia, had retired from public life. 'Alī was thus the fittest candidate left. Notwithstanding the fact, therefore, that the capital was dominated by the insurgents and a free election was not feasible, no one ever objected to the election of 'Alī on that ground — not even Ṭalḥah, Zubair or Mu'āwiyah. Subsequent events show, no doubt, that Ṭalḥah and Zubair were not willing to render allegiance to 'Alī and did so only under compulsion. But their objection was based on the plea that before everything else the insurgents who had assassinated 'Uthmān must be brought to book. They had no quarrel with 'Alī's personality and they undoubtedly considered him the right man for the position.

Dissensions within the house of Islām

With the advent of the reign of 'Alī, there opens a new chapter in the history of Islām. This period of four years and a half was a period of domestic dissensions within the house of Islām. In the internecine warfare that ensued great and prominent figures were involved. This exactly was the warning 'Uthmān had repeatedly given to the insurgents. "Once you draw the sword against me" he had told them, "you will be opening among Muslims a door of dissension that will never be closed." The warning turned out to be true. Till the reign of 'Uthmān there was practically no division in Islām. The disturbance of Ibn Sabā was the handiwork of the hypocrites who, in the garb of Islām, wanted to undermine the power of Islām. Such of the Muslims as he had made common cause with them were their dupes. With the advent of the reign of 'Alī, however, the house of Islām itself was rent in twain. 'Alī thus found himself confronted with difficulties in no way smaller than those which beset his three predecessors. Abū Bakr was faced with the insurrection of Arabia, and 'Umar with the legions of Persia and Rome, while 'Uthmān had to deal with rebels and insurgents. Each one acquitted himself in these difficult times with firmness and resolution. Likewise did 'Alī display his strength of character in the face of domestic dissension among Muslims.

Demand of retribution against 'Uthmān's assassins

Having done their mischief and then elected 'Alī as Caliph, the insurgents left for their respective places, so that they might take the news of their achievement to their headquarters. At the same time, news of the assassination of 'Uthmān spread far and wide. His blood-stained clothes along with the several fingers of his widow were sent to Mu'āwiyah in Damascus. From all sides came the cry for due retribution for the blood of the Caliph. Within the town of Madīnah as well as in its suburbs arose the same cry. But there were great difficulties which cannot be overlooked. The assassination of 'Uthmān was not the work of a few individuals who could be easily secured and executed. There were large bodies of men at the back of the conspiracy in all three important centres, Baṣrah, Kūfah and Fusṭāṭ. It was no easy task to deal with them. 'Uthmān himself hesitated to unsheath the sword against these mischief-mongers. Such a step was sure to lead to a dangerous conflagration. Things had now no doubt changed a little. The insurgents who had risen under the pretext of demanding certain reforms in administration now stood exposed in their true colours. They had stained their hands with blood which was not only innocent but also most precious. According to the law of both religion and morality they richly deserved capital punishment. But to arrest these men and bring them to book would have meant a great and simultaneous disturbance in every corner of the Empire of Islām. The inevitable result would have been the disruption of that empire. This was what restrained the hands of 'Alī. When, after his election, Ṭalḥah and Zubair demanded of him to punish the assassins of 'Uthmān, this was precisely the excuse he put forward. "I am no less anxious about it myself," replied 'Alī, "but I simply cannot help it. It is a critical time, and if there is any disturbance of peace, the Beduins and foreigners will rise in revolt and Arabia will once more relapse into the days of Ignorance. These men are yet beyond our control. Wait and see till God shows me some way out of the difficulty."

Appointment of new Governors

It is not unoften that there arise complications in situations which make it impossible for two men with the best of intentions to arrive at the same conclusion. 'Alī was now face to face with such complications. On the one hand a vast number of people demanded that the assassins of 'Uthmān should be duly punished. On the other, the political situation was growing so complex that any attempt to take up the sword against those men was sure to endanger the peace of the whole empire. There is not a shadow of doubt that 'Alī himself was anxious to visit the assassins of 'Uthmān with due retribution. But he deemed it advisable first of all to ensure the solidarity of the empire. It seemed to him that the first step to be taken in this direction must be to allay the agitation set afoot against 'Uthmān on account of his governors. Perhaps he also harboured some apprehensions from Mu'āwiyah. Consequently he made up his mind to change all the governors. Mughīrah advised him not to take this step. First of all, he advised, let people unanimously accept him as Caliph. He might then order whatever changes he thought proper among the governors. On his return from the pilgrimage to Makkah, Ibn 'Abbās gave similar counsel. He particularly told him not to interfere with Mu'āwiyah. He was not appointed by 'Uthmān and had been holding the office of Governor from the time of 'Umar. He must therefore be left alone. 'Alī, however, did not listen to this advice for reasons known to himself. Possibly he apprehended some danger from Mu'āwiyah and wanted to nip it in the bud. Or, possibly, he adopted the course of wholesale change so that no one might have any cause for complaint. Consequently, he appointed 'Uthmān ibn Ḥanīf as governor in place of Ibn 'Āmir, who was recalled. Qais was posted to Egypt where he succeeded in controlling the situation. The governors of Kūfah and Syria, however, refused to obey orders. 'Alī once more wrote to them urging them to submit. Abū Mūsā, governor of Kūfah, submitted; but Mu'āwiyah, after some time, sent a messenger to the capital with a blank letter. On enquiry, the messenger informed the Caliph that 60,000 weeping men were assembled at Damascus around the blood-stained shirt of 'Uthmān, determined to avenge the blood of the deceased Caliph. He also told 'Alī that they held him responsible for it. "Do they hold me responsible?" asked 'Alī in astonishment. "Do you not see," he added, "it is as yet beyond my power to pursue these assassins and punish them?" When the messenger went out, some people shouted that he must be put to death. The army was close at hand, came the threatening retort of the messenger.

'Alī, like 'Uthmān, was accused, in making the appointments of governors, of partiality in favour of his relations. Perhaps the reason was that he could not repose as much confidence in others and, when the fate of his Caliphate was hanging in the balance, he was justified in doing so. Or, perhaps, he preferred his own relations to conciliate the insurgents whose ringleader Ibn Sabā attached special weight to the family of 'Alī.

War preparations against Mu'āwiyah

'Alī could not possibly afford to ignore the attitude of Mu'āwiyah. A messenger from him had come with a significantly blank letter. He had definitely held out a threat that 60,000 men were ready to avenge the murder of 'Uthmān. 'Alī could not sit still in the face of this challenge. An important province of the empire was rising in revolt. To put this rebellion down was the foremost duty of the Caliph. He delivered a sermon explaining that the attitude of Mu'āwiyah was calculated to undermine the solidarity of Islām. He knew that the seed of rebellion once sown was bound to spread to other provinces. And if each province declared its independence the power of Islām was at an end. Rebellion could not be put down but by resort to the sword. A definite ultimatum had already come from Mu'āwiyah. There was no alternative left but to declare war against him. War preparation briskly began in Madīnah.

'Ā'ishah, Ṭalḥah and Zubair demand retribution for 'Uthmān's murder

This, however, was not the only difficulty 'Alī had to face. Ṭalḥah and Zubair also held, as already mentioned that retribution against the assassins of 'Uthmān should be the first thing that should engage the attention of the new Caliph. 'Alī pleaded before them his inability at that time to proceed against the assassins. But it seems this failed to satisfy Ṭalḥah and Zubair, who left for Makkah. On the way they met 'Ā'ishah, who was returning from the Pilgrimage, and apprised her of the state of things in Madīnah. The capital, they told her, was in critical state and chaos prevailed. The masses could not distinguish between right and wrong, nor could they defend themselves. Consequently, 'Ā'ishah turned back to Makkah with them.

On arrival there all people rallied to them. 'Ā'ishah recited the following verse from the Holy Qur'ān:

> "And if two parties of the believers quarrel, make peace between them; but if one of them acts wrongfully towards the other, fight that which acts wrongfully until it returns to Allāh's command; then if it returns, make peace between them with justice and act equitably" (49: 9).

To Muslims, their lives were meant for God. Before a commandment of God they attached little value to ease and comfort, even to life itself. When duty called them to fight against the unbelievers, they cheerfully laid down their lives in obedience to Divine behest. Now when within the house of Islām itself one group was transgressing to an extent that resort to the sword was indispensable, they were equally ready to come forward with their lives. It was decided that the blood of 'Uthmān must be avenged. To let the assassins go scot-free would be to put a premium on their mischief-mongering. They had killed 'Uthmān; they might thereafter raise their hands against anybody. It was, therefore, absolutely essential to bring them to justice. 'Ā'ishah, it seems, waited for some time in the hope that 'Alī might move in the matter. When nothing was done and, on the contrary, war was declared against Mu'āwiyah, she was disappointed. A consultation was held and it was decided to proceed, first of all, to Baṣrah. This shows that 'Ā'ishah had no ulterior motive and that reform was her only objective. If she had any design on the Caliphate or if Ṭalḥah or Zubair wanted to wrest the Caliphate from 'Alī they had an easy course before them. They had only to march against Madīnah from the side of Makkah. On the north, there was Mu'āwiyah with 60,000 men. There was as yet great agitation against 'Alī. Things had not settled down, and 'Alī's rule had not yet been established abroad. Within the capital itself there was no army. It was all plain sailing, if they had only wished to seize the Caliphate. This, however, was not their object. They contemplated nothing against 'Alī. To punish the assassins of 'Uthmān was all they wanted. Consequently, instead of marching against Madīnah which was easy to capture, they turned towards Baṣrah — this too at a time when fully four months had already elapsed since 'Alī came to power. Their plan was to deal with the seditionists at Baṣrah first and then proceed to Kūfah and Egypt and call the murderers to account.

Purity of their motives

'Ā'ishah, Ṭalḥah, Zubair and 'Alī were but human beings and not infallible. Mistakes they may have committed, but their motives were unquestionable. The first three were certainly out for reform and had no ulterior motives. At the time of 'Uthmān's election Ṭalḥah and Zubair were among the six men whose names were proposed for the Caliphate. But they renounced their claims in favour of 'Uthmān and 'Alī. Even now, after the assassination of 'Uthmān, 'Alī himself had offered to pledge fealty to either Ṭalḥah or Zubair but they had no inclination to shoulder the responsibility of the Caliphate. From the very first day, however, each insisted that the foremost task was to deal with the assassins of 'Uthmān. This was no after-thought. As regards 'Ā'ishah, she could not possibly be imagined to harbour any wish to succeed to the Caliphate. There are people who assert that she had a personal grudge against 'Alī because he did not defend her honour when the hypocrites spread false reports against her. The fact is that when the Prophet consulted 'Alī the latter advised him to ask the maid-servant. If she were to harbour any grudge on this account, she should never have forgiven men like Hassān and Misṭaḥ who had taken a leading part in the slander. But if she had the magnanimity to forgive even those men who had taken a prominent part in sullying her honour, it is ridiculous to allege that for such a trifle on the part of 'Alī she would for so long have nursed a grudge against him. And her conduct on this occasion shows clearly that she bore no such grudge. Her demand was the same as the demand of many other leading men and women. And it was simply to fulfil this demand that 'Ā'ishah, Ṭalḥah, and Zubair proceeded to Baṣrah after waiting for four months during which the Caliph himself did nothing to punish the culprits. Their real object was none other than bringing the insurgents and assassins to book. 'Ā'ishah, Ṭalḥah, and Zubair honestly believed that it was the Muslims' first and foremost duty to punish the miscreants who had murdered the aged and innocent Caliph of Islām in cold blood. The Quranic verse quoted above made it incumbent on them to fight against those who had rebelled against and murdered the Caliph of Islām. A report in the *Muwaṭṭā* of Imām Muḥammad clearly ascribes to 'Ā'ishah the words that it was not proper to neglect the said verse. Her brother Muḥammad ibn Abū Bakr was one of the insurgents but this did not deter her. Her mind was set on the one subject — to carry out the Quranic injunction by fighting against the transgressors and restoring good relations among Muslims. This exactly was the object of Ṭalḥah and Zubair. They may have erred in judgment, but they were certainly inspired by nothing but the purest of motives. Notwithstanding the loss of thousands of lives, their action had on the whole a salutary effect on the political situation. Nevertheless, later on 'Ā'ishah herself regretted this line of action which shows that she realized her error. This only goes to enhance her position in our estimation. These noble souls were so submissive to the Divine injunctions that so long as they believed a thing to be true, they readily underwent every hardship for it and shrank not even from laying down their very lives. No sooner, however, did they realize that their judgment was at fault, then they as readily confessed their mistake. The right course was that, even though 'Alī were committing a mistake, 'Ā'ishah, Ṭalḥah and Zubair should have followed him. In order to punish the insurgents they should not have taken law into their own hands. It was for the authority constituted by law to see that the ends of justice were met. The fact, however, remains that it was an error of judgment inspired by the best of motives, and even God does not make a sin of such error.

'Ā'ishah captures Baṣrah, Rabī '11, 36 A.H. (Oct. 656 A.D.)

In the fourth month of the Caliphate of 'Alī, an army under the direction of 'Ā'ishah, Ṭalḥah and Zubair marched from Makkah towards Baṣrah. On the way they came upon a pond which, some of the party observed, was the pond of Ḥau'ab. Just then was heard the barking of dogs which reminded 'Ā'ishah of a prophecy of the Prophet that the dogs of Ḥau'ab would bark at one of his wives. On this, she at once thought of retracing her steps. Many people, however, came forward to testify that it was not the pond of Ḥau'ab. They also pressed her not to go back. Perhaps her presence might improve the situation, they said. When 'Alī came to know that an army was marching against Baṣrah, he turned that way instead of going to Syria as originally planned. 'Ā'ishah had already reached the destination. On her arrival at the outskirts of Baṣrah, the Governor of the town sent two men to ascertain what had brought the noble lady there. In reply she said that her object was to restore better relations between the Muslims, a duty incumbent on every Muslim, man or woman. She pointed out how the rebels had attacked Madīnah, created disturbance there, killed the innocent Caliph of Islām, pillaged others' property and oppressed people. The Governor, however, refused to surrender the town, and marched forth with his forces to prevent her entry. At last, when the two armies came face to face with each other, 'Ā'ishah once more explained that the object of her visit was nothing but the arrest of the assassins of 'Uthmān. The following few sentences from the speech she made on that occasion speak for themselves:

> "People used to find fault with 'Uthmān and his officers. They would come to Madīnah and consult us. They understood whatever advice we gave them about keeping peace and order. When we considered the grievances they had against 'Uthmān, we found 'Uthmān innocent, God-fearing and truthful, and these agitators, sinful, treacherous and liars. Their hearts concealed one thing whereas their lips gave utterance to another. When they gathered strength, they entered the house of innocent 'Uthmān without any just cause and shed blood which it was not lawful to shed. They plundered what it was not lawful to take. They desecrated the soil whose sanctity it was their duty to respect. Now listen! The work before us which it does not behove us to neglect is to arrest the assassins of 'Uthmān and see that the law of God has its way."

To fight or shed blood was certainly not the object. The only idea was to come to an understanding by mutual discussion. Some of the Baṣrites were impressed and joined 'Ā'ishah. For another day also, the armies remained encamped against one another but it was strictly prohibited to raise the sword. Among the Baṣrites, however, there was a group of mischief-makers. They were on the lookout for an opportunity to stir up trouble. One of them advanced and made an attack. 'Ā'ishah made her army retreat and encamped elsewhere the following day. The mischief-makers, however, did not desist. One of them used filthy language against 'Ā'ishah and cleverly added fuel to the flames. They at last delivered a general attack. 'Ā'ishah had it proclaimed that she did not want to fight. But the presence in the Baṣrah army of the band of mischief-makers made all her attempts to maintain peace and order abortive. The fighting began. 'Ā'ishah's army was compelled to strike back in self-defence. The Baṣrites sustained heavy casualties and sued for quarter. Truce was concluded on the condition that someone should be sent to Madīnah to ascertain whether Ṭalḥah and Zubair had pledged allegiance under compulsion. In case it was so Baṣrah would be made over to them; otherwise they would voluntarily leave the town. The messenger went to Madīnah but opinion there was found to be conflicting. The majority, however, were inclined to think that it was a case of compulsion. In short, no decision was arrived at, and the mischief-makers, finding an opportunity, made a night-attack on 'Ā'ishah. They were repulsed and on October 17, 656, 'Ā'ishah's troups occupied the town.

'Ā'ishah was against fighting

It is obvious from what has been stated above that 'Ā'ishah never wanted any fighting between Muslims. On the other side, however, there had come into being a regular party which, not content with the murder of 'Uthmān, wanted to create a disturbance and undermine the power of Islām. The misfortune was that in order to gain their own ends, they were apparently espousing the cause of 'Alī. In reality they had little sympathy for 'Alī either, as subsequent events will abundantly show. They had, however, mixed themselves up with the army of 'Alī. The fighting at Baṣrah was entirely due to their mischief and so was the battle of Jamal, in which more Muslim blood was shed. It was one of these men that later killed Zubair while he was saying his prayers. These people declared 'Ā'ishah and her associates to be Kāfirs for the only reason that they demanded retribution for the blood of 'Uthmān.

The letter which 'Ā'ishah wrote to the people of Kūfah after her entry into Baṣrah clearly says:

> "On arrival at Baṣrah, we invited the people of the town to abide by the Book of God. The noble elements of the residents welcomed our exhortation but those who had little good in them took the sword against us. They threatened to despatch us as well after 'Uthmān and out of their enmity declared us to be kāfirs, saying unworthy things of us. We recited to them the Quranic verse: Hast thou not seen the people who have been given a portion of the book, and so forth. Hearing this, some of them came round to submission whereas others differed. We let them alone; yet they wielded the sword against us ... For twenty-six days, we invited them to the Book of God, that is to say, barring the guilty ones, all innocent bloodshed should be avoided. They argued against us, yet we entered into a truce with them. They played false and got up an army. God thus arranged for the retribution for 'Uthmān's blood. With the exception of one, not one of these insurgents escaped alive. God reinforced our power with the tribes of Qais, Rubāb and Azd. Now listen! Treat all people well, except the assassins of 'Uthmān until God has made them pay His dues. Do not defend these traitors nor give them quarters."

Another of 'Ā'ishah's letter says:

> "Even then they did not recognize the truth and, not content with this, once in the dark of the night they stole into my camp to kill me. They were yet on the threshold, one man showing them the path, when they met some men of the tribes of Qais, Rubāb and Azd, keeping guard at my door. The wheel of fortune took a turn and the Muslims killed them. God has brought together all the people of Baṣrah to the opinion of Ṭalḥah and Zubair. After retribution, we will grant them pardon."

‘Alī’s attack on Baṣrah and negotiations with Ṭalḥah and Zubair

When ‘Alī came to know that the Makkan army under the command of ‘Ā’ishah, Ṭalḥah and Zubair had gone ahead, he turned towards Kūfah. Abū Mūsā Ash‘arī, Governor of the town, though he had sworn allegiance, did not agree to ‘Alī’s policy. He too was greatly touched by the murder of ‘Uthmān. ‘Alī’s envoys asked him to join the attack on Baṣrah. On his refusal, he was dismissed. ‘Alī succeeded in rallying some following at Kūfah and at the head of twenty thousand men encamped before Baṣrah. Notwithstanding all this, however, ‘Alī was as averse to fighting as ‘Ā’ishah. Immediately on his arrival at Baṣrah he sent Qa‘qā‘ to Ṭalḥah and Zubair. Six hundred men of Baṣrah had already paid with their lives for the blood of ‘Uthmān, he told them. Another battle would mean another six thousand. The fratricidal warfare must, somehow, come to an end. He also emphasized that ‘Alī too would not let the blood of ‘Uthmān go unavenged but was helpless at the time. As soon as circumstances were more favourable, ‘Uthmān’s assassins would be brought to book. Ṭalḥah and Zubair expressed their approval of this and negotiations continued for several days.

Battle of Jamal, Jumāda 11, 36 A.H. (December, 656 A.D.)

As already stated, however, ‘Alī’s army had considerable element of those who were accomplices in the conspiracy and assassination of ‘Uthmān. When they saw that things were tending toward peace, they became alarmed. It meant their own doom. To save their own skins they had to see to it that the Muslims were involved in mutual fighting. They met together to consider this unpleasant development and after consultation among themselves they quietly made a night attack on the troops of ‘Ā’isha, when both armies were sound asleep. In the dark of the night neither party could know who had started the fighting. Each thought the other had played false. 'Alī did his utmost to stop it but fighting went on and Muslim cut the throat of brother Muslim. At dawn, people approached 'Ā'ishah and suggested that her appearance before the contending parties might have a salutary effect. Consequently, 'Ā'ishah mounted a camel after which the battle is known as that of Jamal, i.e., camel — and went about. On the other side, 'Alī sent for Ṭalḥah and Zubair and talked things over with them. What a strange spectacle! People supposed to be enemies met like friends in the very thick of the battle. The explanation is not far to seek. As a matter of fact, there were no personal motives behind the fighting. They only had the good of the Muslims at heart and wanted to see them united. They all hated bloodshed and were free from any selfish ideas. Right in the field of action, the three men whose armies engaged in fighting met one another and, on 'Alī's persuasion, Ṭalḥah and Zubair both left the battlefield. Zubair straightway made for Madīnah. A Sabite was, however, on his heels and when in the desert he drew aside and began to say his prayers this ruffian saw his opportunity. When Zubair went down in the posture of prostration, the fellow pounced upon him and, chopped his head off, took it to 'Alī. What was the reward he got from the latter? "Give the assassins of Zubair the news of hell," said he. Ṭalḥah also was drawing aside from the battle when another ruffian made him the target of an arrow, to which he succumbed. In spite of the officers who did their utmost to cry a halt, the dead and the dying fell in heaps. 'Ā'ishah had the Qur'ān hoisted by way of appeal to stop fighting but the conspirators killed the man who was holding the Holy Book aloft. At last, the centre of gravity of the fighting shifted to where 'Ā'ishah stood. These rogues did not spare even the Prophet's wife. She was made the target of the attack and fierce fighting took place. Men fell thick and fast all around but the cordon formed around her camel was impregnable. At last, when bloodshed exceeded all bounds, someone hamstrung her camel at which the animal dropped down and the battle came to an end. Muḥammad ibn 'Abū Bakr, the brother of 'Ā'ishah stepped forward and asked if she was hurt. After a while came 'Alī too and enquired how she was. Then, with all due respect, he accommodated her in the house of a

Baṣrah chief of her own party and later on gave her safe conduct to Madīnah escorted by forty ladies and her own brother, Muḥammad ibn Abū Bakr. The Caliph in person accompanied her for a considerable distance. She said that she had no grudge against 'Alī, neither then nor any time before that.

Affectionate relations in warfare

From all these events, one thing is clear as daylight. Notwithstanding the fact that the contending armies lay encamped opposite each other and the sword was busy working havoc and men like Ṭalḥah and Zubair were killed, their hearts were full of mutual affection and respect. Nowhere was there a vestige of grudge or ill-will therein. Everybody had the good of Islām at heart. Right in the thick of battle, Ṭalḥah and Zubair met 'Alī as loving friends and accepted his suggestion. At the conclusion of the fighting 'Alī with all honour waited upon 'Ā'is͟hah and behaved as a dutiful son. The battle of Jamal, like that of the first battle of Baṣrah, was due to the machination of the conspirators who wanted to set Muslims against each other and smash the solidarity of Islām. It must of course be admitted that this unscrupulous gang had taken shelter in the army of 'Alī who probably could not prevent it, as is evident from his repeated assurances. At the bottom of this warfare were the machinations of these mischief-makers. They had assassinated 'Ut͟hmān but they were the enemies, not of 'Ut͟hmān alone, but of all Muslims. They joined one party of them in order to destroy Muslims at the hands of Muslims. When the battle was over. 'Alī ordered that no one of the defeated army should be pursued, no spoils of war should be taken, nor should anyone enter the house of another. Of those who fell in this battle on either side, 'Alī observed: "Whosoever joined it out of good motives, no matter on which side, will receive the mercy of God." So far as Makkah, Baṣrah and Kūfah were concerned, the battle of Jamal set at rest the differences amongst Muslims which had arisen in consequence of the murder of 'Ut͟hmān. Syria, however, was still in a state of turmoil, and in order to restore the solidarity of Islām 'Alī now turned towards that part of the empire.

Kūfah as capital and calling Mu'āwiyah to submission

Appointing 'Abd Allāh ibn 'Abbās as Governor of Baṣrah, 'Alī proceeded to Kūfah which was made the capital of Islām instead of Madīnah in the month of Rajab, 36 A.H. As stated before, Baṣrah was a new colony which had sprung up during the reign of 'Umar. History does not chronicle the grounds which weighed with 'Alī in shifting the capital and many are the surmises made in this connection. To our mind, however, the obvious reason seems to have been that Madīnah was too distant from the eastern possession of the Caliphate and Kūfah, being more central, was better to be the capital of the vast empire. Besides, this centre could command greater influence over the Beduin population. There was a certain man, Ashtar by name, who was one of the insurgents against 'Uthmān though he did not take part in his actual assassination. 'Alī kept this man along with himself. When he appointed 'Abd Allāh ibn 'Abbās, Ashtar was again forward with a complaint. "What have we gained," he observed, "out of the murder of 'Uthmān, Ṭalḥah and Zubair? 'Alī is now appointing his relations as governors." Arriving at Kūfah, 'Alī addressed another letter to Mu'āwiyah, telling him that all was now quiet at Baṣrah, and in the interest of the solidarity of the empire of Islām, he too should submit. There was again no reply to the letter. After some time, Mu'āwiyah sent word that his allegiance was bound up with retribution for the murder of 'Uthmān. 'Alī had no alternative left but to declare war against Mu'āwiyah and war preparations were forthwith taken in hand.

Relations between 'Alī and Mu'āwiyah

From the very beginning, relations between 'Alī and Mu'āwiyah seem to have been strained. Mu'āwiyah disliked the very election of 'Alī as Caliph and was in no way prepared to make allegiance. The sincerity of purpose which inspired the opposition by 'Ā'ishah, Ṭalḥah and Zubair was missing in the case of Mu'āwiyah. No doubt 'Uthmān was a very near relation of Mu'āwiyah and he had every right to press with greater force the demand for the punishment of the assassins. But his refusal even to acknowledge the two letters addressed to him by 'Alī clearly shows that he considered 'Alī's inaction in the matter as tantamount to his approval of the murder. This virtually was the verbal reply he sent him. On the other hand, there is no doubt that 'Alī had so far done nothing to crush the mischief-makers, of whom, there was a strong element in his army and who, in fact, were responsible for the battle of Jamal. 'Alī repeatedly pleaded his inability to deal with the assassins. It was not a matter of a few execution of those guilty of 'Uthmān's murder. The real object could not be achieved until the mischief-makers had been thoroughly crushed, their ringleaders executed and their dupes disillusioned. Repeatedly 'Alī put forward the plea that as yet his hands were not strong enough for such action. 'Ā'ishah, Ṭalḥah and Zubair accepted this excuse and gave up opposition. Mu'āwiyah, on the other hand, rather than accept it as true, considered that 'Alī purposely shielded the assassins. Most historians beleive that Mu'āwiyah's demand for retribution for 'Uthmān's blood was not inspired by any high motives. If in his heart of hearts he was not actually an aspirant to the Caliphate, one is, at any rate, constrained to say that his attitude towards 'Alī was from the beginning unfriendly and at last he rose in open revolt against him. In any case, there arose on both sides circumstances which made mutual confidence impossible and for a final settlement recourse was had to the sword.

Battle of Siffīn, Dhul-Qa'dah, 36 A.H. (April 657 A.D.)

At the head of fifty thousand men, 'Alī marched out against Syria. On hearing of this, Mu'āwiyah too mustered his forces, and the two armies met at Siffīn, a place situated on the bank of the Euphrates, toward the south-east of Aleppo and the north-west of Ḥimṣ. 'Alī already had a bitter experience. He issued orders that his men must on no account strike the first blow. He also wished an amicable settlement to be reached through negotiations. Consequently for the first two days, nothing serious took place. 'Alī sent three men to Mu'āwiyah, asking him to come round to submission in the interest of the empire of Islam. In reply, Mu'āwiyah reiterated the demand that he must first punish

'Uthmān's assassins. 'Alī dismissed this as a lame excuse. "It is a lie," retorted Mu'āwiyah, "and the sword shall be the sole arbiter between us." 'Alī divided his army into eight detachments. Only one was to engage the enemy every day. The idea was to avoid a general battle causing unneccesary bloodshed. The new year set in and warfare was suspended during the sacred month of Muḥarram. There were further negotiations for peace, but both parties stuck to their own view-points and peace parleys led to no result. At last, when the month of Muḥarram was over, fighting was resumed. Once again, 'Alī had it proclaimed that it was incumbent on the people of Syria to submit to the Caliph. This, however, failed to create any impression. After some petty skirmishes, there at last came on Ṣafar 11, 37 A.H. (July 29, 657 A.D.) a general engagement. The battle raged the whole day long but the issue was still undecided. It continued the following day but without result. Fighting was carried on even at night and, when the third day dawned, hand to hand fighting was still going on. On the advice of 'Amr ibn 'Āṣ, Mu'āwiyah had copies of the Holy Qur'ān tied to spears and raised aloft, accompanied by the proclamation through the ranks that the Book of God was still there and must be accepted as arbiter. No sooner did this proclamation go forth than there arose the same cry from the army of 'Alī as well. The miraculous power of the Qur'ān forthwith brought the battle to an end. On hearing the call to the Qur'ān, the contending armies immediately sheathed their swords. It is alleged that 'Alī was against the suspension of hostilities, telling his men that it was no more than a stratagem on the part of Mu'āwiyah. The army, however, refused to listen to him. This allegation is absolutely untenable. The general attitude of 'Alī during previous battles and his treatment of his foes after the battle give the lie direct to any such assumption. It has been noted that 'Alī was bitterly opposed to the idea of warfare among Muslims. A man of such a bent of mind could not possibly stand in the way of peace. The truth of the matter is that Ashtar went on fighting notwithstanding the truce. 'Alī sent for him and told him to stop fighting. Victory was at hand, he replied, and he was not prepared to suspend fighting at that stage. And he did not desist until the rest of the army had compelled him to do so. 'Alī then asked Mu'āwiyah what he wanted. Mu'āwiyah proposed the appointment to two arbitrators, one from either side, and whatever their unanimous verdict on the authority of the Qur'ān both parties must accept. 'Alī appointed Abū Mūsā Ash'arī and Mu'āwiyah selected 'Amr ibn 'Āṣ. It was decided that the two, each accompanied by four hundred of his own men should meet in a central place and decide the issue in accordance with the commandments of the Qur'ān. In case the two could come to no agreement, the decision was to lie with the eight hundred men and, whatever the verdict of the majority, it must be binding on both parties. This being settled, 'Alī left for Kūfah and Mu'āwiyah for Damascus. Ashtar alone was dissatisfied at this arrangement.

Desertion of 'Alī's troops

The truce poured cold water on the schemes of the mischief-makers. While yet on the way back to Kūfah, a detachment of twelve thousand deserted 'Alī. When he arrived at Kūfah, the deserters encamped at a place called Ḥarūrā. The chiefs of the Kufite clans of Tamīm, Bakr and Hamdān, were their ringleaders. Apparently, they objected to the arbitration. The decision, they said, lay in the hands of God. What they really meant was that warfare must continue and the verdict of God should be considered to favour whichever side won. As a matter of fact, they aimed at undermining the Caliphate. These were the very men, as already discussed who, when 'Ā'ishah, Ṭalḥah and Zubair came to Baṣrah, called these righteous persons *Kāfirs*. Likewise they declared Mu'āwiyah and his followers to be *kāfirs* and, as such, fighting against them was considered obligatory. 'Alī did not approve of this verdict, saying that though the opponents had rebelled against the Caliphate, they were brother-Muslims and could not be dubbed *kāfirs*. 'Alī did his best to bring them round but to no avail. He dispersed their gathering at Ḥarūrā'. They nevertheless went on their mischief-mongering activities.

The arbitrators' award, Sha'bān, 37 A.H. (February, 658 A.D.)

At the appointed date Abū Mūsā and 'Amr ibn 'Āṣ met at Dūmat al-Jandal, each with his four hundred followers. A discussion took place between the two in a tent and every aspect of the question was duly considered. The final verdict of both was, as reports show, that 'Alī and Mu'āwiyah should both be excluded and another man elected Caliph. It was not, however, within the power of these two arbitrators to elect another Caliph. It was for the general council of Muslims to make such a choice. Both agreed on this decision. When they came out of the tent, 'Amr asked Abū Mūsā to announce his decision first. He delivered the agreed verdict. Then came the turn of 'Amr. It is alleged that he played false and said that so far as 'Alī's dismissal was concerned, he agreed with Abū Mūsā, but as regards Mu'āwiyah, he supported him. The truth of the matter seems to be that the discussion between Abū Mūsā and 'Amr concerned the question of the Caliphate alone, and it was decided that 'Alī and Mu'āwiyah should both be excluded from this office. The question whether or not Mu'āwiyah should remain in office as Governor of Syria was not touched upon. Whatever 'Amr said, therefore, amounted to this that so far as the Caliphate was concerned, neither 'Alī nor Mu'āwiyah should have anything to do with it. As regards the governorship of Syria, however, he was in favour of Mu'āwiyah continuing in office. 'Amr was a companion of no mean position and to ascribe to him treacherous motives is absurd on the face of it. It is nevertheless true that the decision failed to improve the situation in any way or to bridge the gulf of differences. Things remained as they were. So long as Mu'āwiyah was not to submit to the Caliphate, the solidarity of Islām could not be established. Nor could the election of a new Caliph serve any useful purpose. It must, however, be admitted that till the year 40 A.H. when 'Alī was murdered, Mu'āwiyah did not assume the title of Amir al-Mu'minīn, or the Commander of the Faithful. This shows that he was not a claimant to the Caliphate. As regards the allegations that 'Alī cursed Mu'āwiyah, 'Amr ibn 'Āṣ and their associates, whereas Mu'āwiyah cursed 'Alī, Ḥasan, Ḥusain and their comrades, this must be summarily dismissed as a story concocted later on.

Battle against the Khawārij, Shawwāl, 37 A.H. (March, 658 A.D.)

As soon as the decision of the arbitration became known, the Khawārij rose in open revolt. (*Khawārij* is plural of *Khārijī* which is derived from the root *kharaja*, meaning *he went out*). The first *Khawārij* were the 12,000 men who deserted 'Alī and encamped at Ḥarūrā' after which they were called al-*Ḥarūriyyah*. The word *Khārijī* regarding them is, however, used not in reference to their going forth from Kūfah to Ḥarūrā' but because they *went forth* from the community or brotherhood of Islām by declaring those who opposed 'Alī to be *kāfirs*. It was Khawārij really who rent the unity of Islām by calling members of the Muslim brotherhood *kāfirs*, and this disease has now spread to the whole of the Muslim community. Emerging from their strongholds of Baṣrah and Kūfah, they advanced towards Madā'in, in order to take possession of it and establish their own rule there. The Governor of the place, however, got news of this move in time and the attempt failed. From here they proceeded upward and, crossing the Tigris, four thousand of them mustered at Nahrawān. 'Alī, on his side, finding the decision of the arbitration unacceptable, made preparation to invade Syria again. At the same time, he summoned the Khawārij to submission. These, in the course of a harsh reply, called upon 'Alī to confess his own apostasy. In addition to this, they began to disturb the peace of the country and took to plundering. When 'Alī came to know of their activities, instead of marching on Syria he set out against Nahrawān. On arrival there, he sent word to the rebels promising them a general amnesty on the condition that they should hand over all those guilty of plunder and murder. His exhortations at last succeeded. Some of the Khawārij gave up opposition and went back. Some joined the forces of 'Alī. Eighteen hundred, however, did neither and met him in a battle in which they perished.

The Khawārij cause further trouble

This did not put an end to the disturbance of the Khawārij. Those who had left the field of Nahrawān, ostensibly under the pretence of giving up opposition, went to other places and took the conflagration there. They carried on secret propaganda inciting people against 'Alī. These Khawārij did not consist exclusively of those who had created the disturbance during the reign of 'Uthmān. They had even coined a certain creed of their own and given their movement a religious tinge. Nevertheless, as a matter of fact, this disturbance was only another phase of the one in the time of 'Uthmān. These people were the enemies of the empire of Islām and, though apparently their mischief had subsided, they employed all possible underhand methods to undermine the foundations of that empire.

Having defeated the Khawārij at Nahrawān, 'Alī made up his mind to march against Syria. The army, however, wanted to go back to Kūfah and equip itself anew with all the necessaries of warfare, so that it should then be able to proceed to Syria. Consequently, 'Alī returned to Kūfah. On arrival home, however, the army lost its spirit and hesitated to proceed on the Syrian expedition. It seems the mischief-makers had by their poisonous propaganda created disaffection in the army. Besides this, there arose some fresh developments in Egypt which compelled 'Alī to abandon the expedition to Syria.

Mu'āwiyah captures Egypt. Safar, 38 A.H. (July, 658 A.D.)

'Alī had appointed Qais as Governor of Egypt. Qais was a most sober and shrewd statesman. He did not in the least interfere with the party in Egypt which demanded retribution for the blood of 'Uthmān. The party gathered considerable strength, which was attributed by some to the weak policy of Qais. At last 'Alī recalled him, appointing Muḥammad ibn Abū Bakr in his place. Hot-headed man as the new governor was, he adopted a drastic policy of repression as soon as he arrived in Egypt. The result was that in the year 37 A.H., a widespread rebellion broke out in Egypt. Watching these events, Mu'āwiyah ordered 'Amr ibn 'Āṣ to invade Egypt. 'Alī, who was far away, sent Ashtar to reinforce the Governor of Egypt. Before he could reach Egypt, however, he was poisoned by a border chief. 'Amr ibn 'Āṣ defeated Muḥammad Ibn Abū Bakr. Egypt thus came under the sway of Mu'āwiyah and another slice was cut off from the kingdom of 'Alī.

Later period of 'Alī's reign

The loss of Egypt was another blow to the Caliphate of 'Alī. The Khawārij danger had also taken root and rearing its head now in one part, now in another, weakened the Empire. In 38 A.H., Baṣrah was once more the scene of a disturbance. Ibn 'Abbās, the Governor, was at the time on a visit to Kūfah. His assistant, Ziyād, had to take refuge elsewhere. At length, 'Alī wrote to some chiefs who helped Ziyād and the rebels were defeated. But the disturbance, suppressed in one place, reappeared in another. Khirrīt, an influential chief who had till now been faithful to 'Alī and was his ally at the battles of Jamal and Ṣiffīn, was driven to rebellion. 'Alī tried to bring him round but he escaped alone with his associates and, reaching Ahwāz, incited the people there to revolt. Once again the army of Baṣrah put him to flight, but he reappeared and died fighting. This rebellion was thus suppressed, but immediately another sprang up at Kirmān. 'Alī appointed Ziyād to suppress it and he succeeded. His rule was so just and wise that it reminded the inhabitants of the rule of Naushirwān. Difficulties on the Syrian front, however, still existed. Disputes with Mu'āwiyah dragged on and the latter's men reached even so far as Madīnah, Makkah and Yaman. 'Alī despatched troops to these places and re-established his rule there. In the meantime, 'Abd Allāh ibn 'Abbās became displeased with 'Alī and went away to Makkah. Under these embarrassing conditions, 'Alī considered it advisable to conclude a treaty with Mu'āwiyah, by which Mu'āwiyah's rule over Syria and Egypt was recognised whereas the rest of the empire remained under 'Alī. Thus came to an end the conflict between 'Iraq and Syria.

'Alī's martyrdom, Ramaḍāan 17, 40 A.H. (25th January, 661 A.D.)

The conclusion of peace between 'Alī and Mu'āwiyah dealt a death-blow to all the hopes which the mischief-making party, now represented by the Khawārij, had built up; for it was in mutual warfare among Muslims that the secret of their success lay. They were unable to do anything overt, but their underhand conspiracies continued. At last three of them conspired among themselves to take the lives of 'Alī, Mu'āwiyah and 'Amr ibn 'Āṣ, at one and the same day and hour. The design was that one of them should reach Kūfah, another Damascus, and the third Fusṭāṭ, and on a particular Friday during the month of Ramaḍān, just at the hour of morning prayer each one should despatch his victim. 'Amr ibn 'Āṣ happened to be indisposed on the fixed day and did not come out for the morning prayer, and another man was killed in his place. In Damascus, Mu'āwiyah sustained a grievous wound but ultimately recovered. The part of taking the life of 'Alī was allotted to one 'Abd al-Raḥmān ibn Muljam. This man managed to secure two other accomplices in Kūfah. When 'Alī came out for the morning prayer, all three fell upon him. Ibn Muljam was arrested. One assassin was killed. The third escaped. 'Alī was fatally wounded and removed to his house. He sent for his assassin and said to Ḥasan: "In case I die, this man may be executed. But you must see to it that he is in no way tortured, that he is well-fed and comfortably accommodated." 'Alī, succumbed to his wounds on the 17th of Ramaḍān.

'Alī's reign

'Alī died at the age of sixty-three. His reign lasted four years and nine months. During this short period there was no territorial expansion in the empire of Islām. On the contrary, thousands of Muslim lives were lost in consequence of internecine warfare. His reign was a source of trouble to himself as well. As already discussed, however, all this was due not to anything which 'Alī did. It is but human to err or at times to show weakness. If 'Uthmān or 'Alī did at all commit a mistake, it should detract nothing from their dignity as the Prophet's Caliphs. The *K͟hīlafah Rās͟hidah* or the Righteous Caliphate, as the period of the first four successors to the Holy Prophet is known, is sub-divided into four distinct periods and they have four great lessons for the world of Islām. It fell to the lot of 'Alī that he should pilot the bark of Islām in times of the most dangerous internecine dissensions. To maintain a proper control of state administration under such conditions is as difficult as to keep a boat steady on stormy waters. Nevertheless, in spite of all these trying difficulties, 'Alī certainly displayed no shortcoming in acquitting himself as a worthy successor to his illustrious Master, the Great Prophet. In the midst of internecine warfare, 'Alī displayed a high example of affection and sympathy for brother-Muslims which is without parallel. The great charge brought against him is that he took no action against the assassins of 'Ut͟hmān, and that he did not suppress this mischief with a strong and resolute hand. But in the first place, as already shown, he was helpless. And then, he should be exposed to such a charge only if he had dealt differently with the opposition set up against his own person. His handling of the Khawārij insurrection to which he himself ultimately fell a victim was likewise gentle. To suppress open rebellion he had to wage war, but he could never persuade himself, tender-hearted as he was, to pick out these mischief-makers and make an end of them. Like his immediate predecessor, 'Ut͟hmān, the element of fellow-feeling and gentleness was pronounced in the nature of 'Alī, and his dealings with friend and foe were accordingly attuned. His army, no doubt, contained an element of those very mischief-makers. He appointed Muḥammad ibn Abū Bakr, who was one of the assassins of 'Ut͟hmān, as Governor of Egypt. As͟htar also, another of the insurgents of 'Ut͟hmān's time, was one of his trusted lieutenants. But even if these be put down to his account as so many failings, they do not detract from his dignity as one of the greatest sons of Islam. He was after all human and no man is infallible. But it seems probable that even in these matters he was helpless. The opposition of Mu'āwiyah added to his helplessness and strengthened the accusation that he did not wish to punish the assassins of 'Ut͟hmān.

Worldly power and wealth had no more fascination for him than for his three illustrious predecessors. He took pride in the life of simplicity which he led in the life-time of the Holy Prophet. Purity of motives and selflessness were the keynotes of his life. He had no desire for kingship but, when the mantle was cast on his shoulders, he walking in the footsteps of the Prophet, faithfully fulfilled his responsiblity. When he saw that it was impossible to rally the component parts of the empire of Islām to one common centre of the Caliphate, he contented himself with as much unity as could be achieved and did not hesitate to come to terms with Mu'āwiyah. Had there been the faintest desire in his heart for kingship, he would on no account have concluded peace with Mu'āwiyah and thereby laid a new foundation of the unity of Islām. It was this peace concluded by his father which, subsequently inspired Ḥasan to establish peace in the Muslim world by abandoning all claim to kingship, and thus bring the scattered forces of Islam to a common centre. The unity of Islam which 'Alī had at heart was thus accomplished.

No better choice of Caliph could be made

The important fact that should not be lost sight of in forming an estimate of 'Alī is that on assuming the reins of power, he found himself confronted by a most serious situation for which he was not in any way responsible. If he could not check the inevitable course of things, no one else could have done so. In point of knowledge and daring, however, he proved the best possible pilot for the bark of Islām in those stormy days. The two indispensable virtues which qualify a man for kingship over his fellow-men were at the time found in pre-eminent measure in the person of 'Alī. So far as sound judgment and daring are concerned, he had no equal among the then living companions of the Holy Prophet. During the reign of 'Umar, an epoch which stands unique in world history in respect of territorial conquest, 'Alī enjoyed the position of specially trusted councillor of the Caliph. No question of any consequence was settled without his consultation. In personal courage and bravery, he was conspicuous among his contemporaries. It was he who succeeded in capturing the almost impregnable citadel of Khaibar. In the holy wars during the lifetime of the Prophet, he entered the lists in single combats against the most renowned warriors of Arabia and overpowered them. Thus, so far as these two virtues are concerned, the virtues of a sound judgment and courage, the choice of 'Alī as Caliph was the best that could possibly be made. In addition to these he was without a peer in the virtues of piety and tender-heartedness. If the reins of the Caliphate had gone into the hands of a less scrupulous man, it is quite possible that under the circumstances then obtaining, the empire of Islam would have sustained an irretrievable loss. During his reign there was no doubt bloodshed among Muslims. But it must be remembered that whenever he saw the slightest opportunity to avoid bloodshed, he forthwith restrained his hands. He abhorred the idea of division and disintegration among Muslims. This is obvious from the attitude he adopted towards Mu'āwiyah and his followers. When the Khawārij pressed him to declare them as *kāfirs* for having refused to submit to the Caliph, his reply was a flat refusal. "They are our brethen just the same," he said, "even though that they have rebelled againt our authority." The whole of his regime as Caliph was taken up with the suppression of domestic differences, yet, be it said to his credit, he allowed no weakness to creep in the administration of an empire which extended far and wide. Law and order were maintained on the same high level as during the triumphant period of 'Umar.

'Alī's learning

From the earliest days, 'Alī's education and upbringing had been in the hands of one who not only stood on a very lofty moral pedestal but who was also the fountain-head from whom the light of learning spread over the length and breadth of the Arabian Peninsula and even beyond Arabia — viz., the Holy Prophet. 'Alī was only a boy of ten when the sun of Islām dawned and he was among the first to welcome it. In other words, his very intellectual birth took place in the lap of Islam. As he lived under the same roof with the Holy Prophet, he occasionally did the work of a scribe of the Holy Qur'ān. For this reason he had special knowledge of the revelation of its various verses and chapters. He is said to have arranged the chapters in the order of revelation. During the early period of the reign of Abū Bakr, he devoted, according to a report, fully six months to this work. Not only was he a *ḥāfiz*, i.e., one knowing the whole of the Qur'ān by heart; he was also a commentator of high standing. Like Ibn 'Abbās, he enjoyed a special position in having a sound knowledge of the Holy Book. The various Quranic commentaries contain a good many of his explanations. In the preservation of Ḥadīth, too, he had a unique distinction, although out of overcaution he seldom reported sayings of the Prophet. As a *mujtahid*,* he possessed a rare skill and for this gift he was considered the best jurist among the companions. Most difficult and knotty questions were referred to him and his verdict was considered final. It was this deep knowledge of the Qur'ān and Ḥadīth which distinguished him so highly. Otherwise there were no special spiritual secrets which the Prophet confided to him to the exclusion of others. The Prophet's mission was for all alike and he had no secrets. Whoever had the greater opportunity to avail of his company and possessed special gifts of understanding naturally derived the greater benefit from his teachings.

'Alī's devotions

The whole of 'Alī's life was characterised by abstemiousness. From the earliest days he lived in the company of the Holy Prophet, and simplicity and self-denial became second nature to him. His relationship with the Prophet as son-in-law was a guarantee, so to say, that the ease and comfort of life would never have any

---

* A *mujtahid* is one who exerts the faculties of mind to the utmost, for the purposes of forming an opinion in a case of law respecting a doubtful and difficult point. The great jurists of Islām were all *mujtahids*.

fascination for him. To earn his living he did every kind of labour. Till the very last days of the Holy Prophet, he led the simple life of a poor man. He had no servant or maid-servant in his house, and his wife, Fāṭimah, the Prophet's daughter, would grind corn with her own hands. The Prophet once saw him lying stretched in the mosque in the dust and addressed him as Abū Turāb, i.e., the father of dust. From this he came to be known as *Abū Turāb*, a title which was very dear to him. After the Prophet's death, too, 'Alī led the same sort of simple life which distinguished Abū Bakr, 'Umar and 'Uthmān. Even when he became king, he led the same simple life, and not the least change was observed in him. The examples of simplicity presented by the Prophet and his four successors stand unrivalled in the annals of kingship. Monarchs of a vast empire, they led the lives of hermits and they never cast a glance at the worldly riches which were laid in heaps at their shoes. Kingly palaces and regal robes came their way but these four kings, temporal as well as spiritual, ever took pride in the cottages they lived in and in the rough, coarse clothes they wore while they worked and laboured for their daily bread. They had no guards at their doors. 'Umar, 'Uthmān and 'Alī, one after another, fell victims to the assassin's knife, but not one of them cared to make special arrangements for his personal safety. Their lives were simpler than those of common people and, like them, they would go to the mosque for the five daily prayers, unaccompanied by any bodyguard. For their own persons, they had no police or military guard. But for the welfare of the state they were so watchful that the smallest incident on a most distant frontier would forthwith engage their attention. For the good of their subjects, Muslim or non-Muslim, they worked day and night; but for their own sake they had not a thought to spare. Passion for the service for their fellow-men was ingrained in their very natures. Their hearts were devoted to the love of God and their bodies to the service of man.

Index

A

'Abd Allāh ibn 'Abbās, 125, 145, 165, 176, 183.
'Abd Allāh ibn Abī Quḥāfah, Abū Bakr, 1–55; early life, 1; conversion and services, 2, 6, 7; is persecuted, 4; flight to Madīnah, 5; Imām in prophet's illness, 8, 56; elected as Caliph, 9, 10; statesmanship, 11; golden rule of government, 13, relations with 'Alī, 13; relations with Fāṭimah, 160; unexampled obedience to Prophet, 15; places national solidarity before all, 22; object of expeditions despatched, 25; conflict with Roman Empire and Persia, 28; motives of, in fortifying frontiers, 30, 31; illness and death, 42; simplicity of his life, 43; orderes collection of written fragments of Qur'ān, 44; enforces collection of zakāt, 46; bases his government on counsel, 47; establishes ruler's true position, 48; treatment towards enemies, 49; strength of character, 49; appearance and character, 50; also see 56, 57, 59, 60, 67, 80, 116, 120, 156.
'Abd Allāh ibn 'Āmir, 128, 165.
'Abd Allāh ibn Sa'd, 124, 125, 129, 135.
'Abd Allāh ibn 'Umar, 110, 125, 148.
'Abd Allāh ibn Zubair, 125.
'Abd al-Raḥmān ibn 'Auf, 42, 82, 93, 120, 121, 122, 162.
'Abd al-Raḥmān ibn Muljam, 184.
Abrahah, 2.
Abū Bakr, see 'Abd Allāh.
Abū Dharr, 133.
Abū Huraīrah, 1 *f.*
Abū Jahl, 54.
Abū Lahab, 117.
Abū Lu'lu', 93.
Abū Miḥjan, 97.
Abū Mūsā Ash'ari, 128, 136, 165, 173, 179.
Abū Quḥāfah, 1, 3.
Abū Sufyān, 55, 116, 117.
Abū Turāb, 157.
Abū 'Ubaid, 68, 69.
Abū 'Ubaidah ibn Jarrāh, 79, 80, 82, 83, 85, 103.
Abyssinia, emigration to, 4, 117.
Adhān, 55.
'Adiyy, 52.
Afghānistān, 151.
Aḥmad, 117.
Ahwāz, 89.
'Ain al-Tamr, 40, 42.
Ajnādain, 42, 77.
'Alā ibn al-Ḥaḍramī, 28.
Alexandria, 87, 88, 152; library of, 88.
'Alī, 155–189; early life, 155; conversion, 155; ambition as a boy, 156; flight to Madīnah, 156; marries Fāṭimah, 157; martial exploits, 157; as preacher of Islām, 159; relations with first three Caliphs, 160; becomes Caliph, 161; faced with dissensions, 162, 163; appoints new Governors, 164; faced with opposition from 'Ā'ishah, Ṭalḥah, Zubair and Mu'āwiyah, 166–167; attack on Baṣrah and negotiations with Ṭalḥah and Zubair, 173; averse to fighting, 173; in the battle of Jamal, 173; affectionate relations

with those who fight against him, 175; relations with Mu'āwiyah at Ṣiffīn, 177; appoints arbitrators, 179; deserted by Khawārij, 181; insurrections and their suppression, 184; is slain, 184; his reign, 184; his learning, 187; his devotions, 188.
'Ammār ibn Yāsir, 111, 137.
'Amr ibn 'Abd Wudd, 158.
'Amr ibn 'Āṣ, 79, 80, 82, 85, 86, 87, 88, 108, 111, 124.
'Amwās, plague of, 85.
Anbār, 40.
Anṣār, 10, 11.
Anṭākiyah (Antioch), 42, 83.
Apostasy movement, 19.
'Aqbah ibn Mu'aiṭ, 117.
Ardan, 77, 78.
Armenia, 151.
Arqam, see Zaid ibn Arqam.
Arṭabūn, (Aretion), 80, 87.
'Ashrah Mubashsharah, 121.
Ashtar, 176, 179, 183, 185.
Asia Minor, 83, 123, 151.
Aswad 'Ansī, 15, 17.
Ayād, 76.
'Ā'ishah, married to Prophet, 4; age at marriage, 5; with Ṭalḥah and Zubair demands punishment of 'Uthmān's assassins, 166; proceeds to Baṣrah, 166; against bloodshed, 170; captures Baṣrah, 171; averse to fighting, 170, 171; letters to Basrites, 172; in the battle of Jamal, 173, 174; 'Ali's respect for —, 174.
Ayla, bishop of, 86.
Āzarbaijān, 92, 151.

B

Babel, 73.
Badr, 6, 55, 119, 158.
Bahman, 70.
Baḥrain, 27, 29, 37.
Bahrasher, 73.
Bai'at al-Riḍwān, 119.
Banī 'Abd al-Qais, 28.
Banī Asad, 26.
Banī Bakr, 27, 28.
Banī Ḥanīfah, 27.
Banī Hāshim, 53, 117, 155.
Banī Quraizah, 158.
Banī Sa'd, 158.
Banī Salīm, 24.
Banī Taghlib, 18, 19, 40, 76.
Banī Taim, 1.
Banī Tamīm, 18, 26.
Banī Ṭay, 26.
Banī Umayyah, 116, 117.
Banī Yarbū', 18, 26.
Banī Zuhrah, 53.
Barā' ibn Mālik, 27.
Barqah, 124.
Baṣrah, 76, 126, 169, 173.
Beduins, 20, 132.
Bilāl, 111.
Bi'r Rūmah, 118.
Buṣrā, chief of, 40.
Buwaib, 70.
Buzākhah, 26.

C

Caesar, 78, 82, 87; see Heraclius.
Caliph, as defendant in court, 105.
Caliphate, ruler's position in, 13, 126, 127; wars of, 30–39, 62–72; democratic spirit of, 104, 105; governors under, 125–126; a continuance of Prophet's life, 149; four periods of, 185.
Chaldea, 34.
Chosroes, bracelets of, 75.
Christians, relations of, with Muslims, 70.

Constantine, church of, 82.
Cyprus, 123, 151.

D

Dabā', 28.
Damascus, 42, 77.
Decree of God, 85.
Democracy, 104–106, 126.
Dhāt al-Salāsil, 37.
Dhu-l-Qaṣṣah, 23.
Ditch, battle of, 7.

E

Egypt, 81, 86, 124, 152, 182.
Elephant, year of, 1 *f.*

F

Fadak, 50.
False prophets, 16–19.
Fāris, 92.
Fāṭimah, (Prophet's daughter) 14, 157, 160.
Fiḥl, 77, 97.
Firozān, 92.
Fusṭāṭ, 87, 126.

G

Ghaṭafān, 26.
Gregory, 124.

H

Ḥaḍramaut, 25, 28.
Ḥafīr, 37.
Ḥafṣah, 134, 153.
Ḥakam, 117.
Ḥalb, 80, 83.
Ḥamzah, 54.
Ḥanif, 52.
Ḥarūrā' Ḥarūriyyah, 181.
Ḥasan, 157.
Ḥassān, 168.
Ḥau'ab, 183.
Hawāzin, 24.
Heraclius, 41, 77, 80; see Caesar.
Hijrah, 2 *f.*
Ḥimṣ, 78, 79, 83.
Ḥīrah, 37, 68.
Ḥudaibiyah, 7, 56, 119, 158.
Ḥulwān, 75.
Ḥunain, 8, 159.
Hurmuz, 67.
Hurmuzān, 89–91.
Ḥusain, 157.

I

Ibn al-Daghnah, 4.
Ibn Muljam, see 'Abd al-Raḥmān.
Ibn Sabā, 130, 131, 135, 139, 163.
'Ikrimah, 24, 26, 28, 97.
'Irāq, see Mesopotamia.
Isfandyār, 92.

J

Jābiyah, 81.
Jabalah, 111.
Jaish al-'Usrah, 120.
Jalūlā', 75.
Jamal, battle of, 173.
Jarīr, 70.
Jarjomah, 80.
Jasr, 69, 96.
Jazirah, 76, 82, 83.
Jerusalem, 81; treaty of, 81.
Jizyah, 38, *f.n.*, 62–66, 79, 80, 92, 108.

K

Ka'bah, 155.
Khabbāb, 53.
Khadījah, 4, 155.
Khaibar, 56, 158.
Khālid ibn Sa'īd, 41.
Khālid ibn Walīd, 18, 24, 26, 27, 37, 40, 42, 67, 77, 78, 81, 82, 84, 85.
Khirrīt, 183.
Khurāsān, 92, 151.
Khūzistān, 88.
Khawārij, 182–184.
Kirmān, 93, 183.
Kūfah, 70, 76, 127, 131, 136, 176; made capital, 176.
Kunyah, 1, *f.n.*

L

M

Madā'in, 71, 73, 74, 181.
Madīnah, 5, 6, 21, 22, 23, 24, 25, 54, 118, 135, 136, 138, 140, 141, 157, 163, 176.
Mahrah, 24, 28.
Mahrān, 70.
Makkah, 6, 19, 55, 118, 156, 159.
Makrān, 92.
Mālik ibn Nuwairah, 26.
Manādhir, 110.
Marwān, 141.
Mesopotamia ('Irāq), 29, 31, 67, 72, 73, 76, 85.
Mosul, 76.
Mu'ādh ibn Jabal, 78, 85, 102.
Mu'āwiyah, 82, 123, 127, 131, 133, 136, 138, 162, 163, 165, 196, 180, 182, 183, 184.
Mughīrah ibn Shu'bah, 89, 93, 127.
Mughīrah ibn Zarārah, 101.
Muhājir, 24, 28.
Muhājirīn, 10, *f.n.*
Muḥammad ibn 'Abd Allāh, the Holy Prophet, plans to assassinate and flight, 5; last illness of, 8; death of, 9; burial of, 12; revolution brought about by, 20; arranges for education, 20; prophecies of, 79, 81; directions of regarding plague, 85; abuse of, 107; mosque of, 118; wars were defensive, 159–160.
Muḥammad ibn Hudhaifah, 135.
Muḥammad ibn Muslim, 137.
Mujtahid, 188, *f.n.*
Mundhir, 27.
Muqauqis, 87.
Musailimah, 15, 17, 24, 26, 27, 28.
Muslim, — and Christian relations, 79, 82; — sense of duty, 98; — ladies participating in war, 80; — soldiers, 96–99, 100, 103, 112.
Muslims, treatment of, towards enemies, 79, 82; wealth had no attraction for, 100; fought against odds, 99; respected agreements, 103.
Muthannā, 31, 36, 37, 67, 68, 70.

N

Namar, 76.
Namāraq, 68.
Nahrawān, 181.
Na'īm, 53.
Nihāwand, 92.
Nu'mān, 90, 92.

P

Persia, Muslim conflict with, 28; aggression of, 33–35; helps Caliphate rebels, 36–37; seeks revenge, 60; bent upon destroying Arabia, 61, 68–69; revolution, 122.

Q

Qādisiyah, battle of, 72–73, 96, 101.
Qais, 182.
Qamūṣ, (Khaibar fort), 158.
Qa'qā', 72, 75.
Qinnasrīn, 80.
Qubā, 54.
Quraish, 11, 118, 132.
Qur'ān, collection of, 44–46; standardized, 133–135, 153; various readings in, 133–135; chronological order of, 160; stops fighting between Muslims, 178.
Quzā'ah, 24.

R

Rabdhah, 24, 133.
Rām Hurmuz, 90.
Ray, 92.
Roman Empire, constant source of trouble to Muslims, 15; Muslim conflict with, 28–36, 57–67.
Ruqayyah (Prophet's daughter); 118, 119.
Rustam, 61, 68, 72, 102.

S

Sa'd ibn Abī Waqqās, 71, 73, 76, 97, 105, 121, 122, 127, 162.
Sa'd ibn 'Ubādah, 10, 159.
Ṣafā, 54.
Sahl ibn Ḥunaif, 157.
Sa'īd ibn Zaid, 43, 52.
Sajāh, 18, 29, 35, 40.
Sajistān, 92.
Sayyid, 157.
Shahr Barāz, 93.
Shahr ibn Bāzān, 17.
Shuraḥbīl, 26, 97.
Shustar, 90.
Ṣiffīn, battle of, 177.
Slavery, 109.
Suez Canal, 88.
Surāqah, 75.
Syria, 15, 34, 39, 124.

T

Tabūk, 8, 40, 56, 120, 159.
Takrīt, 76.
Ṭalḥah, 117, 121, 139, 175; — and Zubair, 93, 121, 144, 162, 166, 167, 174.
Thaqīfah banī Sā'idah, 10, 57.
Thaur, 5.
Tigris, 79, 73.
Tripoli, 124.
Ṭulaiḥah, 15, 18, 22, 25, 26, 35, 96.
Turkistān, 151.

U

'Ubaidah, 158.
Ubayy ibn Ka'b, 105.
Ubullah, 37, 76.
Uḥud, 7, 55, 119, 158.
Ullais, 37.
'Umān, 24, 27, 28.
'Umar ibn Hishām, 54.
'Umar ibn Khaṭṭāb, 52–115; early life, 52; conversion, 52; help rendered, 55; — and the Prophet's will, 57; elected Caliph, 57; frontier

policy, 57; struggle with Persia and Rome, 57; founds Baṣrah and Kūfah, 76; journey to Jerusalem 81; respect for church, 82; journeys to Syria, 82, 83, 86; ban against advance on Persia removed, 91; orders vacating plague-stricken area, 86; slain by a non-Muslim, 93; reasons underlying conquests of Umar's reign, 93; wealth had no attraction for, 100; democratic spirit of, 104; simple life and concern for the ruled, 106; treatment of non-Muslims, 107; condition of women, 109; gradual abolition of slavery, 109; works of public good, 111; propagates Islamic teachings and knowledge of Qur'ān, 112; soldier and administrator, 113; true successor of Prophet, 114.
Umm Ḥabībah, 143.
Umm Kulthūm ('Umar's wife), 112, 157, 161.
Umm Kulthūm (Prophet's daughter), 119.
Umm al-Khair Salmā, 1, 4.
Usaid ibn Ḥuḍair, 43.
Usāmah, 15, 16, 24, 41, 47, 111, 137.
'Utbah, 76, 89, 117.
'Uthmān ibn 'Affān, 116–154; early life, 116; conversions, 117; emigration to Abyssinia, 117; services, 118; 119; elected Caliph, 120; suppresses Persian revolt, 122; repels Roman attack on Syria, 123; repels Roman invasion on Egypt, 124; extends empire of Islām in all three directions, 122, 123, 124, 125; causes of discontent, 125; appointment of Governors, 127; places authentic copies of Qur'ān, in great centres, 133, 134 135; orders enquiry into grievances, 136; calls Governor's Conference, 137; maltreated by seditionists and imprisoned in his house, 142, 143, 144; slain, 146; sacrifices his life for unity of Islām, 147, takes nothing from public treasury, 149; review of his reign, 151; administration, 152; standardization of Qur'ān, 153; manners and morals, 153.
'Uthmān ibn Ḥanīf, 165.
'Uyainah, 26.

W

Waḥshī, 27.
Walīd, 128.

Y

Yamāmah, 27.
Yaman, 24, 28, 159.
Yanbū', 88.
Yarmūk, 78, 80, 97.
Yazdejird, 70, 74, 75, 89, 92, 101, 122, 123; see also Chrosroes.

Z

Zaid ibn 'Amr ibn Nufail, 52.
Zaid ibn Arqam, 3, 54.
Zaid ibn Thābit, 46, 105, 143.
Zainab, 157.
Zakāt, 21, 23, 46, 47, 133.
Ziyād, 183.
Zubair, 13, 121, 139, 173, 175, see also Ṭalḥah.